Knowing Indonesia

Knowing INDONESIA

Intersections of Self, Discipline and Nation

Edited by
JEMMA PURDEY

© Copyright 2012

All rights reserved. Apart from any uses permitted by Australia's Copyright Act 1968, no part of this book may be reproduced by any process without prior written permission from the copyright owners. Inquiries should be directed to the publisher.

Monash University Publishing
Building 4, Monash University
Clayton, Victoria 3800, Australia
www.publishing.monash.edu

Monash University Publishing brings to the world publications which advance the best traditions of humane and enlightened thought. Monash University Publishing titles pass through a rigorous process of independent peer review.

National Library of Australia Cataloguing-in-Publication entry:

Title: Knowing Indonesia: Intersections of Self, Discipline and Nation / Jemma Purdey, (editor).

ISBN: 9781921867484 (pbk.)

Series: Monash Asia Series.

Notes: Includes index.

Subjects: Anthropology--Indonesia; Indonesia.

Other Authors/Contributors: Purdey, Jemma, 1974-

Dewey Number: 305.895

www.publishing.monash.edu/books/ki-9781921867484.html

Design: Les Thomas

Printed in Australia by Griffin Press an Accredited ISO AS/NZS 14001:2004 Environmental Management System printer.

Contents

Contributors vii

Introduction. ix
Knowing Indonesia from Australia
Jemma Purdey

Morally Engaged. 1
Herb Feith and the Study of Indonesia
Jemma Purdey

Ways of Knowing Indonesia. 17
The Personal Journey of an Academic and Activist
Lea Jellinek

(Indonesian) History and its Uses .37
Theory, Lessons, Activism and Policy
Robert Elson

The Politics of Studying Indonesian Politics 53
Intellectuals, Political Research and Public Debate in Australia
Edward Aspinall

Contending Perspectives in the Australian Academy. 77
A View from Indonesia
Bob S. Hadiwinata

Finding a Middle Way. 97
The Future of Indonesian Studies in the Western Academy
Heather Sutherland

Shared Problems, Shared Interests 123
Reframing Australia–Indonesia Security Relations
Richard Tanter

Index 157

Contributors

Jemma Purdey is Adjunct Fellow in the School of Political and Social Inquiry and formerly ARC Post-doctoral Fellow in the Centre for Southeast Asian Studies, Monash University. She is author of *Anti-Chinese Violence, 1996–1999* (Singapore: ASAA Southeast Asia Publications series with NUS Publishing, 2006). Her biography of Herb Feith was published in 2011: *From Vienna to Yogyakarta: The Life of Herb Feith* (Sydney: UNSW Press).

Lea Jellinek has worked for 35 years as a consultant anthropologist in Asia for agencies such as the World Bank, UN, AusAID, German Aid and Asian Development Bank, presenting the voice of the poor to decision-makers and evaluating how development programs have affected their lives. Her book *The Wheel of Fortune: A History of a Poor Community in Jakarta* (Sydey: Allen & Unwin, 1991) describes the life history of a low-income inner-city community in a rapidly changing Jakarta. Dr Jellinek helped initiate an NGO that focused on micro-credit and good governance, working with groups of poor women in five districts of Jakarta. Currently Lea is co-founder along with her partner Ed Kiefer of a village development program (Sukunan Bersemi) that aims to provide a model of sustainable living for other Indonesian communities to emulate.

Robert Elson is Professor of History at the University of Queensland. His main research interests include the modern and contemporary history of Southeast Asia, especially Indonesia; Indonesian political thinking, leadership in Indonesia; changing identity in Indonesia; the social and economic history of Southeast Asia; social and economic change in nineteenth and twentieth century Java; colonialism and its impact in Southeast Asia, especially in Indonesia; and the economic history of peasant production in Southeast Asia, 1800–1990. He is author of *Suharto: A Political Biography* (Cambridge: Cambridge University Press, 2001) and *The Idea of Indonesia: A History* (Cambridge: Cambridge University Press, 2008).

Edward Aspinall is a Professor in the Department of Political and Social Change, School of International, Political and Strategic Studies, College of Asia and the Pacific, ANU. He is the author of *Opposing Suharto:*

Compromise, Resistance and Regime Change in Indonesia (Stanford University Press, 2005) and *Islam and Nation: Separatist Rebellion in Aceh, Indonesia* (Stanford University Press, 2009).

Bob Hadiwinata is Associate Professor, International Relations Department, University of Parahyangan, Bandung, Indonesia; an Alexander von-Humboldt Research Fellow on civil society and democracy; and a member of Aceh Study Group, East-West Center, Washington. He is the author of *The Politics of NGOs in Indonesia: Developing Democracy and Managing a Movement* (London: Routledge Curzon, 2003), and co-editor (with Christoph Schuck) of *Democratization in Indonesia: Challenges of Consolidation* (Baden-Baden: Nomos Verlag, 2006).

Heather Sutherland is Professor of Non-Western History at the Vrije Universiteit, Amsterdam. She is author of *The Making of a Bureaucratic Elite: The Colonial Transformation of the Javanese Priyayi* (Singapore: Heinemann Educational Books (Asia) for the Asian Studies Association of Australia, 1979).

Richard Tanter is Senior Research Associate, Nautilus Institute, and Professor in the School of Political and Social Studies at The University of Melbourne. His recent publications include '"Just in Case": Extended Nuclear Deterrence in the Defense of Australia', *Pacific Focus*, Vol. 26, No. 1 (April 2011); *Masters of Terror: Indonesia's Military and Violence in East Timor in 1999* (co-edited with Gerry Van Klinken and Desmond Ball), Lanham, MD: Rowman & Littlefield, 2006; *About face: Japan's remilitarisation*, Austral Special Report 09-02S, 19 March 2009.

Introduction

Knowing Indonesia from Australia

Jemma Purdey

It is so terribly important that we should admit that we have a dickens of a lot to learn, not only about but from Asians (Feith, 10 September 1952).[1]

This book explores the deeply complex and intersecting influences on the ways in which Indonesia has been studied and 'known' in Australia from the 1950s until today. These influences fall under three linked themes: nation and policy, discipline and institution, and self and morality. As political scientist Simon Philpott writes, '[k]nowledge arises from a complex interaction between individual authority, institutional authority and scholarly discourse' (Philpott 2000: xvii).

Approaches to the study of Indonesia by scholars within the Australian academy come out of a variety of scholarly disciplines and theoretical perspectives, or what Clifford Geertz terms, 'branch[es] of knowledge of teaching' (1995, 96). The study of 'Indonesia' as a field emerged from area studies and comparative government within the American social sciences in the post-war years and was by its design a multidisciplinary endeavour. Geertz described his first engagement with the field of Indonesian studies, under the banner of a hybrid social science team of scholars in 1952, as an experiment trying to make sense of 'what other conceptions of knowledge, of knowing, and of the uses of knowledge could be brought into play' (1995, 104). Scholarship related to the use of knowledge and the role of the intellectual by major twentieth century social science theorists, including Weber, Foucault and Said, inform this exploration of the interpretations and 'ways of knowing' applied to the study of Indonesia. Practitioners have in the past made attempts to reflect on the nature of their 'knowledge' of Indonesia. In particular, debate related to historiography in Indonesian

---

[1] Herb Feith, Letter to Dr Hans Leyser, 10 September 1952, Herb Feith Papers, Monash University archive, MON 78.

studies has a long trajectory (Benda 1962; Smail 1961; Reid 1981), and a conversation about the role of values and its impact on the work of the Indonesianist is similarly not new. For example, Indonesianists such as John Legge and Benedict Anderson are among those who have had a long interest in the subject. In 1973, Anderson wrote, 'That academics are not simply specialists in particular fields of knowledge but also members of specific cultures and social orders, is something at once obvious and yet too frequently ignored, not least by academics themselves …' (Anderson 1982, 69).

The contributors to this book include Indonesianists working within the Australian, Dutch and Indonesian academies, and from the disciplines of anthropology, political science and history. They respond to questions about the ways in which these influences – the nation, discipline and the personal – impact on how we 'know', represent and write about Indonesia today, with particular focus on the Australian academy. They engage with debate as old as the field of study itself, asking where the study of Indonesia should sit within the academy. Is it within existing categories and structures: area studies or the disciplines? Or is there a possible 'third way' of framing our knowledge about Indonesia that is more reflective of the globalised nature of our world? They grapple with questions raised by Anderson and others over decades related to the ways our personal approach, our own sets of values and conceptions of morality impact on how we approach and know Indonesia; asking whether there is a place for activism alongside rigorous scholarship. The book reveals the diverse ways in which knowledge of Indonesia has been and is being attained in the Australian academy in particular, but also elsewhere in the developed world, where disciplinary training but so too personal affect and influences of national policy are relevant.

Herb Feith as a starting point

The initial proposal to bring together Indonesianists on this theme had at its heart the example of Australia's foremost scholar of Indonesia, Herbert (Herb) Feith (1930–2001) and his almost lifelong engagement with Indonesia as a scholar and an activist. He is author of the definitive account of Indonesia's period of parliamentary democracy in the 1950s (Feith 1957; 1962) and pioneer of the study of Indonesian politics in the Australian academy. After his death in 2001, his importance to the field and to Australia's relations with Indonesia was recognised by the Minister for Foreign Affairs (DFAT 2001). While I was researching a biography of Herb Feith (Purdey 2011), Indonesia historian Heather Sutherland put it to me that the initial point of engagement of the scholar with their subject, in this case Indonesia, impacts upon their way of 'knowing' it: analysing, writing and teaching it. Examination of the personal, 'self', or to use Anderson's terms, 'specific cultures' and 'social orders', emerged as a third theme through which to approach the study of scholarly engagement with Indonesia.

Each of the contributors to this volume knew Herb Feith as a peer, teacher, colleague and friend. In proposing the conference panel that led to this book, they were asked to consider questions Herb asked himself about how we as scholars engage with our subject. An understanding of journeys undertaken by individual scholars within this field as they have come to 'know' Indonesia, and critical analysis of the field as they see it today, provides valuable insight and will stimulate debate about future directions for study. Again, a focus on Herb Feith was a more than useful place to start this investigation.

Herb's initial 'engagement' with Indonesia had a moral compulsion behind it. In June 1951 and at the age of 20 a recent graduate from Melbourne University, he responded to a call from Indonesians to join them in building their new nation. Indonesia lacked skilled people to fill civil service and professional positions vacated by the Dutch colonial authority. The premise of the Volunteer Graduate Scheme under which he worked was that Australians would be placed in jobs and locations where their skills were most needed and that they would work under the same conditions as their Indonesian colleagues. The objective was, therefore, one of deep engagement in the communities in which they worked. How did that commitment flow to his scholarship and that of others who followed him? How does the way in which we as scholars first 'engage' with Indonesia impact on the way we then interpret and know it?

Herb Feith was often at the forefront of debate related to complexities associated with the role of the Western scholar as analyst and expert on the non-West, and how to balance scholarship with a moral obligation. In Chapter 1 of this book, I explore Herb's complex approach to his scholarship and his moral compulsion to activism throughout his career, during which he initiated debate and deeper thought around the role and responsibility of the intellectual in his fields of study: Indonesia and the

Third World. A participant in the wave of studies in the late 1950s of non-Western societies and comparativism and modernisation theory, but also of the 'Kahinian' school of historical method and democratic liberalism in Cornell's Modern Indonesia Project, Herb occupied a unique position at the nexus of the dominant ways of knowing the non-West at that time. This perspective meant that although he took up comparativism in his work, he was also critical of its application. Moreover, his experience in the 1950s as an Australian volunteer graduate working for the Indonesian civil service meant he was keenly aware of the pressures and influences from governments on their scholars. In 1964, he wrote disparagingly of the tendency within the studies of non-Western societies for the scholars' only frame of reference being their own nationalities, and their objective the provision of recommendations for policy. He called for them to see themselves first 'as intellectuals, rather than as Americans, Frenchmen or Australians and that they should make a serious effort to develop relations of full understanding with intellectuals of the countries they are studying' (Feith 1964). This remains a central issue tackled in recent publications exploring the development of the field (Kratoska et al. 2005).

Key debates around interpretation and approach to 'Indonesia' within the academy were often reflected in Herb Feith's work. An early example of this critical perspective, his debate (Feith 1965) with Harry Benda in 1964–5, is examined here by Bob Hadiwinata in Chapter 5. This became a pivotal exchange in relation to the direction of Indonesian studies, opening vital debate about universality of values embodied in democracy and cultural relativism in studies of the non-West. Later, in his 1974 review of Rex Mortimer's provocative *Showcase State* and later debate with Jamie Mackie (Feith 1979), Herb challenged scholars in Indonesian studies whom he believed were being too much persuaded by the New Order's apparent economic successes. In the late 1970s and 1980s, as the New Order regime took hold, many Indonesianists, including Herb Feith, sought theoretical and moral solutions outside the conventional disciplines of political science and Asian studies. In 1982, Herb Feith initiated the first Peace Studies course at an Australian university. The question – how to write as 'foreign' analyst while also giving space to the moral questions – greatly preoccupied Herb Feith in his work on Indonesia and on the study of the 'Third' or 'developing' world more generally all his adult life.

Herb Feith's knowledge of Indonesia was in large part a product of his many friendships, interactions with Indonesians and with foreigners like himself, who were engaged deeply with it. He was clearly buoyed by contact with others – he loved to listen, to probe and question. This was the way he gained a great deal of his 'knowledge'. Herb's 'insight' was largely achieved by way of his interpersonal skill-set – or 'craft skills' as he called them – not primarily from books and models (although he would process what he learned in a very systematic and structured form). This helps to explain his need to visit Indonesia often, to talk to people there, 'to witness' in order to be free to 'know' what was happening. Herb's ability to 'connect' with people from all walks of life, and in various cultural contexts, is important in understanding his approach to his work and activism.

In many ways the example set by Herb Feith and other early scholars of Indonesia beginning in the 1950s and 1960s – one involving prolonged periods of living and travelling in Indonesia in an effort to fill the void of knowledge about our large and complex neighbour – is a pattern of engagement that has continued to dominate. In Chapter 2 Lea Jellinek, who was a student of Herb Feith in the 1970s, shares the story of her 'deep' and embedded engagement with Indonesia from the beginning. Knowledge of the language, culture and society through close interaction was then and is still perceived to be a most effective means for achieving meaningful scholarship in this field. For how long, however, is this approach sustainable? At a time when interest in Indonesian studies is declining across the Australian academy, while political and public engagement with our nearest neighbour expands (Pietsch et al. 2010; Lindsey 2010), the time is right for reflection and, if necessary, reconceptualisation of the study of Indonesia in the Australian academy.

Scholarly engagement with a neighbour: a brief history

Today the field of study of Indonesia within the Australian academy is recognised as world leading. Since the late 1940s, the bilateral relationship between Australia and Indonesia has oscillated between viewing our closest neighbour and indeed the region as a whole as a threat or as an opportunity, and back again. This changing status has often been reflected in shifting interest from students and levels of research funding. The national and political imperative of the bilateral relationship greatly impacts on the study of Indonesia in our schools and universities. However, it can be argued that they are not overwhelmingly decisive in terms of its future. The history of this field of study in Australia reveals that it was the initiative of individuals and groups of concerned Australians, more than politicians and bureaucrats, who laid its foundations and engendered an autonomous and, in many ways, humanist approach to the scholarship.

While the formal study of Indonesia in Australian universities can be traced back to the 1950s, as studies by Walker (1999), Legge (1976) and Thomas (2010) show us, its origins lay decades earlier in the awareness-raising and lobbying of public intellectuals, scholars and some politicians in the 1920s, but particularly, from the late 1930s – around the importance of knowing the region in which we are placed, until then ignored in favour of Europe. In his 1936 book *Possible Peace*, William Macmahon Ball condemned Australia's lack of knowledge of Asia as a combination of 'ignorance and apathy' more appropriate to 'desert tribesmen' with a 'low state of mental growth' than to citizens of a modern democracy. The clear national imperatives of the time, including trade and a growing urge to mark out Australia's place as a nation in its own right, guided this push. However, for individuals like Ball and groups agitating for the development of the field at this time, knowledge of Asia was also seen to serve a broad social purpose. In Australia, this 'campaign' to know our neighbours was led by individuals associated with the American-based Institute for Pacific Relations, like Ball, Ian Clunies Ross, Jack Shepard, Max Crawford and the organisation Australian Institute of International Affairs (AIIA), which began publishing its *Austral-Asiatic Bulletin* in 1937. These academics and public intellectuals saw their roles as much in terms of educating the public about the region as lecturing to the elite. They saw themselves as shapers of public opinion and government policy about Australia's place in the world. In 1939, they were given a considerable boost from one of Australia's most senior and well-respected public servants with considerable international experience, Sir Robert Garran. Garran wrote an article for the February 1939 edition of the *Austral-Asiatic Bulletin* in which he called for the establishment of a school of Oriental studies based on the premise that our 'national recovery … depends on international recovery … [which is] not a job for any country by itself; it is a job for countries in cooperation' (Garran 1939). As Garran saw it, Australia could potentially have a special role as 'interpreter of the East to the West and of the West to the East'. His vision for a college or institution for the study of the 'East' or 'Orient' was multidisciplinary and comprehensive, involving exchanges of academics and students between Australia and Asia. Garran expanded on Ball's linkage between peace and knowing our neighbours, comparing the cost of such an institution with current spending on defence. He appealed to the policy-makers: 'Is it not common prudence to supplement this expenditure by a comparatively trivial amount towards the removal of some of the chief causes of war' (Garran 1939).

After the Second World War, the international politics of the region and Australia's own foreign policy changed entirely. The relationship Australia had with its great and powerful friend America was as strong as any in international relations. In the region, Australia's mission was now one of engagement, for it was keenly aware, as David Walker puts it, that 'Survival now seemed to demand a neighbourly response to Asia …' (Walker 2003, 340). Australia gave its wholehearted support to the Colombo Plan in the late 1940s partly for geo-strategic reasons, but more than that it also saw the project as a means for defining itself within the region. Walker explains, 'In doing good deeds, we hoped that we were not like other Europeans, burdened by the excesses of empire, or even like the Americans with their truculent sense of mission' (2003, 340).[2] In an early Cold War context, America charged forward, establishing centres for the study of Asia and the developing countries in what was a convergence of its national priorities to 'know' these places in the spirit of modernisation and 'progress'; what Cumings (1997, 10) refers to as a 'new era of reformist thinking on an interdisciplinary basis' within its academy. In contrast, the first such institutions in Australian universities were not founded until the late 1950s, almost 20 years after Garran's call.

Timing and scale

In his memoir *Available Light*, American anthropologist Clifford Geertz reflected on the beginning of his career.

> I have, in any case, learned at least one thing in the course of my scholarly career: it all depends on timing. I entered the academic world at what has to have been the best time to enter it in the whole course of its history; at least in the United States, possibly altogether (Geertz 2000, 3–4).

---

[2] The Colombo Plan was a scheme under which young Asians studied in Australia before returning with their skills to contribute to their own nation's development. The encounters between Australians and Asian youth mostly from Southeast Asia and South Asia were also instrumental in shaping public perceptions of the region and creating personal links into these cultures and societies.

Compared to the United States academy in the immediate post-war years, which Geertz remembers so fondly as a source of opportunity to study and get to 'know' other societies and cultures, the Australian universities were slow to react to the new world order. Nothing akin to the US Defense and Education Act was forthcoming from the government until much later, although this was not through want of trying on the part of those like Macmahon Ball, whose own Asia knowledge was employed directly by the government in the immediate post-war period, and who stressed this message to his students at the University of Melbourne in the late 1940s and early 50s. In its April 1946 edition, *Austral-Asiatic Bulletin*'s editors highlighted the situation of Indonesia as the most urgent of the current problems 'agitating' in the Pacific (*Austral-Asiatic Bulletin* 1946). Nevertheless, despite the urgency of foreign policy issues and pressure from some within the academy, direct government intervention and emphasis on the study of our neighbours and their language did not eventuate until the relatively late timeframe of 1956 to 1958.[3] Australian government funding was finally dedicated for centres for language and Indonesian and Malay studies at Universities of Sydney and Melbourne and Canberra University College (later incorporated with the Australian National University), with each institution more or less left to design its own model.

This relative lag in institution and capacity-building in Australian universities in area studies, and Indonesia in particular (Reid 2009), is contrasted with the high levels of public interest in the situation in Indonesia itself after its declaration of independence in the late 1940s.[4] The support of Australia's waterside workers for Indonesia's declaration of independence in 1945, and opposition to forced repatriations of Indonesians exiled in Australia during the war, excited wide public interest extending to university campuses. At Melbourne University in particular, this interest together with Macmahon Ball's influence (he was a professor of politics from 1949) led to an initiative among students there to live and work in Indonesia. This was inspired by calls from Indonesian students for assistance to build their nation and excited by the prospect of doing something useful. In 1951 a group of students from Melbourne University from across various faculties founded an organisation called the Volunteers

---

[3] For a detailed discussion on the history of Indonesian language teaching in Australia see Thomas, Paul. (Forthcoming). *Talking North: The Journey of Australia's First Asian Language*.

[4] See Mortimer, 1973b, for discussion of how this limited the significance of the comparative politics and modernisation theory models.

Graduate Scheme, which a year later gained the official recognition of both the governments of Australia and Indonesia. Earlier, the students had taken advice from Macmahon Ball and others on how to lobby both at home and in Indonesia, but it was their own endeavour.

It was largely made possible by the work on the ground in Jakarta by Herb Feith, a Melbourne University graduate and a student of Ball who went to Indonesia on his own initiative in 1951. From 1952 onwards, a steady stream of young Australian graduates worked in Indonesia, mostly in the civil service. They learned the language and gained insight and knowledge of the country from the unique position of working alongside Indonesians under equal conditions. In the 1950s and into the 1960s, they became some of Australia's best informed and first 'Indonesianists'.

In 1956, when the Australian Government eventually provided funding for departments of Indonesian and Malayan studies at three universities, the sums of money involved were moderate. Melbourne University employed a single staff member to teach language and existing academic staff contributed to the teaching program. There were also some resources to build library collections. This could not compare with the funds being poured into 'area studies', including Indonesian studies, in the US at this time. In addition to direct government funding, this included the Ford Foundation's investment of over $270 million in research training and building research 'centres of excellence' in the 1950s and 1960s.

As a beneficiary of one of the earliest programs funded under the US scheme, Geertz counted himself lucky: 'And once again, I caught the wave. An interdisciplinary research team, handsomely funded by the Ford Foundation in the open-handed way that foundation funded ambitious, off-beat enterprises in its heroic early days …'(Geertz 2000, 9). Geertz and the team from Harvard University's Department of Social Relations lived in East Java from 1951 to 1954 at the same time that Herb Feith was living and working in Jakarta as a civil servant in the Ministry for Information's foreign language division. Herb returned again in 1954 for a further two years to research his dissertation, once again employed with the ministry as a civil servant, teaching English to supplement his small income. Comparing these two young researchers – who both went on to be world leaders in their field – illustrates the differences in terms of timing, scale and support for the study of Indonesia between America and Australia in the early 1950s.

Over the next decades, as Indonesian studies developed in the Australian academy into a vibrant and world-class field, scholars were attracted from overseas, and it grew many of its own. Herb Feith and others like him who encountered Indonesia first as volunteers, evolved into one of the dominant groups within the field in Australia. Their early moral commitment to Indonesia imbued their scholarship with lifelong dedication to the nation and its peoples, and profoundly shaped the field more broadly.

Seventy years on from Macmahon Ball's critique of its knowledge of Asia as that of 'desert tribesmen', Australia's knowledge of its neighbours within the academy and more widely too, is sophisticated and in many cases world leading. To get a sense of where Indonesian studies is situated in Australia after more than 50 years of teaching and research, a search of theses produced at Australian universities listed on the Australian Library Collections Database (1954–2008) using the keyword 'Indonesia' found 2254 masters and PhD theses. The first is dated 1954 (Feith's 'Wilopo Cabinet' MA at Melbourne University), but almost 50 per cent (1091) of these were completed in the 11-year period 1996–2007.[5] The listed theses ranged across the sciences, engineering, medical research and linguistics as well as the humanities and social sciences. These results mirror those at one institution, the University of Melbourne. In the period 1973–1996 only nine PhD theses were completed; for the period 1997 until 2006, this expanded to 46 theses in total (Coppel 2006).

In addition to the relatively recent surge in postgraduate research on Indonesia, two other interesting trends emerge from the combined data. Of the 46 theses completed at Melbourne University in the period 1997–2008, all but nine were by people with Indonesian names. As the report's author writes: 'The list demonstrates a dramatic growth over the last decade in the number of PhD theses completed as well as in the proportion of their authors originating from Indonesia' (Coppel 2006). The third trend is similarly interesting, and reveals much about the future direction of research in the field of Indonesian studies in Australia. A further search of the Australia-wide database using keywords 'Indonesia' and also 'Islam', identified 58 theses (a relatively small percentage of the overall number), of these 39 were completed in the period 1996–2007. The data tells us that more PhDs and Masters theses have been produced in this decade than at any other time, but that most of them were written by Indonesians; and that there is also a trend towards studies of Indonesia that include Islam in their focus. Whilst this is not in itself a cause for concern for the

---

[5] Keywords used were 'Australian'; 'Theses'; 'Indonesia'. Accessed 15 January 2008. N.B. There is some repetition.

present state of the field, when these findings are read together with data compiled by Hill (2012) on the state of Indonesian language teaching in Australian schools and universities in the period 2001–2010, showing a national decline in enrolments by 40 per cent, we must be duly concerned about the future of Indonesian studies in the academy.

The future considered

The absence in Australia of non-government foundations that provide funding for Asia-related research like the Ford Foundation and Luce Foundation[6] in the United States, means that scholars in the academy rely almost entirely on the government for their significant research funding. The administering body, the Australian Research Council (ARC), holds annual competitive grants rounds for the entire academy, from which it distributes a variety of different types of grants and fellowships. The peer-review structure under which these grants are awarded is a complex web of interaction across and between boards of academics, based on discipline, and government apparatchiks pursuing national policy priorities. Besides the scholarly and intellectual value, rigour and potential of the applicants and their proposed research project, this system requires the demonstration of its application and relevance to a set of National Research Priorities and to the national interest more broadly, although this was slightly modified in 2011. As Ed Aspinall discusses in Chapter 4, in some respects this consideration may have resulted in Indonesia-related research being promoted ahead of others, although the number of successful grants as an overall percentage would counter this.

In recent years, major reports on Australia's Asia knowledge and its future have been produced by stakeholders from within the academy. These reports warn that Australia's Asia knowledge base is in jeopardy (ASAA 2002; 2007; Hill 2012). The ASAA reports include data about the number of ARC-funded 'Discovery Grants' (three years in duration and the premium research grants available for scholars in Australia) by country or region of study. They show that Indonesia-related research is, after China, the second-highest 'country' awarded in the period under study, 2002–05. In 2006, however, the position of Indonesia-related research dropped to equal fourth alongside East Timor. These numbers have since returned to more 'normal' levels. What is concerning is that the numbers are extremely

---

[6] Ford Foundation gave $US25 million in the period 1999–2003; Luce Foundation gave $US12 million, in 1999–2002.

small to start with. In 2002, five grants were awarded; 2003, nine; 2004, six; 2005, nine; 2006, three; 2007, seven; 2008, eight (this is less than 1 per cent of total awarded grants for 2008) (ASAA 2007; ARC 2008). There are many possible explanations for the small numbers of Indonesia-themed grants awarded, including low application rate and quality compared with other proposals. However, this data does not stand alone. The ASAA's 2002 report, which was directed at government, raised the alarm. It warned that the ranks of scholars within the field would be depleted in the next few years by retirement of those scholars and researchers who were part of the boom in the 1960s and 1970s, and that they were not being replaced by universities eager to make budget cuts; and that in the previous 10 to 20 years Australia had not sufficiently invested in the renewal of its Asia knowledge resource (Lindsey 2010, 2007; Hill 2007, 2012). Hill's 2012 report on the state of Indonesian language teaching in Australian universities further reiterates these concerns. The report demonstrates statistically how the decline in numbers of students studying Indonesian as part of their degrees will impact in the short to medium term; with some states failing to have Indonesian programs in any universities by as early as 2017 (Hill 2012, 22).

A 'community of assessment'

While funding issues, declining student numbers and, following terrorist attacks in Indonesia since 2002, the Department of Foreign Affairs and Trade warnings against travel to Indonesia (see Hill 2012, 26) have impacted on the growth of the field in Australia,[7] arguably a further and important set of structures and restraints on the direction of future research on Indonesia are those from within the academy itself. These structures and systems include access to funding, peer approval and support, and thereby promotion and wider influence. In Australian Indonesianist Robert Cribb's article 'Circles of esteem' (2005), he highlights the internal structures and systems within the academy, and particularly Indonesian studies, and exposes the patterns of interaction and influence. It is, Cribb argues, a structured system of rules governing interaction and the exchange of research in which conferences and publications and their citation are its key vehicles. Cribb's 'circles of esteem' are akin to what Arjun Appadurai

---

[7] In May 2012 DFAT changed its travel advisory for Indonesia from a level 3 or 4, 'reconsider the need to travel' for all the country, to a level 2, 'exercise a high degree of caution' for most of the country with some areas excepted.

calls, 'a community of assessment', which decides whether knowledge is new and compliant with the protocols in the field (Appadurai 2000, 9). A decision to step away from this system or to operate outside it will result in the marginalisation of your work.

Such a system of protocols within the field of study of Indonesia includes deep local knowledge as a consequence of immersion in the language and place, regardless of discipline. As Daniel Lev put it when introducing the edited volume of papers *Interpreting Indonesian Politics*, published in 1982, 'there are few false notes in these papers … [T]he basic reason, I suspect, is that all but one of the authors had done extensive field research in the country and knew the country as well as any foreigner can.' This meant, he went on, that 'All were aware … of just how complex and hard to reduce Indonesia is; none was about to play fast and loose with Indonesian realities …' (Lev 1982, 10). In his article analysing the responses of Australian scholars to the West Papua struggle against the central government, Indonesian scholar Freddy Kalidjernih (2008), supports such a 'standard' for 'knowing' Indonesia. He argues that the absence of this 'deep' local experience results in a diminished claim to expertise on Indonesia issues, even though they may be international in orientation. He warns, 'If this group of scholars [non-traditional Indonesianists, that is, without formal training in Indonesian studies] does not have sufficient astuteness, but only knowledge and experience of Indonesian social and political issues, their criticism of the Indonesian government will endanger Australia–Indonesia relations' (Kalidjernih 2008, 89). As Kalidjernih observes and both Hadiwinata and Aspinall contend with in their chapters in this book, 'traditional' Indonesianists are no longer on their own in making comment and influencing policy on West Papua and other issues in Australia, but that nevertheless, there is inevitably tension and conflict between these groups of scholars (Kalidjernih 2008, 87).

Although various criticisms of this type of argument exist,[8] the question with which they are all preoccupied is who has the 'right', the expertise, the 'knowledge' among Australians to provide authoritative assessments of Indonesia? If it is, as Kalidjernih asserts, only those with deep local, social and linguistic knowledge of the people and place, as numbers of Australians

---

[8] In his book, Philpott focuses an Orientalist lens on the study of Indonesian politics in the West and challenges Lev's approach and that of Kalidjernih's lauded 'traditional' Indonesianists as a 'naïve realist interpretation'. It presupposes, Philpott argues, that an outsider, appropriately trained and immersed in Indonesian culture, can have even better insight and objectivity than an Indonesian herself. (Philpott 2000, 132).

with Indonesian language training declines,[9] the question becomes who will fulfil this role in the Australian academy in generations to come? As Aspinall ponders in his chapter here, and others do elsewhere (Heryanto 2002), it may rightly rest with Indonesian academics themselves.

Themes

The chapters in this book explore the ways in which the themes outlined above have intersected and produced different ways of interpreting and representing 'Indonesia'. Highlighting the importance of the individual scholar's initial point of engagement with their subject and particularly the example of Herb Feith in the Australian academy, the book opens with my chapter related to Herb Feith's particular struggle between his scholarly and moral motivations in his approach to knowing Indonesia. I argue that his initial engagement with Indonesia as a volunteer graduate influenced the ways he interpreted Indonesia and communicated it through his writing, teaching and actions thereafter. Significantly, this was always a tension that brought considerable difficulties to his work. Highlighted here, too, is Feith's importance as a role model for Indonesianists in the Australian academy, who were both challenged and led by his commitment to this approach.

In Chapter 2, Feith's former student Lea Jellinek presents a similarly personal narrative of her more than 30-year-long engagement with Indonesia in which she examines her constant struggle between the worlds of academic analysis, consulting and activism. Jellinek details her approach to knowing her subject – Indonesia's urban poor – beginning with her disillusionment with the conventional methods in academic research in the 1970s, and later in her roles as consultant for international NGOs and aid organisations in the 1980s and 1990s. As a student at a university where 'Asianists' resided within their disciplinary departments, Jellinek's approach to her research was, she believes, better suited to the 'area studies' model popular on and off in many parts of the Western academy over the past 50 years. Her commitment to knowing Indonesia, as she puts it, in a way that might assist her in solving the problems she sees there, is based on experiential learning over time with long and deep in-country experience,

---

[9] In Australia in 2010, 1100 Year 12 students studied Indonesian. This is half the number of a decade before (cited in Lindsey 2010, 40). Furthermore, as Hill pointed out, 'There are fewer Year 12 students studying Indonesian in 2009 than there were matriculating in the language in 1972' (Hill 2012, 25).

coupled with a multidisciplinary approach to scholarship on Indonesia, poverty, economics and culture.

As with Jellinek, questions about balancing scholarship with an impetus to activism are the subject of Indonesia historian Robert Elson's Chapter 3. He poses the provocative question: 'Can historians really be "a powerful positive force in society"?' Through an examination and close reflection of his approach to his own work and many years of experience in his field, Elson concludes that the scholar should honour his discipline (in this case as historian) and the rigorous pursuit of 'contingent truth' above all else. Elson argues that a 'middle ground' can be found between interpretation and relativism and the search for the facts, and it is by adhering to the strictures within the conservative discipline that the historian will fulfil his social responsibility. He describes the scholars' role as that of 'skeptical watchdogs' surveying their areas of 'specialised truths'.

Ed Aspinall shifts the discussion to also focus on the third theme under consideration, nation and policy. He presents an analysis of the unique position of the study of Indonesian politics within the Australian academy, as imperatives related to the national and public create a complex set of sometimes competing and sometimes complementary influences. Aspinall begins by examining the long-held debate between an area studies and disciplinary approach to the study of Indonesia. He presents a close analysis of the study of Indonesian politics in the Australian academy, considering the 'academic political economy' in which the debate over the future of area studies is played out. Aspinall sees Australia's unique geo-strategic position and its strong, internationally renowned scholarship, as a fillip for the ongoing future of a deep, multidisciplinary areas studies approach to the study of Asia, and Indonesia in particular. He provides us with a complex structure or frame by which to understand this rich and varied field of practice. In the field of Indonesian politics in particular, the intersections of national policy as they influence public opinion and educational planning and funding, with the theoretical and personal 'politics' or, to use his term, 'affect' of individual scholars are especially evident. The foreign policy imperative of Australia's relationship with Indonesia means that works of scholarship by Australians on Indonesia's politics is given a greater role than it might be given in other countries. Like Elson, Aspinall tackles questions about a scholar's social responsibility in balance with her obligation to scholarly rigour, concluding that there may always be inescapable tensions and conflicts, which are based not only on the personal but also on the national influence on this particular field.

Following on from Aspinall's analysis of Australian scholars' approaches to Indonesian politics, in Chapter 5, Bob Hadiwinata presents a critical perspective of such debates and struggles in the Australian academy as he sees them from Indonesia. He argues that, while the approaches of Australian Indonesianists were always and continue to be both scholarly and grounded in the academic disciplines due to the complex relationship between our two countries, elements of political activism and cultural relativism are unavoidable. His study of two separate debates over approaches within Indonesian studies – one theoretical and that took place 50 years ago, and the other political and contemporary – demonstrates that this is a highly dynamic field within the academy, and is accommodating of a wide variety of approaches; and that while the emphasis of these debates has shifted, we can recognise a continuity of particular tensions within the field along the fault lines of discipline, nation and self.

In Chapter 6, Heather Sutherland raises epistemologically based questions about the study of Indonesia itself and also institutional questions such as: 'Where should we as "Indonesianists" sit within the academy?' She provides a historical summary of the rise of 'area studies' in the West after World War Two, beginning with her own experience in Australia in the 1960s and later in the US and in the Netherlands. Her chapter, like Aspinall's in part, deals with the ongoing and 'recurring debate about the relationship between area studies, with their multidisciplinary focus on a specific place, and the established disciplines as defined by methodology and institutionalised into secure departments'. Using the Dutch academy as a comparative example to the situation in Australia, Sutherland details how recent trends there show a combined drop in both national funding and interest in 'Indonesian studies', arguing that the future for the field lies in engagement with the disciplines. Sutherland proposes a compromise solution, a 'middle way' through this, which does not mean abandoning the specialist knowledge about a country made possible by 'area studies', but rather 'embedding' Indonesian studies within the wider programs on Asia, 'globalisation' or the non-West.

In sympathy with Sutherland's views on the changed future for the study of Indonesia in the Western academy, Richard Tanter argues in Chapter 7 for an approach to knowing Indonesia through a global understanding of the problems and types of issues facing its people and all humanity. Like Aspinall, Tanter recognises that Australia's relationship with Indonesia is imbued with a heightened significance in the broader context of Australia's foreign and security policy. He tackles the particular question here of how Australia's security and foreign policy relationship with Indonesia has been configured and, in turn, has impacted on how we have studied and come to know it. Tanter issues a challenge to academics, media professionals and civil society alike to rethink how we define the Australia–Indonesia relationship in order to shed new light on our shared interests and shared problems in a globalising world, where issues like climate change require a new non-state-centric approach. He argues that 'the question of how we in Australia think about Indonesia politically – not just analytically – is now very firmly on the agenda'.

Conclusion

The slow and in large part unstructured and independent beginnings of Indonesian studies in Australia (Reid 2009; Thomas 2010), meant that the field emerged amid great diversity in disciplinary and personal approaches to scholarship. Early on, its scholars developed a degree of autonomy and, although greatly preoccupied with concerns about Australia's relationship with Indonesia and with educating Australians about Indonesia, they maintained a non-parochial approach. This autonomy, it can be said, is guarded by each and every scholar who works in a foreign country, although it is not always easy to maintain. There is no evidence, nor indeed vocal suspicion in the Australian academy of what James H. Mittelman has described in the American academy as 'post-9/11 infringements on the free exchange of ideas' and 'Intrusions on academic freedom', specifically in the field of international studies (Mittelman 2007, 363). Nevertheless, there are causes for concern. Increasingly we see that the independence to choose research topics and to travel to Indonesia for fieldwork is challenged by foreign policy and national interest priorities of the Australian government in a way that has rarely been seen in the history of engagement since the 1930s.

The motivation for individuals to study Indonesia in the past often came from personal experiences, interactions, an awareness or concern for their neighbours or fascination with their rich culture. These traits remain within the general nature of Indonesian studies in the Australian academy, although these too, as the contributors to this book show us, are under challenge as Indonesia features less in Australian public and intellectual consciousness as an opportunity for learning, and more as a threat to be feared (Lindsey 2010).

As the contributors to this book confirm, across 'Western' scholarship, area studies as a field of study and public examination is necessarily being reconceptualised and repositioned as it faces the realities and challenges of globalisation. As Barbara Andaya has observed, for Indonesianists and all of those engaged in the close study of 'other' nations, 'the great challenge will be to balance a participation in global conversations with the specific, pressing and often quite different needs of localised research' (Andaya 2002, 284).

References

Andaya, Barbara Watson. 2002. 'Review: Southeast Asia, Historical periodisation and area studies', *Journal of the Economic and Social History of the Orient*: 45, 2: 268–287.

Anderson, Benedict. 1982. 'Perspective and method in American research on Indonesia'. In *Interpreting Indonesian politics: Thirteen Contributions to the Debate*. Ithaca, NY: Cornell Modern Indonesia Project, Southeast Asia Program, Cornell University, 69–83.

Appadurai, Arjun. 2000. 'Grassroots globalization and the research imagination', *Public Culture*. Vol. 12.1: 1–19.

Asian Studies Association of Australia (ASAA). 2002. *Maximizing Australia's Asia Knowledge: Repositioning and Renewal of a National Asset: A Report*. Bundoora: Asian Studies Association of Australia, 2002.

Asian Studies Association of Australia (ASAA). 2007. *Suez to Suva: ARC Asia Pacific Futures Research Network*. 'Suez to Suva' website, Bibliometric data. Accessed 3 March 2008. Available from: http://www.sueztosuva.org.au/biblio.

Austral-Asiatic Bulletin. 1937. 1 (1). 'Review' (April).

Austral-Asiatic Bulletin. 1946. (April).

Australian Research Council (ARC). 2008. Discovery Funding Outcomes for grants commencing 2008. Accessed 3 March 2008. Available from: http://www.arc.gov.au/ncgp/dp/dp_outcomes.htm.

Benda, Harry J. 1962. 'The structure of Southeast Asian history', *Journal of Southeast Asian History* 3: 106–138.

Benda, Harry J. 1964. Review of *The Decline of Constitutional Democracy in Indonesia*, 'Democracy in Indonesia' in *Journal of Asian Studies* (May): 449–456.

Coppel, Charles, 2006. *Melbourne University Indonesia Forum Annual Report*.

Cribb, Robert. 2005. 'Circles of esteem, standard works and euphoric couplets', *Critical Asian Studies* 37 (2): 289–304.

Cumings, B. 1997. 'Boundary displacement: Area studies and international studies during and after the Cold War', *Bulletin of Concerned Asian Scholars* 29: 6–26.

Department of Foreign Affairs and Trade (DFAT). 2001. Media Release 'Australia

Indonesia Institute establishes scholarship in honour of Herb Feith' (27 November). Available from: http://www.dfat.gov.au/media/releases/foreign/2001/fa170_01.html.

Feith, Herbert. 1957. *The Indonesian Elections of 1955*. Ithaca, NY: Modern Indonesia Project, Southeast Asia Program, Department of Far Eastern Studies, Cornell University.

Feith, Herbert. 1962. *The Decline of Constitutional Democracy in Indonesia*. Ithaca, NY; London: Cornell University Press.

Feith, Herbert. 1964. 'Some political dilemmas of Indonesian intellectuals', Paper presented at conference of the Australian Political Studies Association, Canberra.

Feith, Herbert. 1965. 'History, theory and Indonesian politics: A reply to Harry J. Benda', *Journal of Asian Studies* 24 (2) (February): 305–312.

Feith, Herbert. 1974. 'Review of *Showcase State: The illusion of Indonesia's "accelerated modernization"* ', by Rex Mortimer, editor, *Bulletin of Indonesian Economic Studies* 10 (3) (November): 114–118.

Feith, Herbert. 1979. 'From Sukarno to Suharto: A reply to Jamie Mackie', in Jamie Mackie et al., *Contemporary Indonesia: Political Dimensions*, Monash University: 15–20.

Garran, Sir Robert. 1939. 'A School of Oriental Studies', *Austral-Asiatic Bulletin* (February–March): 15.

Geertz, Clifford. 1995. *After the Fact*. Cambridge, Massachusetts: Harvard University Press.

Geertz, Clifford. 2000. *Available Light: Anthropological Reflections on Philosophical Topics*. Princeton, NJ: Princeton University Press.

Heryanto, Ariel. 2002. 'Can there be Southeast Asians in Southeast Asian Studies?'. *Moussons* 5: 3–30.

Hill, David T. 2007. 'Return to Asian Studies', *Australian* (23 May). Accessed 3 March 2008. Available from: http://www.theaustralian.news.com.au/story/0,20867,21776842-12332,00.html.

Hill, David T. 2012. *Indonesian Language in Australian Universities: Strategies for a Stronger Future*. National Teaching Fellowship: Final Report, Murdoch University, February, (http://altcfellowship.murdoch.edu.au/Docs/ALTC_NTF_Indonesian_in_Australian_Universities_FINAL_REPORT.pdf).

Kalidjernih, Freddy K. 2008. 'Australian Indonesia-specialists and debates on West Papua: Implications for Australia–Indonesia relations'. *Australian Journal of International Affairs* 62 (1): 72–93.

Kratoska, Paul H; Raben, Remco; Schulte Nordholt, Henk, editors. 2005. *Locating Southeast Asia: Geographies of knowledge and politics of space*. Singapore: Singapore University Press; Athens: Ohio University Press.

Legge, J D. 1976. 'Southeast Asian history and the social sciences', in *Southeast Asian History and Historiography: Essays presented to D. G. E Hall*, edited by Cowan, C D; Wolters, O W. Ithaca, NY: Cornell University Press: 388–404.

Lev, Daniel S. 1982. 'Introduction'. In *Interpreting Indonesian Politics*, edited by Anderson, Benedict; McVey, Ruth. Ithaca, NY: Cornell Modern Indonesia Project, Southeast Asia Program, Cornell University: 9–14.

Lev, Daniel. 2005. 'Conceptual filters and obfuscation in the study of Indonesian politics', *Asian Studies Review*, December: 345–356.

Lev, Daniel S; Ruth McVey, editors. 1996. *Making Indonesia*. Ithaca, NY: Southeast Asia Program, Cornell University.

Lindsey, Tim. 2007. *Lingua Franca*, Radio National (24 March). Accessed 3 March 2008. Available from: http://www.abc.net.au/rn/linguafranca/stories/2007/1878187.htm.

Lindsey, Tim. 2010. ' "Preposterous Caricatures": Fear, Tokenism, Denial and the Australia–Indonesia Relationship'. *The Price of Fear: Dialogue 2010* 29 (2): 31–43.

May, R J; O'Malley, W J, editors. 1989. *Observing Change in Asia*. Bathurst: Crawford House Press.

Mittelman, James H. 2007. 'Who governs academic freedom in international studies?' *International Studies Perspectives*. 8, 4: 358–368.

Mortimer, Rex. 1973b. 'From Ball to Arndt: Liberal impasse in Australian scholarship on Southeast Asia', in *Showcase State: The Illusion of Indonesia's 'Accelerated Modernisation'*. Sydney: Angus & Robertson.

Philpott, Simon. 2000. *Rethinking Indonesia*, Basingstoke: Macmillan.

Pietsch, Juliet; Clark, Marshall; He, Baogang. 2010. 'Generational change: regional security and Australian engagement with Asia', *The Pacific Review* 23 (2) (May): 163–181.

Purdey, Jemma. 2011. *From Vienna to Yogyakarta: The Life of Herb Feith*. Sydney: UNSW Press.

Reid, Anthony. 1981. "Alterity" or "Reformism": The Australian frontier in Indonesian studies', *Archipel* 21: 7–18.

Reid, Anthony. 2009. 'Indonesian studies at the Australian National University: Why so late?', *Review of Indonesian and Malaysian Affairs* (RIMA), 43, 1: 51-74.

Reid, Anthony; Marr, David, editors. 1979. *Perceptions of the past in Southeast Asia*. Singapore: Heinemann.

Smail, John. 1961. 'On the possibility of an autonomous history of modern Southeast Asia'. *Journal of Southeast Asian History* 2: 72–102.

Thomas, Paul. 2010. 'Menzies "Bahasa": The Cold War and the introduction of Indonesian to Australian tertiary institutions in the 1950s', Centre of Southeast Asian Studies, Seminar Series, 2 September.

Thomas, Paul. (Forthcoming). *Talking North: The Journey of Australia's First Asian Language.*

Walker, David. 1999. *Anxious Nation: Australia and the Rise of Asia, 1850-1939,* University of Queensland Press.

Walker, David. 2003. 'Afterword'. In *Australia's Ambivalence Towards Asia,* edited by D'Cruz, JV; Steele, William. Clayton: Monash Asia Institute: 335–341.

Chapter 1

Morally Engaged

Herb Feith and the Study of Indonesia

Jemma Purdey

> Advocacy and activism do not diminish the validity of one's scholarly research. On the contrary, activist scholarship reminds us that all research is inherently political – even, and perhaps especially, that scholarship presented under the guise of 'objectivity', which is really no more than a veiled defense of the status quo (Sanford 2006, 14).

After Herb Feith's sudden death in November 2001, through the facility of cyberspace, his fellow Australian Indonesianist Anthony Reid and Indonesian journalist and writer Goenawan Mohamad, engaged in a dialogue of sorts. It was Reid's heartfelt tribute to Feith relayed from Los Angeles that Mohamad picked up when preparing his weekly *Tempo* column, which he devoted to Feith. Both men were old friends of Feith and students of his work. In his email posting Reid wrote:

> He seemed to know everybody worth knowing in Indonesia and what's more to be loved by them in a way that opened every door … he gave an ethical quality to the whole Indonesia-Australia (or north-south, as we now say) relationship which made it seem perfectly right that we were as committed to this project as they were. The huge and growing differences of wealth, education, and perspective seemed minor in light of his self-forgetting passion. Of course these differences weren't really minor, and most of us couldn't really overcome them especially in later years. But I am sure that whenever I was in 'the field' I had

the model of Feith in my brain as the way it morally could and should be done.[1]

Goenawan Mohamad included a part of Reid's testimony in his column, then went on,

> The ethical character and spirit of selflessness – which did not formulate 'the Other' as something captured in the knowledge of 'the Self' – is not something that can be readily obtained and achieved. Social sciences (particularly the humanities) are not an easy scientific process, because they always exist within various ambivalences and tensions. There is always a problem between 'knowing' and 'mastering', between 'detachment' and 'ambivalence', between 'relativism' and 'anti-relativism' (Mohamad 2001).

The tributes made by Reid and Mohamad to Feith's ethical character, his morality and its impact, not only on them but on the study of Indonesia, mirrored the sentiments of many others of his colleagues. This was the sense that Feith's ethical and moral model, although increasingly difficult (if not impossible) to replicate personally and professionally within the institutions and disciplines within which they worked and the world in which they lived, was an ever present challenge, and was provocative; a model for scholarly engagement to strive towards.

From his earliest encounter with the idea of 'Indonesia' in the late 1940s as an undergraduate deeply involved with questions about world peace, the liberation of oppressed peoples and an intellectual engagement with these issues, Feith's passion for Indonesia, its politics, people and its future was infectious. By the force of his personality, his intellect and also critically, his timing, Feith's influence on the development of the study of Indonesia in the Australian academy in the 1960s, 1970s and 1980s was foundational. Of course, he was not alone and the field would have not have evolved without the likes of J. D. Legge, J. A. C. Mackie, Heinz Arndt, Anthony Johns in the beginning, and so many more since. Feith was but one important figure in this history. What is intriguing about him, and was made even more apparent after his death, is that Feith's contribution to the field as a scholar and researcher, as important as it was, is rarely separated from his role as an advocate and activist.

---

[1] Anthony Reid, Email correspondence to Indonesian studies online group, 16 November 2001.

Where did it come from?

In a letter to Feith in 1959, his father Arthur Feith repeated a by now familiar opinion (to Herb, that is) on his son's future prospects and career direction. He wrote:

> You know that Mum and I have never thought that you are cut out for an academic career but if academic – teaching would be much more in your line than research. I don't mean to say that you cannot do a good job researching, but your organisational abilities and your skill in handling people would not get full scope in the sort of research one does in Canberra, research in a library. Besides, after three years at Cornell, won't you be fed up with this type of work? Even when you accepted the Cornell fellowship I had similar doubts; it has no doubt increased your skill for research work but even so I cannot see this as the field where your natural gifts can be put to best advantage.[2]

Feith's journey to scholarship and academia was not inevitable. Clearly a great intellect, he excelled at school and in his undergraduate degree. However, as his father observed, Feith also had an often overriding impulse to action – a drive, which again his father worried, would not necessarily be accommodated from within academia.

The Feith family came from a Central European Jewish culture of intellectualism, music and multilingualism, although these were rarely attained by way of formal education. Feith's father, a businessman, was largely self-educated (he left school aged 14 years) and his mother, Lily, trained as a radiographer's assistant. There was no 'tradition' of higher education in either family. As they understood it, this was not the only way to deep intellectual experience. Rather, for the Feith household back in Vienna and here in Melbourne, it was a part of their everyday life – reading Arthur Koestler, George Orwell and Karl Kraus was as commonplace for the young Feith as Ginger Meggs comics and *Boys Own Adventure* magazines may have been for his childhood contemporaries in Melbourne in the 1940s. Alongside this intellectualism was always a life of action. For Arthur and Lily, this was in the necessary world of business – from which they made their living – but also as members of clubs, committees

---

[2] 'Letter Arthur Feith to Herb, Betty, David Feith', 19 September 1959, Herb Feith Papers, MON 78, Monash University Archive.

and through their general community involvement. This compulsion to act as well as reflect and intellectualise was something Feith would inevitably bring to his career as a scholar and more specifically, to his approach to the scholarship itself.

As a child who had escaped the horrors of Holocaust Europe and yet who was from the earliest times and despite being worlds away in Melbourne, intellectually and emotionally aware of them, Feith grew up with a particular sense of his role in the world. As he wrote in diary notes in the late 1980s, 'I grew up feeling I was a special person with a special calling, with a special moral responsibility ...'[3]

Understanding 'moral engagement' in Indonesian studies

> Denouncing injustice and oppression is not a naïve, old-fashioned anti-intellectual concern or a superannuated totalizing vision of Marxism. On the contrary, it is a vital historical task intellectually, because globalisation has become synonymous with military intervention, market-driven poverty, and ecological destruction (Bourgois 2006, x).

Today, academic arguments around questions of morality, authorial values imbued within scholarship and challenging objectivity and 'scientific' evaluation, are commonplace in the social sciences and humanities disciplines. This includes the post-modernist critique that such a position is unavoidable and inherent to the process. As Jean Bethe Elshtain argues in an essay for the volume *In Face of the Facts*, 'Description ... is always from a point of view and hence is always evaluative: it cannot help but be moral in some sense or secrete moral notions and ideas' (1998, 43). For others, the notion of moral engagement in scholarship is a much more an active and goal-driven process. As anthropologist Athena McLean defines it, 'The morally engaged researcher does not simply hope the community does well, but actively seeks to improve its position through "responsible criticism"' (2007, 280). Burma researcher Monique Skidmore is even more insistent of this for those carrying out social science research in situations and countries suffering under authoritarianism and violence, 'In such conditions of repression, terror, and civil war, there seems to me to be no ethical alternative to becoming engaged' (2006, 54).

---

[3] Handwritten notes, 20 June 1989, Herb Feith Papers, National Library of Australia Manuscripts, MS 9926.

It is from within the social science and humanities disciplines, notably anthropology, history, cultural studies, gender studies and literary theory that some of the deepest reflection, debate and often, discipline redefining writing and theorising is done around these questions (Sears 2007, 39–58). As disciplines where scholarship itself is deeply narrative and description based, where representation of other peoples, cultures and times is their raison d'être, these debates around ethnography and objectivity, the relationship between a researcher and their subject and the conditions within which they produce their work, have preoccupied scholars for more than 40 years now. As John Legge put it in 1976; 'The problems of values are not new problems' (Legge 1976, 404).

A practice of reflexivity like this which tackles questions about the values, social and national backgrounds of researchers and its impact on their perspective and approach has however, little tradition in Indonesian studies. Little progression has been made from the work of John Legge, Rex Mortimer (1973) and Benedict Anderson (1982) in the early 1970s, to apply these questions to the field as a whole in more recent times. In Anderson's essay 'Perspective and method in American research on Indonesia' he writes: 'That academics are not simply specialists in particular fields of knowledge but also members of specific cultures and social orders, is something at once obvious and yet too frequently ignored, not least by academics themselves' (1982, 69). Mortimer's essay, 'From Ball to Arndt' published in *Showcase State* (1973) took the form of something like a genealogical approach to the ways in which a field or discipline of study develops – its history. The anthropologist Kay B. Warren, referring specifically to her discipline but making the argument for social science more broadly supports this approach, 'The generation one belongs to is a crucial but often neglected aspect of anthropological analysis and our experience as teachers' (Warren 2006, 215).

The 1970s was a decade of significant reflection, self-critique and debate within the field of Indonesian studies in Australia in particular. These were critical debates – engaging with the ideological and theoretical arguments of the time, but which as Warren argues in relation to the American Social Sciences, led to a cleavage between academics and activists that 'overdetermined norms of inclusion and exclusion in research networks …' (Warren 2006, 215). So too, in the Australian academy by the mid-late 1970s these cleavages were deeply drawn between those Indonesianists who were considered sympathetic to the New Order government and those who opposed it – both highly homogenous and unfair classifications, but nonetheless soon rigidly aligned along institutional lines and it can be said, around particular personalities and their affiliations. To some extent the legacies of this acrimony, although no longer relevant in political terms, remain present and have in part inhibited reflexive thinking from within the field of study upon itself.

In her 1995 essay 'Change and continuity in Southeast Asian studies' Ruth McVey observed about the field of Southeast Asian studies more generally:

> ... I am struck by how little has really changed in the way in which we study Southeast Asia. For in spite of the questioning of America's role, and of the internationalization and diversification of scholarship, the mental framework within which most of our research has been carried out has remained largely the same (McVey 1995, 1).

As an interdisciplinary field, Indonesian studies relies on Indonesianists bringing such critique from their disciplinary viewpoint to bear on their Indonesia-related work. Exemplars of this include Anthony Reid's 'Alterity' essay (1981), Smail's 'autonomous history' (1961), Geertz's various more recent essays on ethnography, a volume edited by Audrey Kahin and Benedict Anderson, *Interpreting Indonesian Politics*, published in 1982, and more recently Simon Philpott's (2000) critique of Indonesian politics. These contributions have served our field very well and, as Laurie Sears and Carlo Bonura argued, 'The vitality of area studies, its reflexivity or ongoing reconsideration of core theoretical conclusions depends on communication with other interdisciplinary concerns ...'(2007, 20). Just as Sears and the contributors to their edited volume *Knowing Southeast Asian Subjects*, argue for re-investigation of the broader area of 'Southeast Asian studies', the particularities of the study of the complex and now more than 60-year-old 'Indonesia' in our Australian academy in particular, and in the West more generally, warrants deeper reflection on its own.

As a now mature field of study in Australia with a significant international reputation, which is facing challenges perhaps not for its survival, but certainly regarding its prominence and about its perceived relevance; questions about who does it, why they are attracted to it, the ways in which we do our research, write and present our work, need to be asked and answered. Will this be a dynamic and questioning field of study in the future?

As demonstrated in the testimonies for Feith by Reid and Mohamad mentioned here, the emphasis on his moral engagement with Indonesia and his pursuit of peace, highlights this characteristic (albeit in one pioneering figure) as one important element of what we do or strive to do as Indonesia scholars. Indeed, as Victoria Sanford observes, '… advocacy and activism, if not the initial impetus for research in zones of social conflict are its inevitable outcome when one achieves an understanding of the everyday lived experience of violence and survival' (2006, 14).

Will there be space for personalities and provocateurs like Feith in Indonesian studies in the Australia academy in the future? His example raises questions too about how to value the importance of teaching, mentoring and relationship building, in addition to research outputs in the form of writing. These are questions for current practitioners in the field, and so encourage a revised or new self-consciousness about how we do our Indonesia-related research and writing (Warren 2006).

A lasting engagement

As Feith's biographer, it seemed to me that I was in a position to investigate some of these questions of generation and the relationship between a scholar's initial or first engagement with his subject – Indonesia – and its impact on the life and work that follows. How does our personal story and experience influence our analysis of another political system, culture and society? As one of his former students, Jean Gelman Taylor has observed, the Indonesia Feith studied in the late 1950s and taught at Monash in the early 1960s, 'was Indonesia now and looking forward. He did not look back' (Gelman Taylor 2012). It was in many ways an inherently optimistic and forward-looking approach born of the time at which he commenced his engagement with the new nation state.

As my discussion above about the ways Feith was perceived by others and how he saw his own role from an early age shows, his was a deeply embedded commitment to ethical and moral values from childhood until his death. He was an exemplary person in this regard and so therefore perhaps an unsuitable example for reflecting of the field as a whole. Critically, however, in his chosen profession as an academic researcher, as for most of us, his was never a straightforward or even comfortable role. It is not possible to describe this journey at any length or completeness; rather the focus is on Feith's initial engagement with Indonesia and its impact on him, and the early challenges he faced to find a balance between the roles of scholar and activist, revealing a pattern of discomfort and tension that would endure personally and professionally, and both inspire and provoke his peers in the field of Indonesian studies.

In 1951, Feith's decision to go to Indonesia as a 20-year-old, had a moral impetus. A call from Indonesian students to assist their new nation, relayed to a small group of active, politically and morally aware Melbourne University students, planted the seed. Feith's critical early impressions and reactions in his first months in Indonesia from June 1951 remained central to his lifelong engagement with it. He immediately adored the vibrancy and passion of the newly independent nation, and particularly apparent among the cohort of people he engaged with, the high degree of intellectualism and, simultaneously, spiritualism. However, in these early months he struggled to come to terms with the class disparity and deep poverty in society, and the corruption and laziness in politics and the bureaucracy within which he worked. In his frank exchange with an old friend back in Melbourne, his moral position at that time comes through and serves as indication of the existential but also practical challenges he was facing:

> It is wickedness, moral wickedness that causes the terrible inequality here, the terrible indifference of the rich to the sufferings of the poor. Although this level of looking at it obviously doesn't exclude the other socio-political level, it is itself terribly real and not to be forgotten … It all presents terrible problems: how far to go to show one's moral indignation at it all, how far to fit in; how far to work for social equality in an organised systematic way and how far to be uncalculatingly true to one's momentary passion and desire to witness. These things are indeed often on my mind, and I'm far from having got far with solving them. But I'm fairly sure these are things where ethical norms are though necessary, yet in a way inadequate in themselves.[4]

In his first year in Indonesia, Feith suffered from depression and the physical manifestations of that, which was exacerbated by exhaustion brought on by overwork. The state of the world around him replete with its poverty, inequality and oppression proved overwhelming for the still young and unworldly idealist. The effects of such deep emotional, moral and also physical stress, first manifest here in his early twenties, would reappear in his forties and fifties with similarly debilitating effects.

From his first months in Indonesia he had great difficulty working out precisely how to engage – whether to detach as observer, or to engage deeply,

---

[4] Letter from Herb Feith to Eric. 15 August 1951, Herb Feith Papers, Monash University Archive.

morally and emotionally with the subject. They remained lifelong questions. These concerns were first manifest in his negotiation of his position as both employee of the Ministry of Information (Kempen) and foreign researcher and also in his personal relationships with members of the national bureaucratic and political elite. In assessment of his masters thesis on the Wilopo Cabinet submitted to Melbourne University's Politics Department in 1953, although his examiners agreed that the research was first class and its descriptions of unrivalled detail and close insight, they were also united in their criticism of the absence of sharper critique and analysis. As he had as a government employee and research student in the 1950s and again as a graduate and young scholar in the 1960s, Feith struggled to identify and choose the correct mode of delivery for his analyses and writing on Indonesia; to know when it was 'appropriate' to reveal his moral position and when to subsume it in favour of more objective analysis. This was made even more problematic by the increasingly chaotic and critical political situation in Indonesia at various times, particularly early in his career. As Monique Skidmore writes about her work on Burma, 'To be an engaged scholar under conditions of authoritarianism and in a climate of fear is not an easy decision to make' (2006, 50).

Self-identification and its impact on approaches to the subject

Feith described himself as a scholar-activist. Since his youth he was actively committed to causes. His friends at Melbourne High School and Melbourne University knew this about him, and soon after arriving in America at Cornell University it became a central element of his identity among his growing network there. In 1959, then living in Ithaca, Feith wrote a letter to the editor of the *New York Times* about the displacement of ethnic Chinese from rural areas in parts of Indonesia. It was an act which drew the attention of his fellow Indonesia scholars in America and their admiration. His friend and fellow Indonesianist, Clifford Geertz, wrote to him,

> For someone whose work depends so much on maintaining workable relationships with Indonesians, I think such a clear stand on principle represents a level of morality which is, in my country at least, rather rare nowadays, to put it mildly … I don't want to be too sticky: enough to say that its initial effect on me was to make me feel guilty that I had not had the same impulse to make the same sort of public condemnation of

a set of policies to which the term fascistic can be given in a quite literal, non-name-calling sense.⁵

Geertz's admission of feeling guilt for not acting as Feith had echoes 40 years later in Reid's testimony. His strong values and activism based on them was critically important to Feith's sense of identity, his ego. However, it was not long before he too was challenged by precisely the constraints Geertz gave him praise for overcoming or ignoring in 1960, and the reality of his situation as a scholar and the expectations of him as an objective social scientist came to bear.

This moment of realisation probably came in 1964 when while editing the second edition of the volume *Governments of Southeast Asia* for which Feith wrote the Indonesia chapter, his mentor, supervisor and friend, George Kahin found himself in the fairly unusual position of reprimanding and faulting his former student:

> This is going to be a difficult letter for me to write ... My major concern is that there has crept into your writing a tendency towards value judgements and moralising, which, while perfectly appropriate to certain kinds of writing ... seems to me to have no place in the kind of book we are collectively writing ... There is, I feel (and so do Jamie [Mackie] and Dan [Lev]), a degree of partisanship in your writing ... moral judgements are infused which bend much too far away from the actual base which you are in a position to lay.⁶

Feith took this criticism and advice in his stride and responded to it with apologies and corrections. As the political and social conditions in Indonesia fell deeper into crisis in the next couple of years, Feith's analysis was sharp, and not without judgement, particularly where Sukarno was concerned. Greater challenges, however, lay ahead.

Now established in the Politics Department at Monash University as one of Australia's foremost experts on Indonesia at a time of critically poor relations between the two countries, and of heightened anxieties about the communist threat in the region, Feith became a public commentator and

---

⁵ Letter Clifford Geertz to Herb Feith, 6 May 1960, Herb Feith Papers, Monash University Archive.
⁶ Letter George Kahin to Herb Feith, 22 October 1963, Herb Feith Papers, Monash University Archive.

thereby became increasingly aware of his Australian identity and its national preoccupations. In August 1965, he gave a seminar at the World Council of Churches conference on 'Christian Responsibility in World Order' in Sydney, about 'the moral dilemmas involved in Australian decision-making in relation to Indonesia and Malaysia and on the question of how one is to judge a regime like Indonesia's which tends to produce confrontations of its neighbours as part of its internal dynamics'.[7] A few months earlier, Australia had deployed its first battalion of combat troops to Vietnam, and at the time of the conference, the earliest anti-war and anti-conscription demonstrations were taking place. In the coming months, successor to Prime Minister Menzies, Harold Holt, would announce an escalation in Australia's troop commitment to Vietnam, including conscripts, and pledge support for the American's with the infamous phrase, 'All the way with LBJ'.[8] Within such an atmosphere of anti-communism and growing fear in relation to 'Asia', for Feith questions about how to analyse the Indonesian situation and represent it to an Australian public were increasingly pressing preoccupations.

In February 1966, Feith wrote and published an article in the Australian journal *Nation*, which lays bare the extent of his dilemma – by then 15 years long – about how to balance a scholarly analysis of Indonesia with a moral one. In his essay on the alleged coup and mass killings of communists in Indonesia since the previous October, Feith presented the 'analysis' and 'moral' positions starkly as A and B arguments. The decision to choose such a format or methodology for this piece was because, he later admitted, he wanted to reach an Australian public that was anti-communist; that supported the defeat of the Sukarno government and of the Indonesian Communist Party. Whether those who read the piece were more open to the B argument, which Feith intended should prevail (humanitarian approach, anti-violence regardless of who is the victim), as a consequence of giving the A (anti-communist side) its airing, is unknown. However, the article elicited a devastating response from some of his Indonesianist colleagues at Cornell, who had only recently 'finished' their preliminary report into the coup and its aftermath, in which they pointed not to the communists for responsibility, but to the army. As George Kahin wrote to him soon after receiving the piece from Feith sent by post, he found it difficult to believe that the author of this article was one and the same as the author of the 1959 *NYT* letter. Benedict Anderson and Ruth McVey, the authors of the preliminary report into the

---

[7] Herb Feith Papers, National Library of Australia Manuscripts, MS 9926.
[8] Holt said this when visiting Washington, 30 June 1966.

alleged coup circulated among a select group of academics and journalists the same month, reacted even more strongly, comparing Feith's essay to that of apologists for the Third Reich. The ferocity of the criticism was unexpected and shocking but Feith did not entirely concede to their condemnation. He defended his motives as sound, although in the end misplaced. However, this exchange, at this moment in time, coupled with the findings of his own research and witnessing of the repression in Indonesia over the next 12 months, represented a turning point for Feith.

As Edward Said explains in his memoir *Out of Place* (1999), cataclysmic events combined with personal witnessing can have life-changing effects. Said wrote, 'I was no longer the same person after 1967; the shock of the war drove me back to where it had all started, the struggle for Palestine' (293). Over the course of the next years, as Feith personally witnessed the plight of the political prisoners and the tightening grip of the military on Indonesian politics, he ended his long struggle to balance the moral with the analytical in written scholarship. Although demonstrably capable of presenting brilliant work, he was no longer satisfied of its importance or relevance on its own. Again, the characteristic that was most critical to how he saw himself and for which he wished to be seen by others – his moral position and advocacy for good – faced its gravest challenge. It was not something he could or would forgo. But of course, such a decision was not without cost. After the late 1960s, Feith did not write anything about Indonesia considered by his peers to be of great significance to the study of Indonesia. Although he was content with his choice, it was not without some regret. His bouts of depression often triggered such reflections and regret about what 'big ideas' he might have had, and the intellectual difference he might have made.

Writing a life: that which cannot be left apart …

> A tension exists … between speaking the truth and deploying that truth in an argument for social change (Hopgood 2006, 5).

Feith was keenly aware of what he described as his 'moral responsibility' and 'special responsibility', probably for most of his life. He was also aware in his lifetime that others regarded him in this way. In 1977 Jamie Mackie named him as being among the 'saintly people'. One can only wonder at the effect that such a description and awareness of the way he was perceived by others had on his expectations of himself. How could one live up to such high expectations?

In early 2005, in my email correspondence with Indonesianist and biographer Daniel Lev, he gave me, Feith's biographer, this advice, 'The problem is, as I have discovered in writing a biography of Yap Thiam Hien, the late human rights lawyer, psychologies are complex and worrisome and filled with traps and uncertainties, and yet cannot be left apart.'[9] In many ways, trying to understand and write about Feith's moral engagement with his scholarship and particularly with his primary subject for study, Indonesia, is also a psychological investigation, for which few of us are equipped and yet, unavoidable. Following a session with his psychologist in 1989, Feith himself reflected on his engagement with Indonesia and was extraordinarily frank, 'One of the things I cherish about being in Indonesia is being always able to do good to people. The other aspect of that is the high status I have there – some of it directly because of those actions of doing good …'[10]

Feith was aware that most humans are a mass of contradictions. How does this expression of ego and self-pride sit alongside the common sentiment expressed by others about his saintly altruism? This starkly honest self-proclamation or admission is precisely an example of Daniel Lev's worrisome traps and uncertainties involving unknowable human psychologies. Lev's own personal set of question marks around his old and close friend involved such a quandary of how to reconcile the entirely selfless, generous and moral man he knew well, with the flicker of self-promotion and aggrandisement in Feith he very occasionally caught glimpses of.

Conclusions: the need for provocateurs

As a scholar who engaged in activism Feith was not unique, and on the surface he did not seem to be particularly prominent outside of his own networks. When I surveyed the extent of his activism in terms we might understand as 'actual deeds' in the form of lobbying, organising, publishing of essays and so on, the results are surprisingly limited. However, those actions he did carry out in this way – letters to the editor, submissions to parliament, marching in demonstrations (although rarely organising them), policy recommendations and essays on topics ranging from the need for post-war emergency relief for German refugees in Europe, opposition to the New Order, East Timor, and nuclear proliferation – were simply the tip of

---

[9] Dan Lev, Email correspondence with author, 12 March 2005.
[10] Handwritten notes, 20 June 1989, Herb Feith Papers, National Library of Australia Manuscripts, MS 9926.

the iceberg. Lying beneath these visible and vocal 'activist events' was Feith's deeply embedded commitment in all he did as teacher, researcher and scholar and university administrator to consideration of moral questions. This is something that is not always quantifiable in terms of recordable 'events'. As a former mentee Richard Tanter explained, the means of Feith's influence took various forms and worked, '[s]ometimes overtly, in speaking of paths to peace in particular horrors of this world, [but] more often indirectly, by demanding both attention and intellectual honesty to the problem at hand. Always by listening and making space for the other to speak' (Tanter 2002).

My informants, Feith's friends, and colleagues in particular, repeatedly described to me what can only be explained as his almost 'spiritual' or 'moral' presence and power in his relations with people. There was something about his very being that people responded to and described as Feith's 'saintliness' or, more specifically, as contained in his ability to listen, to show genuine concern and to empathise. In this way his influence was transmitted through simple contact, conversation and displays of concern. Of course, this was not how everyone regarded it, particularly among his colleagues within the field of Indonesian studies. Lack of action in such a world meant a declining status and therefore influence in real terms. For some, Feith's prioritising, from the mid-1970s on, of moralism at the expense of 'action' in the form of writing, organising and researching was a loss and disappointment. The tension he experienced personally and professionally throughout his career and near lifelong engagement with Indonesia as subject of study and 'home', was projected into and onto the field of Indonesia studies and served to provoke.

Herb Feith's trajectory, his historical pathway as a social scientist working on Indonesia during periods of authoritarian rule and violence, is unique to him as an individual. However, the way in which his approach has been highlighted as exemplary by his peers begs for reflection on our field more widely.

References

Anderson, Benedict. 1982. 'Perspective and method in American research on Indonesia'. In *Interpreting Indonesian Politics: Thirteen Contributions to the Debate*, edited by Anderson, Benedict; Kahin, Audrey. Ithaca, NY: Cornell Modern Indonesia Project, Southeast Asia Program, Cornell University: 69–91.

Bourgois, Phillipe. 2006. 'Foreword', *Engaged Observer: Anthropology, Advocacy and Activism*, edited by Sanford, Victoria; Angel-Ajani, Asale. New Brunswick: Rutgers University Press, 2006: ix–xii.

Elshtain, Jean Bethke. 1998. 'Political theory and moral responsibility'. In *In Face of the Facts: Moral Inquiry in American Scholarship*, edited by Wightman Fox, Richard; Westbrook, Robert B. Washington, DC: Woodrow Wilson Center Press; Cambridge: Press Syndicate of the University of Cambridge: 40–56.

Gelman Taylor, Jean. 2012. 'A complicated life', *Inside Indonesia* (January–March): 107. Accessed 12 March 2012. Available from: http://www.insideindonesia.org/stories/review-a-complicated-life-03031500.

Hopgood, Stephen. 2006. *Keepers of the Flame: Understanding Amnesty International*, Ithaca, NY: Cornell University Press.

Legge, J.D. 1976. 'Southeast Asian history and the social sciences'. In *Southeast Asian History and Historiography: Essays Presented to D. G. E. Hall*, edited by Cowan, C D; Wolters, O W. Ithaca, NY: Cornell University Press: 388–404.

McLean, Athena. 2007. 'When the borders of research and private life become blurred'. In *The Shadow Side of Fieldwork: Exploring the Blurred Borders between Ethnography and Life*, edited by McLean, Athena; Leibing, Annette. Malden, MA: Blackwell: 262–287.

McVey, Ruth. 1995. 'Change and continuity in Southeast Asian studies', *Journal of Southeast Asian Studies* 26 (1) (March): 1–9.

Mohamad, Goenawan. 2001. 'Herb', *Tempo* 12/11 (November 27 – December 3).

Mortimer, Rex. 1973. 'From Ball to Arndt: Liberal impasse in Australian scholarship on Southeast Asia'. In *Showcase State: The Illusion of Indonesia's 'Accelerated Modernisation'*, edited by Mortimer, Rex. Sydney: Angus & Robertson: 101–130.

Philpott, Simon. 2000. *Rethinking Indonesia*, Basingstoke: Macmillan.

Reid, Anthony. 1981. ' "Alterity" or "reformism": The Australian frontier in Indonesian studies', *Archipel* 21: 7–18.

Said, Edward. 1999. *Out of Place: A Memoir*. NY: Knopf.

Sanford, Victoria. 2006. 'Introduction'. In *Engaged Observer: Anthropology, Advocacy and Activism*, edited by Sanford, Victoria; Angel-Ajani, Asale. New Brunswick: Rutgers University Press: 1–15.

Sears, Laurie J. 2007. 'Postcolonial identities, feminist criticism and Southeast Asian studies'. In *Knowing Southeast Asian Subjects*, edited by Sears, Laurie J. Seattle/Singapore: University of Washington Press in association with NUS Press: 39–58.

Sears, Laurie J; Bonura, Carlo. 2007. 'Introduction: Knowledge that travels in Southeast Asian area studies', In *Knowing Southeast Asian Subjects*, edited by Sears, Laurie J. Seattle/Singapore: University of Washington Press in association with NUS Press: 3–32.

Skidmore, Monique. 2006. 'Scholarship, advocacy and the politics of engagement in Burma (Myanmar)'. In *Engaged Observer: Anthropology, Advocacy and Activism*, edited by Sanford, Victoria; Angel-Ajani, Asale. New Brunswick: Rutgers University Press: 42–59.

Smail, John R W. 1961. 'On the possibility of an autonomous history of modern Southeast Asia', *Journal of Southeast Asian History*, 2, (2): 72–102.

Tanter, Richard. 2002. 'In memory of Herb Feith', Author's Blog (27 July). Nautilus Institute, RMIT.

Warren, Kay B. 2006. 'Perils and promises of engaged anthropology: Historical transitions and ethnographic dilemmas', In *Engaged Observer: Anthropology, Advocacy and Activism*, edited by Sanford, Victoria; Angel-Ajani, Asale. New Brunswick: Rutgers University Press: 213–227.

Chapter 2

Ways of Knowing Indonesia

The Personal Journey of an Academic and Activist

Lea Jellinek

For the past 40 years, Indonesia has played a central role in my professional and personal life. In 1969, I caught a cargo ship from Brisbane to Jakarta and island hopped from Java to Timor. I travelled by bus, train, boat, car, horse-cart, bicycle and on foot. My adventures continue to this day as I hunger for greater understanding of a culture that is geographically and emotionally close to me and yet very different from my own.

Indonesia still surprises and evades me, and its magic and charm keeps me coming back for more. In coming to know Indonesia, it is through relationships and personal involvement that I have learned the most. I believe there can be a productive synergy between the detachment of the academic and the committed involvement of the activist. In this chapter I look at my years as student, volunteer, consultant and action researcher, and how these experiences shaped my ways of knowing Indonesia.

Early experiences

As an undergraduate at Monash University in the 1970s, I was introduced by Herb Feith to the study of Indonesia. His influence on my life path was profound. Feith's passion, enthusiasm and personalised approach encouraged me to push beyond what I found to be an otherwise mostly uninspiring university experience.

I love books, but as an undergraduate student at times I felt overwhelmed. There was so much to read and so little of what I read related to what I was trying to understand – ordinary peoples' lives, the context within which these people lived and the daily challenges they faced. I remember the sense that the masses of books, piled high on the towering shelves, could fall down upon me. Maybe it was my rural upbringing and intensely social primary education at a two-room, one-teacher school, or my background as a child of Czech non-English-speaking migrants and my frustratingly slow reading. At any rate, the elements that had intrigued me about Jakarta and the villages of Java were not reflected in the literature.

The literature as it was in the early 1970s described Indonesian culture, history, geography, politics and economics, but rarely gave detailed integrated pictures of the lives of the urban and rural poor – the majority of the Indonesian population and the people I was most interested in. I was keenly motivated, and so I wondered why the library material did not resonate. In hindsight, the answer is probably that the experiences of the poor do not lend themselves to being recorded in the academic literature. The poor mainly have oral traditions, rarely leaving written records or letters. Their bamboo houses are flimsy and don't make it into the archaeological record. Scholars are understandably reluctant to venture into these untidy, often toxic communities where research is time consuming and difficult. Since the mid-1980s, more researchers ventured into the field to record the lives of the urban poor, but to this day it remains a marginal and difficult area of study.

At the end of my undergraduate studies in 1971, Feith encouraged me to go to Indonesia as a volunteer and provided me with the opportunity to teach sociology and political science at the University of Indonesia in Jakarta. There I found academics and students to be remote, theoretical, statistically oriented with vocabularies full of big and abstract words, and closed in their willingness to learn from and communicate with uneducated people. More rewarding were my personal explorations of Jakarta. I found myself welcomed into the city centre or kampung of Kebun Kacang, where I began listening to people and the stories of their lives, their histories and their concerns. This proved to be a life-changing experience.

As a graduate student in the mid-1970s I returned to Jakarta with a desire to understand poverty. I had read the literature on urbanisation, migration to cities, social networks, housing in shanty towns, informal sector employment, the impact of politics and big business on the poor, growing inequality and politicisation and rebellion. I had found insights into the predicaments that faced Jakartans in unlikely places. Booth (1902), Mayhew (1861) and Stedman Jones (1971) writing about nineteenth century London shed light on the lives of migrants and peddlers in the kampung

I was studying in Jakarta. Some of the writing that inspired me included Oscar Lewis's portraits of the poor from Latin America (1961; 1966; 1976) and the importance of community networks (Lomnitz 1977); Terry McGee (1969; 1977) on Asian cities and the informal sector, and Clifford Geertz (1963a; 1963b) on Javanese peddlers and his description of the elaborate sharing systems in Javanese wet rice cultivation. I wondered which of these areas was the most important for understanding poverty, and which would provide a framework and discipline for my study.

It was not clear which department or discipline at university I should work within. My study and my interests were not confined within any of the singular disciplines of history, geography, politics, anthropology, economics or sociology. My interests lay across all of these – what we now term 'area studies' – but interdisciplinary studies were not common in Australian universities in the 1970s and 1980s, a period when Australian academia suffered from a 'hardening of the categories'.

Observing one community in depth over an extended period of time was not something that many academics were able to do. Pressures of limited time and finances meant most doctoral candidates completed their research in one session of fieldwork, producing a snapshot in time. I was finding that my observations varied greatly from one visit to the next. I wanted to put all these snapshots together to get a meaningful picture of change. Inspired by Oscar Lewis and his longitudinal studies of families in Mexico and Puerto Rico, I decided that I wanted to study one community over time through the lenses of many disciplines.

Studying over time: the urban kampung, Kebun Kacang

Over a period of 10 years, I collected many case studies of individuals and families in Kebun Kacang – a community the affluent world called an 'urban slum' (Jellinek 1991) – in what is now central Jakarta. To me it was a lively and even attractive, dense village. I had been welcomed into the kampung by Ibu Bud, a petty trader who invited me to share her life. I lived in her household of three wives and one husband. This type of extended family was not atypical among the Indonesian urban and rural poor. The arrangement had its own logic and benefits, with Ibu Bud receiving considerable support from the other wives (Jellinek 1977; 1988).[1]

---

[1] Herb Feith supported my activities in Kebun Kacang. Every so often, an envelope of cash would appear for me to distribute to those most in need. I knew Herb had sent it. His

People in the kampung were essentially rural villagers living in the city. Every third house had some type of cottage industry or trade employing family members or others who had come from their home village to the city. One relative invited another to the town and they lived together in communal lodging houses or settled nearby and supported one another helping with work and shelter (Jellinek 1978). The kampung was a mosaic of kinship clusters and village ties.

Instead of the widespread poverty I had expected, I found many people earning more than they ever had before, and certainly more than they would have earned in their rural villages. Many sent substantial sums back to rebuild houses and educate children. In the city, they progressively rebuilt their shanty houses into more substantial dwellings. Over time, they began to be able to afford consumer goods. Soon televisions, motorcycles and even cars began to appear in the kampung.

Growing prosperity brought about increased jealousy and individualism. Those who had acquired more wanted to keep their wealth for themselves and found it difficult to do so within the traditional Indonesian culture of sharing (*bagi bagi rejeki*) and togetherness (*rukun*). Within 10 years, a growing gap appeared between those who had accumulated wealth and those who had less. As the disparity increased, the more affluent became increasingly reluctant to share or loan money to neighbours or kinfolk. They wanted more privacy and distance from their neighbours. Some began to build houses of brick rather than the standard bamboo. Increasingly, physical barriers separated people. The evolving architecture of the kampung mirrored the social and psychological changes that were taking place.

By the late 1970s, political and economic forces began to destroy the way of life of central city kampung dwellers. The informal sector livelihoods that had been so important were in decline. Traders were being pushed off the footpaths as roads were widened and traffic increased. Kampung dwellings were standing in the way of planned multi-storey office blocks, hotels, embassies, malls and supermarkets. In the eyes of Indonesian politicians and decision-makers, kampung were an embarrassing anachronism to be eliminated as the modern city developed. The new city of Jakarta was being created in the mould of modern cities around the world and the kampung were to be pushed aside.

---

heart and mine went out to the *orang kecil*, who were, at that time, often accused of being communists.

Rapid change over time was a major theme. In the 1930s Kebun Kacang was a garden of peanuts and spinach (the literal translation is garden of peanuts) with fewer than 10 houses. Between the 1950s and 1970s, many jobs emerged in construction, cottage industries and petty trade. In the early 1970s, during the oil boom in the Indonesian economy, kampung dwellers also experienced an economic boom and were able to earn good incomes and build homes. Ten years later, as the modern economy encroached, government and business pushed for the elimination of the kampung. From the 1990s, thousands of kampung were demolished and replaced by multi-storey commercial developments. Homes, communities, and livelihoods were lost. In many parts of central Jakarta, urban kampung living became a thing of the past.

Kebun Kacang was demolished in 1981 and replaced by multi-storey flats, which provided housing for only 21 per cent of the original inhabitants. Most of the remainder moved to other kampung on Jakarta's periphery. The now inner-city flats were surrounded by tall buildings, highways, malls, offices and traffic jams. The qualities of Indonesian peasant culture that had so attracted me in the 1970s – the harmony, togetherness and communalism – were disappearing. In a rapidly urbanising environment, they were transforming into the previously alien values of individualism and capital accumulation.

By intensive study of the Kebun Kacang kampung in a multidisciplinary and holistic way over more than 10 years, I was able to identify some of the major trends affecting many poor urban communities. I know I would not have been able to understand the poor of Kebun Kacang through the lens of a single discipline or by focusing upon any one aspect of their lives or at one point in time. I needed to understand their families, household and neighbourhood relationships, the community in which they lived, their aspirations and basic needs as well as the social, economic and political factors that impinged upon them from the outside world. The life patterns observed in Kebun Kacang during the 1970s and 1980s repeated themselves again and again in many kampung in Jakarta and other major cities of Indonesia as well as in other parts of the post-colonial developing world.

Qualitative and quantitative research

I have learned that many Indonesians dislike formal questionnaires and surveys because they evoke the language of distrusted officialdom. At first I went about trying to document everything and collect data from every household. But when I sensed their discomfort, even shock, I stopped this approach. Formal interviewing techniques were treated with suspicion and respondents answered in a way they thought the interviewer wanted. In trying to please, they gave misleading answers. People from the villages responded better to questions asked in a natural way in the course of everyday life: preparing food, eating, walking, or trading in the market. Effective interviews had to be 'open-ended' discussions without too many direct questions. In order to understand what was important in people's lives, I found it more effective to let them direct the conversation. If I directed the discussion, then I was determining priorities that may not have been their own. Although this may seem inefficient, it was when people went 'off the track' that the richest insights were gained. To me this is a key to qualitative research.

Qualitative research explores the subtleties and complexities of people's lives, their interactions with others, their thoughts and behaviours. It is often considered inferior to quantitative research, which focuses on simpler factors that are more easily measured by means of formal questionnaires, simple yes/no answers and the collection and analysis of statistics. The two methods of research are complementary. Qualitative research provides an in-depth picture of people's lives and helps to determine which questions are appropriate. Quantitative research deals with variables that can be precisely measured, but results in a more general picture of how many people fall into a particular category.

A problem with quantitative research is that it is often done in isolation of qualitative research, with questions being asked of informants that are of no or marginal relevance, resulting in unhelpful data. I argue that qualitative research (getting to know you) should precede quantitative research (getting to know how many there are of you) if the latter is to be useful. Case studies provided by qualitative research can stand alone because they provide a colourful picture that can be verified to be more general or not by follow-up surveys.

In 2000, I came across the concept of action research (Greenwood and Levin 1998) and it was exciting to discover an approach to research that came naturally to me. My way of understanding Indonesia was to go to the field, observe and respond, and over time think deeply about my experience. Then, I sought literature and information that resonated with my experience. I started with an experience that moved me and drew me to where I wanted to focus. This is far more attractive to me than reading, hypothesising and then going to the field with questionnaires to collect data.

I believe field experience should be a substantial part of undergraduate study at the earliest stages. Experience is a powerful motivator for learning. Reading, writing and manipulating symbols can become a refuge from the untidy storms of real life. It is not enough to be immersed in symbolic representations of reality, as I fear too many academics are. We must encourage our students and ourselves to take time out from computers, libraries and classrooms in order to experience – not just read about – the wider human condition and the environment of the planet.

Self, personality and research

I have discovered that oral history comes naturally to me. I enjoy talking to people and delving into their lives. I am endlessly curious and intrigued by their stories. I like to be surprised by their secrets. I like to use my senses and feelings to try to understand their world. The scholarly term used for this is 'embodied research'.

Some people find my prying and prodding annoying, but there are many who welcome my interest and attention. Very early on, I was taken by the openness and tolerance of Indonesians who were keen to embrace me as a family member. By the age of 20, I had been 'adopted' by Indonesian families both rich and poor. This gave me a perfect vantage point for listening to and observing family members and feeling the texture of daily life.

In the past, I have preferred to move instead of sit still, talk instead of listen. I tend to be an explorer who jumps into situations and blurts out an idea rather than carefully thinking about it. I often process my ideas by expressing them in interaction with others rather than sitting alone and reflecting. I learn best through direct experience and interaction with others. The most well thought out research methodologies may miss the point that the enthusiasm you bring to your research and your personality are possibly the most important factors in qualitative data collection.

If we think about the self as an instrument of research, then we can also think about how unknown cultures become known through comparison with one's own. In trying to come to understand the mysteries of the Javanese, I have spent much time thinking about myself and my own culture. My understanding of the Javanese has been generated by finding points of similarity and difference.

In significant ways I resonate with my subjects' culture – the warmth and welcoming openness of the 'little people' living in extended families at close proximity with each other, is similar to what I experienced as a child.

My mother's sister and her husband (my father's brother) lived with us and were an extra set of parents for me. Along with grandma and my siblings and cousins (who felt like siblings) we structurally resembled the extended families I came to know in the kampung of Jakarta. And, like Indonesians who have guests constantly dropping in, we had hordes of Jewish Czech-speaking visitors who arrived for coffee and cakes each weekend. In this sense, I felt at home in Indonesia.

In terms of personality, I could not imagine more difference than that between myself and my Javanese friends. Where I have been hurried, they have been endlessly patient. Where I have asked too many questions, they have refused to probe for such a style is felt to be rude and offensive. Where I have been (from their perspective) coarse and crude, they have been supremely polite. Where I have been an extrovert, they have been shy. Where I am somewhat oblivious to boundaries and propriety, they are highly sensitive. Where I like to debate every issue and idea, they may be offended by too much candour and discussion. Where I have a thick skin and am not easily hurt, their faces fall with the slightest offence. Where I am transparent and open, their thoughts and feelings are often hidden. Interestingly, while a Javanese would be considered offensive if they addressed someone with excessive candour and directness, I am tolerated because I am an outsider.

The ethics of consulting

After earning my PhD I was lured into the glamorous world of consulting for large international aid agencies, for example, the World Bank, Asian Development Bank and AusAid. I had many assignments with these prestigious organisations, and I enjoyed the pay and the status. In the early days, I believed that my work would benefit the 'little people', but I gradually came to feel that this was not the case. Ensconced in luxury hotels, I dipped in and out of the world of the poor as I benefited from high fees and generous expense accounts. The people we were supposed to be helping – what did they get? Too often it was only promises and rhetoric. Aid organisations often did not deliver what I had hoped for or recommended.

As an anthropological consultant, the time I would spend on any one project was usually brief – up to three months. Often anthropologists were brought in late, to look at the impacts of a project in progress. The anthropologist was needed to officially assure the donor organisations that there would be no negative social impacts, in other words to rubber stamp their projects.

I encountered numerous problems with aid projects. The team leader of most aid projects was usually an engineer or an economist, often without local knowledge or language capacity. Plans and targets were frequently designed by engineering firms in offices far away (sometimes in Western countries). During the planning, feasibility and implementation phases of a program, different firms took up different parts of the project and there was little communication between them. Agencies within the Indonesian government wanted to control a project and refused to work or cooperate with other government agencies because they wanted to monopolise donor funds. Donations intended to benefit the poor were often largely absorbed by consultants, advisers and government officials, many of whom had little contact or understanding of the people they were supposed to be helping.

Projects were often developed by specialists who did not have an integrated understanding of how the different program parts (housing, health, education, water supply, income generation) fitted together in village life. For example, in Aceh after the Boxing Day 2006 tsunami, many houses were designed, built and located without consideration for livelihood needs, space for cottage industries, livestock, trade, or vegetable growing. The specialists (architects) in the housing section typically did not communicate with income-generation specialists, who were brought in only as an afterthought.

I saw my job as going into the field and collecting as much information as possible about the communities and their needs and demonstrating how the proposed project would or would not satisfy these needs. Most aid agencies, however, did not want to go into such detail. They were often focused on technologies and constructions that were highly visible, quick to implement and objectively measurable.

In emergency situations, pulling people out of harm's way, treating the injured and building temporary shelters is important. This crisis phase is usually followed several months later by a community development phase. Aid agencies often don't know how to elicit information from aid recipients about their needs and wishes. The task of reconstructing people's lives and communities involves many more options and choices, and is much more challenging and time consuming than the first immediate task of saving lives.

The big aid organisations did not seem to appreciate my 'ways of knowing' Indonesia. They spoke the language of statistics, spreadsheets, logframes and objective indictors that had less meaning to me. I was told that my research had low reliability because it provided knowledge of only one community or was based on detailed interviews with individual people. These critics do not appreciate that in-depth case studies of people and communities over time often shed light on widespread trends occurring in many communities, not just the one being observed. One community is often a microcosm capable of revealing what is happening in many.

I came to believe that pursuing the life of a development consultant was unethical. The knowledge that had been given to me by kampung people was building my career, providing me with prestige and improving my bank balance. It is true that particular friends from among the poor with whom I maintained lifelong relationships benefited from my assistance with housing, education and medical attention. But I worried that most of the urban and rural villagers were benefiting little. Even the thought that I had empowered them to better understand their world and their governance could not compensate for the gross inequality of our lives. I had become relatively rich and famous through knowing them, but for most, their lives changed little, and this troubled me.

From academic to activist

My desire to improve the lot of Jakarta's urban poor ultimately led me away from academia to activism. My first taste of this came at the conclusion of my work in Kebun Kacang in 1981, when I contacted government ministers in the Department of Housing and encouraged them to try to understand the nature of life in Jakarta's kampung. From the fortunate position of being able to move easily between the kampung poor and the governing elite, I was able to encourage and facilitate kampung dwellers' demands for more generous compensation for their housing and land.

In the late 1990s, I helped start a micro-credit program, the 'Women's Barefoot Bank' in Jakarta (Jellinek 2001). I also facilitated the creation of a non-government organisation (NGO) composed of social workers that conducted research among kampung dwellers during the Asian economic crisis of 1997–99. By working with young committed Indonesian social workers, I gained insights into the joys and pitfalls of setting up an NGO, especially around issues of funding transparency and accountability (Jellinek 2005).

Our research highlighted the critical role played by social networks and the informal sector that enable the poor to survive economic downturns

(Jellinek et al. 2002). While better-off people relied on cash for their survival, the poor turned to friends, neighbours and relatives to help them survive the economic downturn. They pooled their resources – time and labour – and worked together sharing outputs. While big companies went bankrupt and the middle classes lost their jobs, the poor continued to work in informal sector jobs such as small trade, small-scale building, cottage industry, becak driving or scavenging. Ironically, prosperous times may lead to the breakdown of the social fabric that enables the poor to survive times of difficulty.

Sukunan: a model for village waste management

In 2003, my partner Ed Kiefer and I were living in Yogyakarta, Central Java while employed as the resident directors of the Australian Consortium for 'In-Country' Indonesian Studies (ACICIS) supervising Australian university students studying Indonesian language and culture. The noise from traffic and the mosque coming from outside our home was often so loud that inside the house we could not hear our conversation. We were often awakened in the midst of a night's sleep by the roar of motorcycles. The blades of a newly installed white ceiling fan in our bedroom grew a black moustache within a week. Walking along a river gorge in the city, we found ourselves dodging rubbish dumped from the banks above. Crossing roads on foot was dangerous. We were unable to find any place to get away to anything approximating unspoiled nature, or even away from the sound of traffic and the smell of burning rubbish.

At home in Australia, my partner Ed lived in a healthy rural environment with a composting toilet, stand-alone solar electricity and solar hot water and grew much of what he needed. He felt that my urban poverty focus in Indonesia was a losing battle because urban environments were so severely polluted and the crowded urban poor had little time to think of anything beyond daily survival. He argued that I could be more helpful working with people in less despoiled rural environments and trying to help preserve and protect them. Ed believes in healthy living with regular exercise, a good diet and environmental responsibility. At our home in Yogya, he separated our household waste for recycling, and food waste was composted for use in the garden and potted plants.

We met Iswanto at a student gathering at Gajah Mada University. He lived in the nearby rural village of Sukunan, where farmers were concerned about the plastic waste accumulating in their rice fields and interfering with their crops. Iswanto visited our home and observed our meticulous waste separating, recycling and composting. Iswanto decided he would try some of Ed's methods in his own home. So the program began.

Iswanto had been burning his waste in a drum outside his home before he saw Ed's careful management of waste. Sukunan is located just outside the city limits of Yogyakarta and had no government waste collection system. Most of its inhabitants buried, burned or dumped their waste along the pathways, on vacant land or in the river. Iswanto told us that the Polytech of Health where he had studied and where he now taught advocated the burning or burying of plastic waste. He was unaware that burning plastic produced toxic gases, and surprised when our advice was confirmed on the internet.

Iswanto was well connected within its leadership group, even though he was not a native of the village. Together with Iswanto, these leaders came to the view that waste management was a major priority. He personally adopted techniques of waste separating, recycling and composting and introduced these ideas to his night watch team – a group of neighbourhood men who guarded their hamlet at night. This team included Sukunan's headman and other leaders.

At a village meeting, most attending agreed that they needed better waste management. The main concepts of waste management were subsequently introduced to each of the six hamlets by headmen, women's groups and youth leaders. Many methods were used to encourage people to participate. A competition was held among young people to paint colourful recycling drums. Children ran races carrying different types of waste to be placed in the correct drum. Parents cheered on the sidelines. Women formed a choir to sing about caring for their village and the importance of cleanliness. Important guests from newspapers and universities were invited to view and write about these activities.

The program evolved organically, step by step, as we came up with new ideas. Unlike big aid programs, there wasn't a master plan, a clear target or a budget that had to be spent at a certain time. We hoped that people would adopt better waste management ideas and practices. At first we relied on local headmen and women's groups to convey these ideas, but soon realised that without practical demonstrations door-to-door and face-to-face, poor uneducated people had difficulty understanding what was expected of them. At the same time as we were getting this realisation, Sukunan was becoming famous as the one village in Indonesia doing household separation and recycling of waste.

Within two years, Sukunan had received over 5000 visitors from governments, universities, NGOs and other villages to learn about waste separation, recycling, handicraft and compost making (Bambang 2004; Jakab 2006; Webb 2007). The outside world admired Sukunan but insiders faced many challenges. Few people wanted or were able to work as motivators in the community. The burden fell to a few active individuals who were overworked and could not serve as volunteers for long. They needed financial support to feed themselves and their families. When we tried to pay them, the rest of the community objected because of the tradition of not paying locals for working to improve their own community welfare.

The challenges

Women were expected to do most of the household waste separation but did not fully understand the program. They were left out of the decision-making, which was largely done at men's meetings. However, decisions the men made were not passed on to the women even though the women's groups (PKK and Dasawisma) were said to be critical channels for communicating to most of the community. Once the separated waste had been pooled and sold, most women did not know what was done with the money. The village headmen decided how it was spent.

Young people did not know how to communicate. They would gather in youth meetings to discuss the program and remained silent throughout. A tradition of discussion and debate did not exist. Young people feared saying something wrong when talking to the elders. *Sungkan*, a strong sense of shyness, *malu* (embarrassment) and *isin* (reluctance) inhibited young people from taking an active role in the program. Only a few emerged, and all of the burden fell on their shoulders. When we gave them a wage, there was resentful gossip in the community.

Guests flooded into Sukunan. Iswanto, the main figurehead and only person who knew how to speak to the public, was overworked. He was supposed to be teaching students at the Polytech of Health and caring for his young family, but found little time for either. In 2006, we invited him to visit Australia for three months for further training in waste management and environmental issues. This gave Iswanto many new ideas but again took him away from Sukunan, his family, and his job at the Polytech where he was much needed. Iswanto had become well known as the pioneer of the Sukunan program and he was struggling to cope with fame and the new demands on his time and energies.

Iswanto returned to Sukunan in May 2006 10 days before the Bantul earthquake. Sukunan was not far from the epicentre, and 90 of its 250 houses were damaged. The focus of the community and the leaders of the waste management program shifted to coping with the disaster and then to rebuilding homes. Initially there was harmony, but when money from government and aid agencies came up for grabs, togetherness turned to competition, jealousy and hate. The team leaders were dismayed and exhausted by this ugliness and soon burned out. Yet visitors continued to come and wanted lessons about waste management and handicraft making.

Crisis

Sukunan experienced stagnation between 2007 and 2009, overwhelmed by the challenges of recovering from the earthquake, finding good leaders, learning communication skills, and involving women and young people. Changing patterns of thought and behaviour seemed beyond reach. We held interactive meetings to help people reorient and decide on new or different plans and priorities for their village. Many questions came to mind. Had we failed to help the community to formulate a vision or make a community development plan? Perhaps the original program had been too top-down or monopolised by a small group of leading men in one corner of the village? Perhaps the program had lacked transparency and proper accounting? Perhaps we needed to focus more on women, children, farmers and/or youth?

Although lacking energy to carry on, the original leaders were not willing to let go of their status and control. They said they wanted others – young people and women – to be involved, but when we tried to facilitate educational and motivational meetings the old guard objected, claiming we had no right to intrude, as we were outsiders. This was very disheartening, and for a time I thought our program had failed.

I turned to others for help and advice. I had invited a young woman from Jakarta – Wati – to become involved with educating women and children. She struggled for two years against great resistance. I also turned to leading NGO figures in Yogyakarta to ask them what to do. They advised that the Sukunan program was experiencing a normal plateau after four to five years of functioning well. Few programs, they suggested survived to this point. They also pointed out that Sukunan's early excessive fame contributed to this stagnation. The people who started the program had become celebrities prematurely. Some were too proud of their achievements and were not open to new ideas and suggestions.

Regeneration

In frustration, we encouraged the groups that felt excluded to experiment in new directions. Two young men, Muji and Hari, gave women in one neigbourhood of Sukunan intensive door-to-door training in household waste management. Wati set up classes for the children of Sukunan, introducing them to games, songs, theatre, English language and environmental ideas. She also invited mothers to attend cooking, sewing and English language lessons. We funded travel to Bali for nine leading farmers to learn about biogas production, worm farming, compost making and organic farming.

To my surprise, by 2010 things started to change. A new generation of women and young people began to become increasingly involved. Muji's efforts in extending waste management skills door-to-door in one neighbourhood paid off three years later. Under the leadership of an educated woman, Ibu Rini, 45 women in that neighbourhood cooperated together to make and sell compost. They were the talk and envy of most people in Sukunan who admired how the women worked together each week, raised money from the sale of their compost and were able to go on bus trips to the beach or other interesting places each year.

Guests continued to arrive to see the famous village of Sukunan. It seemed as if there was no other village in Indonesia doing waste management. Although practice of in-house separating of waste was not perfect in Sukunan, government officials, academics, NGOs, women's groups, students and villagers continued to visit. By 2011, an estimated 20,000 people had visited Sukunan. It was not unusual to see four large buses lined up with crowds of visitors walking in groups around the village. The guests brought in money and fame, and distracted Sukunan from the many serious unresolved problems of effective village-wide waste management. We tried to challenge the old guard to spread the program beyond the village centre, and to train the young to become better environmental educators and practitioners.

In 2011, Sulung became the new village headman. He had been the young man in charge of Sukunan's workshop that had made drums and composters from 2004 to 2010. Wati, the Jakartan woman brought in to help educate women and children married Hari, who was invited by the Ministry of Environment to extend ideas from Sukunan's waste management program to many parts of Indonesia. Hari and Wati jointly became hamlet leaders. A new generation was emerging, although the former pioneers continued to play a critical role.

Muji, the former undervalued youth leader and door-to-door teacher in Sukunan, became a teacher of waste management to institutions such as Gajah Mada University and the Yap Eye Hospital. Iswanto continued to travel the length and breadth of Indonesia for the Ministry of Environment and Ministry of Marine Affairs to promote a broad range of environmental management ideas. He no longer played a dominant role in the Sukunan program, letting others take the lead.

Ripples

Most impressive of all were other villages that were implementing environmental programs inspired by the Sukunan model. In 2011, I visited several villages around Bantul, all of which openly acknowledged that their waste management ideas came from Sukunan. They had visited Sukunan some time between 2005 and 2009 and invited members of Sukunan, often Iswanto, Hari or Muji, to come to their communities and present their ideas.

Jumali, the head of Salakan village admitted that he had stumbled across Sukunan's colourful rubbish bins while mulling over what to do with the problem of waste in his village (Jellinek 2011b). This fortuitous event had meant that his village, which had been severely damaged by the earthquake of 2006, was able to help rebuild itself by collecting, separating and selling waste, making compost, growing and selling seedlings, and planting and selling organic chillis and eggplants. The women of Salakan also made handicrafts á la Sukunan (Jellinek 2011a). Similar stories emerged from many other villages I visited. Each had learned from Sukunan and then went on to adapt the program to its own needs. One of the highlights was the evolution of a waste bank and waste cooperative modelled on Sukunan. These were introduced to the refugee settlements of the volcano victims of Mount Merapi (Jellinek 2011d; 2011e).

In September 2011, a Waste Bank Congress sponsored by the Indonesian Ministry of Environment was held in Yogyakarta to which newly established waste banks throughout Indonesia were invited to share their challenges and experiences (Jellinek 2011c). Prior to this, the regency governments of Yogyakarta and Bantul had been promoting the spread of waste management to other villages. They are providing facilities such as waste bins, motorcycles for collecting waste, composting equipment and waste storage facilities. The Yogyakarta government had placed billboards near the city centre requesting citizens to be responsible with their waste. The city slogan was changed to 'A civilized person separates their waste and puts it in its place' (*Orang beradab memilah dan menaruh sampah pada tempatnja*).

The program we had started went well beyond our expectations. It moved from one village to 150 other villages (each of these villages have on average from 1000 to 2000 people). The program moved from a poor village where most people were uneducated and worked as farmers and labourers to one of the most prestigious universities and eye hospitals in Indonesia.

Conclusion

Concern and sadness about the great damage brought by modernisation to Indonesia has meant that I cannot simply observe and document. I feel that I should play an active role. The transformation of Java from rural tranquillity to urban chaos between 1970 and 2000 encouraged me to turn towards ecology and psychology – disciplines I had not even considered in the 1970s. I believe many Indonesians are not coping well with the rapidity of change and the loss of their culture and environment. I want to understand what motivates people to change their behaviour. How can people who are focused on income earning be motivated to develop a broader sense of wellbeing, which includes caring for the quality of their own lives and their environment?

I became disillusioned with the formality and impersonal nature of the institutions of aid and academia. I believe that we need to create a good model working with poor people who are prepared to do the hard, time consuming, often dirty and meticulous work. These 'little people', not the politicians or academics or aid agencies, provide the motor for progress. But the 'little people' need the assistance and advice of students, academics, NGOs, entrepreneurs and politicians.

We need knowledgeable and talented outsiders who are prepared to go and live in community and spend their time, money and effort sharing their ideas with local people. In Sukunan, it has taken at least eight years for villagers who lacked knowledge, confidence and the ability to communicate to successfully run the program. It takes a combination of top-down and bottom-up processes to get a program working in the field.

The main lesson I learned from Sukunan is that one has to be patient. We cannot predict where a program will go or how long it will take. Change can be imperceptibly slow but it does happen. We need people to try things out, make mistakes and then try again. Failures will occur and we need to learn from these. All we can do is open doors and create opportunities and encourage people to take up new practices. We need to share networks, contacts and information as widely as possible. We need financial support and careful monitoring of funds. We should not insist that funds be spent quickly or according to a timetable. Success may bring its own pitfalls: swollen heads or competition for acclaim. We need to forgive and move on. When others copy us and even become better than us, it is the biggest honour. Imitation is the sincerest form of flattery.

My way of knowing Indonesia has been to identify a place, get to know its people, find out about their past and identify their key problems. My aim has been to understand and then facilitate new possibilities for better and more fulfilling lives. This has given rise to active involvement and commitment to change. From interaction with the world I have gained my major insights.

References

Bambang, C. 2004. 'Villagers join hands to save the Earth'. *Jakarta Post* (12 June).
Senohadi, Y. 2005. 'Iswanto, pendekar sampah dari Sukunan'. *Sinus* (March).
Booth, C. 1902. *Life and Labour of the People in London*, London: Macmillan
Geertz, C. 1963a. *Peddlers and Princes: Social Development and Economic Change in Two Indonesian Towns*. Chicago and London: University of Chicago Press.
Geertz, C. 1963b. *Agricultural Involution: The Processes of Ecological Change in Indonesia*, Berkeley, Los Angeles and London: University of California Press.
Greenwood, Davydd J; Levin, Morten. 1998. *Introduction to Action Research*, Thousand Oaks California: Sage Publications.
Jakab, C. 2006. 'Case study: Rubbish as a resource in Indonesia', *Global Issues Natural Resources*, Macmillan Library: 27.
Jellinek, L. 1977. 'The life of a Jakarta street trader'. In *Third World Urbanization*, edited by Abu-Lughod, J; Hay, R. Maaroufa Press: Chicago.
Jellinek, L. 1978. 'Circular migration and the Pondok dwelling system: A case study of ice-cream traders in Jakarta'. In *Food Shelter and Transport in Southeast Asia and the Pacific*, edited by Rimmer, P J. et al. Research School of Pacific Studies, ANU: Canberra: 135–54.
Jellinek, L. 1988. 'The changing fortunes of a Jakarta street trader'. In *The Urbanization of the Third World*, edited by Gugler, J. New York: Oxford University Press.
Jellinek, L. 1991. *The Wheel of Fortune: The History of a Poor Community in Jakarta*, University of Hawaii Press: Honolulu.
Jellinek, L. 2001. 'Jakarta Women's Barefoot Bank'. *Inside Indonesia* 66 (April–June): 9–10.
Jellinek, L. et al 2002. *My Neighbour, Your Neighbour: Governance, Poverty and*

Civic Engagement in Five Jakarta Communities, Department for International Development (DFID) of the British Embassy: Jakarta.

Jellinek, L. 2005. 'Collapsing under the weight of success: An NGO in Jakarta'. In *Urban Poverty: Practitioners Influencing Policy*, edited by Nelson, Nici; Jones, Sue. Intermediate Technology Press: London.

Jellinek, L. 2011a. 'Novi Aryani: A passion for handicrafts from waste', *Jakarta Post* (12 September).

Jellinek, L. 2011b. 'Starting from zero', *Jakarta Post* (12 September).

Jellinek, L. 2011c. 'Becoming a model', *Jakarta Post* (12 September).

Jellinek, L. 2011d. 'Tobadiono: Developing his village', *Jakarta Post* (17 October).

Jellinek, L. 2011e. 'Junaidi: Crazy about waste', *Jakarta Post* (25 October).

Lewis, O. 1961. *The Children of Sanchez: Autobiography of a Mexican Family*, Harmondsworth: Penguin Books.

Lewis, O. 1966. 'The Culture of Poverty', *Scientific American* 215 (4):19–25.

Lewis, O. 1976. *Five Families: Mexican Case Studies in the Culture of Poverty*, London: Souvenir Press.

Lomnitz, L A. 1977. *Networks and Marginality: Life in a Mexican Shantytown*, New York: Academic Press.

Mayhew, H. 1861. *London Labour and the London Poor* (4 volumes), London: Griffin, Bohn and Company.

McGee, T G 1969. *The Southeast Asian City: A Social Geography of the Primate Cities of Southeast Asia*, London: Bell and Sons.

McGee, T G 1977. 'The persistence of the proto-proletariat: Occupational structures and planning for the future of Third World cities'. In *Third World Urbanization*, edited by Abu-Lughod, J; Hay, R. Chicago: Maaroufa Press: 257–70.

Stedman Jones, G. 1971. *Outcast London: A Study in the Relationship Between Classes in Victorian Society*, Harmondsworth: Penguin.

Webb, C. 2007. 'Saving the environment: It takes a village', *Jakarta Post* (11 November).

Chapter 3

(Indonesian) History and its Uses

Theory, Lessons, Activism and Policy

Robert Elson

Perhaps to the cynic I may appear naive, but I passionately believe that historians can be a powerful positive force in society. As George Santayana famously wrote, 'Those who do not remember the past are condemned to repeat it.' Sadly, I can think of no more pertinent example of the dangers of forgotten history than is manifest in the vast human tragedy unfolding in Iraq today (Cook 2007).

Can historians really 'be a powerful positive force in society'? What might it mean to make such an assertion? The implication seems to be that historians know the field of their acknowledged historical expertise better and deeper than other people, and that they are therefore better positioned to devise socio-political policies and advice which relate to that field that will more likely prove correct and socially useful than that provided by people without such expert knowledge. I want to argue here that this activist, policy-oriented notion loads more upon the historian than he or she can possibly bear; in an important sense, indeed, it can sometimes entice the historian to relinquish best practice in the pursuit of political preferment and popular renown. For it is my argument that the discipline of doing history is an inherently conservative one, with conservative rather than activist implications, and that the proper public or social role of historians is as watchful critics of over-generalised, misleading, misunderstood or mistaken policy ambitions or activist claims allegedly based upon historical precedent, rather than themselves, *qua* historians, pretending to roles as activists or policy-makers.

Ways of 'doing history'

To make this argument, I want to conduct a kind of 'thinking-out-aloud' exploration of my own historical practice as a historian of Indonesia, insofar as I understand it, interlacing it with some (admittedly old-fashioned, but nonetheless persistent) historiographical concerns and reflections. I will begin with some examples from Indonesian history writing, which I consider to be examples of poor historical practice:

> On one occasion, the prince [Iskandar Muda of Aceh, r. 1607–1636] went out on an elephant catching expedition. His grandfather became nervous and decided to set out to bring him back. The prince, having heard that his grandfather was on the way to the forest, decided to go to meet him with his aide Setia Rimba. Now Setia Rimba had a sore leg, so the prince seated him on a buffalo, while he mounted his horse. After travelling part of the way Iskandar's horse stopped and trembled. A tiger roared nearby. The prince shouted at it: 'Senseless, uncivilised beast, how dare you lie in wait for me. Why couldn't you choose someone else?' The prince gave chase but the tiger escaped. But meanwhile the unfortunate Setia Rimba, left behind seated on his buffalo, suddenly found himself face to face with the tiger, and shouted desperately for help. Iskandar came galloping back on his horse and thrust his spear into the tiger's mouth, slaying it (Hikayat Aceh in Johns 1979: 50).

> We had a precious former day; we had a period of brilliance! ... lives there an Indonesian whose heart does not sigh upon listening to tales of those beautiful times: is there anyone who does not feel the loss of that greatness? Where is the Indonesian whose national spirit does not come alive upon hearing stories of the great kingdoms of Melayu and Srividjaja, of the greatness of the first Mataram period, of the Sindok, Erlangga, Kediri, Singasari, Madjapahit, and Padjadjaran periods – and the grandeur of Bintara, Banten, and Mataram II under Sultan Agung! What Indonesian does not longingly remember his former flag, seen and honoured even in Madagascar, Persia and China? But conversely, too, ought we not to live with the hope and belief that a people who achieved such greatness formerly will surely have the strength to attain as beautiful a future – will surely have the capabilities necessary to rise again to the level of their former grandeur (Sukarno in Paget 1975, 75–80).

The palpable deterioration in living conditions of the Indonesian masses ultimately compelled even the Dutch authorities to institute enquiries at the turn of the [twentieth] century. There were perfectly sound reasons for this apparent altruism. In the first place, industry in Holland was by now sufficiently alert to export prospects to appreciate that, whatever low wages for colonial labour might contribute to the prosperity of the mine and plantation companies, they spelled unnecessarily miserable business for Dutch exporters. In the second place, the general infrastructure requirements of all big European enterprises in Indonesia, which had been met up till then by NEI expenditures raised from termination of the *batig slot* (1878) and from subsequent loan issues, were rising steeply as new industries brought new and more demanding requirements. Hence there was inaugurated in the early years of the twentieth the smugly-styled 'Ethical Policy', under which grants were made from the Netherlands treasury for social capital investment in the Indies … In fact, of course, the expenditures undertaken were all of most benefit to the foreign companies and the colonial administration, in providing improved roads, ports and other facilities, and in providing healthier and harder working labourers and slightly better educated but low level clerical employee (Caldwell and Utrecht 1979, 33).

The problem with this kind of history-writing is that the writers engage their material with a strong sense of what they want to conclude – something that might be termed 'jigsaw puzzle' history-writing. With 'jigsaw puzzle' history-writing, the fascination and interest in the job at hand is not in the solution to a historical problem, but rather in how one gets to the solution, already preordained. The writers know the answer they want, and their interest is not so much what they finally arrive at but rather in how they select and arrange their materials to get to the anticipated solution. They are not so much interested in 'what really happened' – for example, the fact that Iskandar's aide was attacked by a tiger is not all that important – but in 'how things happened as they did' – how the pieces came together to provide the expected, indeed desired, end-product. The solution in each case is clear: Iskandar Muda was a brave and kind ruler; Indonesia has a great and glorious past; capitalism and colonialism are self-interested and necessarily impoverish the masses. The historical puzzle is not in finding a solution but in selecting and appropriately placing the pieces of the puzzle so that this known, preordained solution can be arrived at.

My problem with the 'jigsaw-puzzle' approach to history is that I have a sense that all is not how it should be. I do not think I 'do history' like this, nor do I think it is a proper way to 'do history'. I usually do not have a sense, at least not a strong and determining sense, of what my conclusions might be when I set out. To put it bluntly, what I try to do is to get to 'the truth', whatever that might mean (and I'll say a little more about that presently) – a truth which is not available to me at the beginning of my historical pursuit. But how exactly does what I do, and what I take many other historians to do, differ from 'jigsaw-puzzle' history, and what exactly is it that makes what I do, as I judge it, 'better' or 'more proper' history than 'jigsaw-puzzle' history'?

Truth

The problem of 'truth' is an eternally difficult one. At least one fundamental aspect of the problem lies in the old difficulty of bridging the gap between the historian (in the present) and 'the past'. This, I think, is an appropriate place to bring in E. H. Carr, because he spills so much ink on this particular question in his old, but still eternally useful and brilliant little book *What is History* (Carr 1964). In his first chapter, Carr raises the old problem of fact and interpretation. He argues that there is no such thing as an objective historical fact that lives, as it were 'out there', free of the observer and independent of him/her. 'History', he says, 'means interpretation' (Carr 1964, 23). He goes on to make three points. First, historical facts are always refracted through the mind of the recorder, and have therefore already lost their 'purity', have already been polluted, before they even reach the historian. Second, the historian needs to have an 'imaginative understanding' of the people of the past with whom they are dealing. Third, we understand the past only through the eyes of the present, by which I think Carr means we retrospect our current values and interests into the past, so that certain ages and individuals tend to produce certain types of history.

Now all this is more or less acceptable up to a point, but there are important and difficult problems involved in it, of which the major one is relativism. Carr seems to realise the problem; to realise that he is steering his ship towards the rocks of relativism because of his emphasis on the interpretative, imaginative and time-bound activities of the historian. If there are no 'objective facts', and if the way in which data are selected and ordered is purely a matter of personal interpretation or the arbitrary or deliberate choice of a certain determining theoretical framework, then one ought to argue that history is eventually a matter of invention and artifice, of 'constructedness', and thus not really substantially different from literature or poetry or even some reaches of philosophy. So Carr makes a valiant effort to stave off the problem. He acknowledges that 'the emphasis on the role of the historian in the making of history tends, if pursued to its logical conclusion, to rule out any objective history at all: history is what the historian makes' (Carr 1964, 26). But he certainly does not want to go this far – he does not want to allow that history has 'an infinity of meanings, none any more right than another', nor is he happy with the notion that the only meaning history has is that which can be applied to some present purpose. But how does Carr attempt to escape from the predicament in which he finds himself? Put simply, Carr escapes from his problem by returning to a notion of 'the facts' that he has previously abandoned as excessively empirical. On page 23 he had claimed that 'by and large, the historian will get the kind of facts he wants. History means interpretation'. By page 28, however, more mindful now, perhaps, of the problems he faces, he states that '[the historian] must seek to bring into the picture all known or knowable facts relevant, in one sense or another, to the theme on which he is engaged and to the interpretation proposed'. He goes on then to give an orthodox empiricist account of how most historians write, moving back and forth from their writing to the sources, developing new questions, new insights, new hypotheses and so on, in a kind of dialectical manner – in Carr's words, 'moulding his facts to his interpretations and his interpretations to his facts' (1964, 29). Carr has re-installed the old view of facts which he was wanting to dispose of, that there are 'facts' out there independent of the writer and having some sort of existence apart from his or her mind.[1]

Here we have a real problem. On the one hand, I sense there is something wrong with what I have called the 'jigsaw-puzzle' approach to history-writing, which simply selects the facts that are needed to fit into the predesigned solution. On the other hand, Carr, at least in the first part of his first chapter, has shown the subjectivism inherent in history-writing – that facts are refracted and distorted before the historian gets them, and that he/she dissects and reshapes them even more in using them; that historians using 'facts' are in fact creating rather than simply reproducing them. The problem is that, to my mind, we need to acknowledge the truth of what Carr says about the role of selection and interpretation in history-writing, but

---

[1] For a similar critique of Carr's approach, made from a rather different perspective, see Munslow 1997.

on the other hand we need to realise that history-writing is, or in my mind should be, different from artistic and literary forms which are based on pure invention. What should we do? Is there some sort of middle ground that will give due credit to the role of interpretation and the selection and ordering of 'facts' in history-writing, but which will not deliver us into the hands of complete relativism and constructivism?

The first requirement, it appears to me, is to rescue the notion of 'fact' from the uncomfortable limbo to which it has been consigned by Carr and others. We need to assert that there is some real sense in which the facts are independent of the observer, because if we can't do this, if the fact is no more than invention and entirely subjective interpretation, there is no escape from the problem of relativism, a relativism which does not distinguish between varying accounts or which does so purely, for instance, on the basis of their literary merit. But how can we do this if the data are patchy and distorted, and becomes even more distorted when the historian uses them?

One way is to return to basics and sort out what we really mean when we talk about 'fact'. I argue that when we say 'fact', we really mean a 'proposition' or 'assertion'; 'facts' as historians use them are propositions that contain certain pieces of information, such as 'Sukarno became president of Indonesia in 1945' or 'Suharto died in 2008' or 'The price of rice in Java in 1830 was f3 [3 guilders] a picul'. Now, it seems to me to be an indispensable and distinguishing mark of the work of historians that they be able to say that propositions such as these are in some sense 'true', however qualified that assertion might be, or in some sense 'false'. What does it mean to say this? Essentially, it means that we say a proposition is true if it conveys information that accords with the event or happening (or whatever) of which it is an assertion; we say it is false if it does not so accord. I am aware, of course, that even the casting of 'facts' into the shape of 'assertions' entails some degree of theorising, the employment of a priori assumptions and values, and some inventiveness. Thus, the proposition 'Suharto was more evil than Sukarno' might require some further elaboration, even deconstruction. But the assertion is not in itself thereby unable to be declared true or false.

The bigger and more important question, however, and the place where Carr starts getting himself into difficulties, is the question of how one goes about establishing truth and falsity, especially when the data we have is so distorted, patchy and often unreliable. How can we say with any certainty or meaning that such-and-such is true or false? Even more to the point, how do we know that the result of the way we employ these propositions in writing our history is either true or false?

At this stage, I think we need to distinguish some separate meanings of the word 'truth'. For the sake of the argument, I want to distinguish two simple senses of the word 'truth'. The first is an absolute sense in which a proposition is true by definition. For example, 2 + 2 = 4. Given a certain sense of 2, of 4, of the notion of addition, and of the notion of the consequence of addition, there can be no dispute over the truthfulness of the proposition that 2 + 2 = 4. But this sort of truth is of no interest to historians, since it does not add to their stock of knowledge. Historians are usually concerned with another form of truth, which we might conveniently label as 'contingent truth', that is, when an assertion is true (or false) not by definition but by some other kind of test.

Here we are getting into fairly deep waters. What sort of criteria might serve as a means of establishing that we have arrived at a contingent truth? In my view, we do this by means of what might be called a 'set of general expectations'. If, for example, I drop my pen, I expect, other things being equal, that it will fall to the ground. In social life, in the relations of humans with humans, we develop much bigger, more complex and more sophisticated 'sets of general expectations'. For example, if I give my students the option of sitting a final examination or not, I would expect that most will choose to avoid the trauma associated with examinations. But this notion of a 'set of general expectations' needs closer analysis. How, for example, do I get such a thing? I think I get it from social observation, from self-reflection, from reading, from social theory, from experience with other people, from dealing with different situations, and so on. How precise it is? It is precise to the extent that I would expect certain consequences to occur from a certain happening given certain conditions and contexts. For example, I would expect the pen I dropped to fall to the floor unless, for example, somebody caught it, or it rested on some other object before hitting the floor, or someone removed the floor, or the law of gravity for some reason went into suspension. I would be surprised if the pen suddenly stopped in mid-air for no apparent reason, and I would want to know why. So, to return to the question of contingent truth, when I come to the study of 'the fact', I bring to it my set of general expectations and set them to work. It is this that allows me to assert that a proposition is more or less true or more or less false (that is, the notion of contingent truth); it is also this that allows me to select and arrange my propositions to tell a certain story.

I have recently published a book on the history of 'the idea of Indonesia' (Elson 2008). I know such an idea actually emerged because my 'set of general expectations' gives me no grounds for thinking that all the evidence available for its existence has been fabricated purely to deceive me and others. How do I start finding, selecting and ordering all the masses of data that are available to me to take my research forward? My 'set of general expectations' tells me that one place to start looking is the Dutch-language archives for information, since, other things being equal, relevant information is more likely to be found there, given the fact that the Dutch were the colonial masters in the archipelago in the nineteenth and early twentieth centuries, rather than in the archives of, say, Kenya or Peru. I arrange the material I select in certain patterns; again these are the result of my set of general expectations. I would expect, for example, that under certain conditions some things are more likely to have happened than others and that other things defy credibility, and I arrange my material accordingly.

In other words, the sense in which I write is very similar to the description Carr gives at the end of his first chapter; there is a no clear distinction between a research phase and a writing-up stage, but rather a continual interchange between my data and my writing. I bring my set of general expectations to the selection and ordering of the materials, but I frequently find things that are surprising or do not accord with my expectations. For example, I began my PhD thesis on a region in East Java in the nineteenth century with the expectation that certain kinds of colonial economic intrusion there would lead to peasant unrest and revolt. I was most surprised when I came to peruse the archive documents in the Netherlands only to find, with a single small exception, that this situation had clearly not arisen. My expectation (no doubt informed by a certain fixation with then predominant theories of social action) suggested to me that revolts had in fact taken place but that local Dutch officials had covered them up or ignored them or perhaps not even noticed them. That trail ran cold when I came to realise that many Dutch officials were not averse to reporting such events and, indeed, were prone to report them in excruciating detail when they did break out. Meanwhile, I was left wondering, whether I still had a thesis to write. So I had to go back and revise my set of general expectations, informing them with a much more appropriate and, I hope, much more sophisticated sense of the range of choices available to peasants, and this approach led me to the realisation, among other realisations, that for peasants in certain circumstances revolt was often very much a last resort rather than a first choice. It also meant that I had to go back to the data again with different questions and select different sorts of information, look for different clues, read the materials in different ways. In other words, I learned that history-writing means constantly going back and forth from the writing to the data (itself necessarily a changing field) and vice versa, constantly refining my general sets of expectations, making them more appropriate, more sophisticated and more intricate, and refining at the same time the way in which I put my materials together as a consequence of my more subtle and, I hoped, agile set of general expectations.

'Sets of general expectations'

There are some difficult problems with the view of things I have outlined. One such problem is that of differentiating between different 'sets of general expectations'. Is it the case that one person's set of general expectations is just as valid as everyone else's, and that we have therefore not really escaped from the problem of relativism? I think not. It seems to me that there are means available for testing and correcting and improving our individual sets of general expectations. Some sets of general expectations are better than others and it is precisely this quality which sets off good historians from bad ones and from very good ones and from outstanding ones.

A set of general expectations, for example, which is given to challenge, alive to complexity, and amenable to perceiving links between things that are not immediately evident, would seem to be a better set than one that is dogmatic and simplistic. Thus an explanation of the outbreak of the Indonesian revolution based on a set of general expectations that takes into account social conditions and popular feeling in Java in mid-1945, the operations of the Allied powers, the policies of the Japanese, the opportunities provided by the Second World War, the intransigence of the Dutch, and so on, would be preferable to one that focuses purely on the personality and behaviour of Sukarno. By the same token, a set of general expectations that is internally coherent is preferable, better, and truer than one that is riddled with internal contradictions. In other words, I am arguing that sets of general expectations are not purely matters of whim or arbitrary choice, that some are better than others, and that there can be contests between them that can be resolved.

A second problem might be that our sets of general expectations are no more than particular reflections of our present-day situation, and that when we do history, we simply mould the data of the past to our present conceptions and concerns. There is certainly a sense in which that is true. We have concerns and interests today, as well as ways of discussing and analysing things, which were not a part of the past. We are, for example, much more interested in the fate of women, or of ordinary people, or of peasants, and we indulge ourselves in such notions as 'identity' or 'memory' in ways that would puzzle the early chronicle writers of Indonesia. We also have categories of social analysis such as demographic theory, elite theory, game theory and even critical theory that help us to analyse things in ways these earlier writers would have found unimaginable or nonsensical. At the same time, however, these present-day categories are not altogether delimiting and defining. They do not, of themselves, prevent us from understanding at least something of what a nineteenth century peasant or a revolutionary fighter or a Javanese general felt, or how they might reasonably be expected to have acted in the context in which they found themselves. One of the greatest skills of the historian is to rise above and see beyond the categories of the present day to achieve some understanding of the past. It is difficult to do this, and even more difficult to do it well; we need continually to refine and refurbish our set of general expectations to do it, but it can in principle be done.

Where has all this discussion brought us? I hope it is to see that there is some middle ground between arbitrary relativism on the one hand and the compilation of meaningless empirical 'facts' on the other. The key is to be found in the notion of contingent truth, that is, propositions that are not necessarily true, but can be said to be so on the basis of a set of general expectations that is moulded by the experience of living. The truth of these propositions is always partial and never total, and always subject to modification, elaboration, revision and re-evaluation. What we decide to be true one day we may realise is false the next day. The reason we change our minds is not pure whim or arbitrary choice, but because we realise that our set of general expectations has not been equal to the task of understanding, and that it needs further enhancement and modification. Moreover, it is part and parcel of this argument that the choice of sets of general expectations is not just a matter of invention or whim. Some sets are better, more refined, more sophisticated, more sensitive, more aware than others, and we therefore should choose them rather than less appropriate and clumsy ones. It follows from this, as well, that some histories are better than others and that one can choose rationally between competing histories not just on the grounds of their literary merit or internal logic, but on the grounds of the accuracy with which they deal with the past, and the significance, aligned with accuracy, that they draw from it.

History's uses

If historians can claim to achieve, if only in a provisional, partial and always revisable sense, some significant sense of the truth of the past, does it follow that they have an obligation to use that knowledge in the services of better state policy-making or in the pursuit of activist causes? In other words, should the knowledge of historians have practical and more or less immediate utility? At bottom, this problem of utility comes down to finding answers to two questions. First, does history give us lessons which can be employed in present or future activities? Second, if it does, how should those lessons be applied? And by whom?

One of the challenges of history-writing is to explain, with the greatest possible precision and care, why a particular outcome occurred rather than some other possible outcome; to put the matter in Legge's terms, the special concern of the historian is not with 'the sort of thing that occurred' but rather 'what in fact occurred and with the fact that it happened in one way rather than another and at one time rather than another' (Legge 1976, 399). In other words, there is a certain characteristic particularism about history-writing that might imply that it contains no generalisable principles. That implication, however, is untenable because, as I have argued, the only way historians can arrive at explanations of the historical problems they address is to use working generalisations – what I have termed 'sets of general expectations' – which tell them what they might expect to happen under certain conditions and in certain contexts. That is, we can construct certain expectations about how people might behave in certain circumstances, and how larger social forces might impact upon them. This, of course, is what we do in our normal everyday lives – thus, I expect that if I plunge my hand into boiling water, the hand will, other things being equal, be scalded. History-writing, then, is fundamentally concerned in its very process with generalisation.

The second question is more troublesome: if there are lessons in history, how should they be applied? Can the specialised, detailed, particularised knowledge that historians possess allow them to act as 'a powerful positive force in society'? Some people think so. Some of us might recall the intervention of Geoffrey Blainey in the so-called 'immigration debate' in Australia in the mid-1980s. He based his authority to intervene on his expertise in Australian history. Indeed, he is reported to have said that 'my interpretation was essentially based on my knowledge of Australian history. I was speaking very much as a historian' (in Markus 1985, 10). One lesson of Australian history, if I may so paraphrase Blainey's views, is that there are certain circumstances where you can't put different ethnic groups together. We in Australia are doing this today, he went on, under these certain circumstances, and therefore there will be trouble.

Is this kind of intervention by Blainey, or by historians more generally, socially useful and acceptable? The answer lies in the kinds of claims being made, and for their transferability to other contexts. When we draw a lesson from history we do two things: we accept something about the specific character of a person or event, and we specify certain conditions. For example, when I generalise about people dropping pens onto the floor, I assert something about the nature of objects when constrained by the law of gravity, and I specify certain conditions, for example, that no one will catch the pen before it hits the floor. In order to explain such happenings, I need to have an insight into the character of the thing I am inquiring into and I need to specify closely and accurately the conditions under which it will behave in certain ways rather than others, or not at all. This is where things get tricky, because it is uncomfortably easy to get things wrong, to ignore or not give due weight to certain conditions or to misjudge the character of the thing we are examining. Consequently, in normal life, we use lessons that are partly general and flexible, so that if we do get things wrong, the consequences won't be too bad. We can also apply general rules of thumb (another name for generalised lessons of history) to a large number of situations that confront us daily. Moreover, the more general the lesson, that is, the less the number and specificity of the conditions we attach to it, the more likely it is to be correct, durable and thus socially useful.

Clearly, the more we want to specify a lesson, the more difficult it is to get it right and the more careful and precise we need to be in applying it. This problem is the great danger in applying specific lessons from history to specific present or future circumstances. The more complicated and particular those lessons are, the more easily we get them wrong or misunderstand them, or improperly contextualise them, or misapply them. In other words, if we act to draw lessons from history, we need to do so with great care and only after very thorough examination of the particular character or nature of the person or event under consideration and the particular circumstances under which certain things took place. Otherwise, we run the risk of missing or misunderstanding vital variables that made things turn out this way rather than that way. This is particularly dangerous when the lessons are applied by institutions that affect us all, like governments. It would, in my view, have been disastrous had the Australian government agreed with Blainey about the lessons of Australian history he wanted to promulgate and sought to apply them by stopping immigration from Asia. Similarly, it would be similarly concerning, not to mention cavalier, were Australia to adopt a more relaxed, even encouraging policy towards changes to the territorial boundaries of Indonesia, simply because one scholar drew the lesson that 'the politics of contesting and redrawing political boundaries *never ends*' and because that kind of policy would allow Australia to be 'on the right side of history' (Burchill 2000, italics in original).

Conclusion

We need to be careful about how and where we apply the lessons we have learned, and the more careful the more specific we want to be. But does this prescription then mean that historians have no social responsibility, that even if they discover important lessons they should not attempt to benefit themselves and their societies as well by having those lessons applied in public policy? It all depends on the sort of lesson that the historian wants applied. If the lesson is a generalised one, such as 'reading good literature makes people wiser', I would have no complaint and vigorously fight for the establishment of more and better libraries, schools, universities and so on. But my concern would grow as the lesson to be applied gets more complicated and more specific. I would need to look very carefully at the purported lesson, exactly what it meant and what it specified, be satisfied that it was accurately drawn from the past and applied appropriately and contextually in the present.

My position comes not as a denial of the historian's social responsibility, but rather arises out of the knowledge of just how difficult it is to gain full insight into the nature of things, and to grasp all the sufficient and necessary conditions that makes things turn out in certain ways – in short, my always developing awareness of the essentially contingent, fragile nature of knowledge that the historian establishes. Put another way, it is history's 'inability ever to secure what are effectively interpretive closures' (Jenkins and Muslow 2004, 3). History, it has been said, is among the more conservative of disciplines:

> [C]onservative… in the larger sense of inculcating skepticism about people's ability to manipulate and control purposefully their own destinies. By showing that the best laid plans of people usually go awry, the study of history tends to dampen youthful enthusiasm and to restrain the can-do, the conquer-the-future spirit that many people have (Wood 1984, 10).

Robert Cribb makes the same point more elegantly and restrainedly:

> [H]istorical consciousness refers to the way that knowing about the past expands our sense of the human experience as a basis for which we can plan for the future. The dilemma in every human aspiration is to understand what is possible and what is not possible, so that we know more precisely where to put our efforts, whether on the one hand to

avert catastrophe and to achieve success or on the other hand simply to avoid wasting effort on things that cannot be changed. The social value of history lies in its vast repertoire of complex human experience ... (Cribb 2008, 207–208).

One can so easily get things wrong, or weigh things misleadingly, or ignore nuances and contexts. This knowledge of the characteristic imperfections of the result of our work make me wary about applying complicated, and thus necessarily contestable, lessons from the past to a similar (and perhaps even more) complicated present and future. Doing history means dealing with unending complications, and that inevitably should make the historian a meticulous, cautious, skeptical and, yes, even conservative operator.

Perhaps our greatest social responsibility is to be critical of those who think they enjoy command of such complex lessons in those areas of our own special expertise (and not theirs) and who want to impose them on us all. Historians, precisely by the nature of their engagement with the complexities of truth, at least as I have described it, should be the skeptical 'watchdogs' of their specialised truths. They must engage in matters of public importance, and they must communicate, as best they can, their specialised knowledge by way of careful criticism and incisive commentary. It is there, and not in areas of activism, advocacy and policy-making, which are necessarily less nuanced and more generalised, indeed, often prophetic, and which have a public and unspecialised audience, that historians can perhaps best exercise the vocation of being 'a powerful positive force in society'. Such modesty in engagement might seem unduly limiting, but it is the necessary implication of and most accurately reflects the complex intellectual activity that is history-writing.

References

Burchill, Scott. 2000. 'Australia and Asia: towards new rules of engagement'. Accessed 18 February 2009. Available from: http://www.scottburchill.net/laverton.html.

Caldwell, Malcolm; Utrecht, Ernst. 1979. *Indonesia: An Alternative History*, Sydney: Alternative Publishing Co-operative.

Carr, E H. 1964. *What is History?* Harmondsworth: Penguin.

Cook, Benjamin. 2007. 'Rival imaginings: Nationalism, education and Iraq's Arab Shi'a, 1921–1941'. BA honours thesis, University of Queensland.

Cribb, Robert. 2008. 'Pak Sartono and historical consciousness'. In *Sejarah Yang Memihak: Mengenang Sartono Kartodirdjo*, edited by Nursam, M; Wardaya, Baskara

T; Warman Adam, Asvi. Yogyakarta: Ombak: 206–208.

Elson, R E. 2008. *The Idea of Indonesia: A History*. Cambridge: Cambridge University Press.

Jenkins, Keith; Munslow, Alun. 2004. 'Introduction'. In *The Nature of History Reader*, edited by Jenkins, Keith; Munslow, Alun. London: Routledge: 1–18.

Johns, A H, 1979. 'The turning image: myth and reality in Malay perceptions of the past'. In *Perceptions of the Past in Southeast Asia*, edited by Reid, Anthony; Marr, David. Singapore: Heinemann: 43–67.

Legge, J D. 1976. 'Southeast Asian history and the social sciences'. In *Southeast Asian History and Historiography: Essays Presented to D. G. E. Hall*, edited by Cowan, C D; Wolters, O W. Ithaca, NY: Cornell University Press: 388–404.

Markus, Andrew. 1985. '1984 or 1901? 'Immigration and some "lessons" of Australian history'. In *Surrender Australia? Essays in the Study and Uses of History*, edited by Markus, Andrew; Ricklefs, M C. Sydney: Allen & Unwin: 10–35.

Munslow, Alun. 1997. 'Book review (reappraisal): What is history?'. Accessed 27 June 2008. Available from: http://www.history.ac.ukihr/Focua/Whatishistory/carr1.html.

Paget, Roger K. 1975. *Indonesia Accuses! Soekarno's Defence Oration in the Political Trial of 1930*. Kuala Lumpur: Oxford University Press.

Wood, Gordon S. 1984. 'History lessons', *New York Review of Books* (29 March): 10.

Chapter 4

The Politics of Studying Indonesian Politics

Intellectuals, Political Research and Public Debate in Australia

Edward Aspinall

Indonesia occupies a fraught place in Australian domestic political debate. The country looms much larger on Australia's political horizon than it does in other Western countries (the Netherlands was an obvious exception for a long time, but as the memory of the colonial experience fades, so does interest in Indonesia). In popular Australian political culture, Indonesia elicits a jumble of fear, fascination and hope, mixed, of course, with a great dose of indifference. Over the last two decades alone, it has been seen as, alternately and often simultaneously, a focus of dreams of economic redemption, a key to deeper integration in East Asia, a harsh and repressive military regime that should be within Australia's power to change, a site of chaotic and threatening political disorder 'on our doorstep', a site for emancipatory Australian military intervention, a tropical holiday land where hapless Australian youths are in danger of being swept up into a punitive anti-narcotics regime, and a breeding ground of violent and hostile Islamic terrorists. Underlying all this, it remains a source of inchoate invasion fears for a significant part of the population.

Large sections of the Australian public know Indonesia directly, if only through the experience of holidays in Bali, although a growing number have more intimate knowledge. Yet public perceptions of the country remain generally negative. A 2006 survey of Australians, found that 'Respondents felt that Indonesia was essentially controlled by the military, that Indonesia was a dangerous source of Islamic terrorism and that Australia was right to worry about Indonesia as a military threat' (Cook 2006, 2). Although views were somewhat warmer when a similar survey was conducted in 2010, '[a]sked whether "Indonesia is more of a threat to Australia or less of a threat than it was 15 years ago, or has there been no change", 38 per cent of Australians said there has been "no change" and 33 per cent said it was "more of a threat" ' (Hanson 2010, 6). At the same time, successive Australian governments have viewed building good relations with Indonesia as crucial to Australia's future economic prosperity and security. Australia's largest embassy is in Jakarta, and the city is most frequently visited by Australian ministers and even the prime minister. Moreover, Indonesia is now the greatest recipient of Australian overseas development assistance.

As a result of this context, the scholarly study of Indonesia is potentially more politicised, and fraught in Australia than in other developed countries. A straw poll of practitioners I conducted while preparing this article seemed to confirm this guess. In more or less equal numbers, those I asked to give instant characterisations of the study of Indonesian politics in Australia gave strikingly contrasting answers: some suggested that the field was elitist, narrow and politically disengaged; others said that most Indonesianists were inappropriately activist and politically biased. Different sorts of people gave the contrasting answers, and they obviously had different bodies of work, and individual scholars, in mind. Nevertheless, it was remarkable that there could be such highly charged and such contrasting evaluations.

In this chapter, I suggest that there may be some truth in both such characterisations and discuss public political engagement on Indonesia among Australian academics, focusing especially on scholars who work on Indonesian politics, but also straying into other fields of scholarly endeavour as appropriate. I look at three levels of structure and context that shape scholarly interest in Indonesian politics in Australia: the national political context, the institutional setting of the public university system where most Australian academics work, and what I call the structures of affect which underpin the motivations and drive the interests of most scholars engaged in the study of Indonesia. Although generally hidden behind a screen of appeals to scholarly objectivity and rigour, academics are also 'members of specific cultures and social orders' (Anderson 1982, 69), and to a large extent our enquiries are guided or at least constrained by the assumptions of those cultures and the imperatives of those orders.

I survey varied forms of political engagement and public commentary on Indonesia by scholars, considering how the different structures can produce different sorts of public postures. With some stylisation and even exaggeration, I divide these variants into three main strands. First, a so-called 'Jakarta lobby', emphasising Indonesian security, stability and economic growth, and improved inter-governmental ties, was always weaker among Indonesia specialists than was sometimes suggested in the past. However, a practical and policy-oriented perspective on both Indonesian politics and Australia–Indonesia relations remains influential, and has arguably become even more so since Indonesian democratisation began in the late 1990s. Second are scholars who emphasise human rights advocacy and who view Indonesia through the prism of East Timor and Papua and according to a narrative of 'Australian betrayal' of those struggles. The third, and most numerous, strand consists of academics who hold liberal and progressive political views, are personally fascinated by Indonesian society and are committed to increasing public knowledge of, and sympathy for, Indonesia. Of course, these categories are ideal types, and in practice there are many overlaps, at least between the third group and the other two.

Scholarship on Indonesia in Australia, especially among the third group, is characterised by specialisation, both in terms of scholarly apprenticeship (acquisition of high-level language skills, lengthy fieldwork, etc.) and fields of individual research. Several factors mean that most scholars from the third group intentionally or unintentionally avoid public political debate on Indonesia. A result is that much public debate on Indonesia in Australia is dominated by individuals from the first two groups, who lack Indonesia expertise, and takes the form of a projection of domestic Australian controversy onto an Indonesian canvas.

Political science and the study of Indonesia

A recent and important volume by mostly American political scientists surveys the contribution that studies of Southeast Asia have made to the field of political science (Kuhonta et al. (eds) 2008). The book has many merits, but one thing that will be striking for most Australian scholars of Indonesian politics is how it raises fundamental questions that are rarely asked in Australia about the compatibility of Southeast Asian studies and political science as a discipline. Although Australian scholars do sometimes think about such questions, this book is marked by a seriousness of purpose, almost an angst, that is largely absent from analysis by scholars of Southeast Asia in Australia.

Take, for example, American Indonesianist Donald Emmerson's chapter entitled 'Southeast Asia in political science: Terms of enlistment'. Not surprisingly, Emmerson (like the volume as a whole) mounts a spirited defence of the necessity of area studies knowledge – language, understanding of historical and cultural context and all the rest – in the face of the claims of the proponents of rational choice theory, quantitative analysis and big-N datasets who have dominated most American political science departments over the last couple of decades. He begins his chapter with a quotation from one such author, David Laitin, who suggests that rational choice theories are becoming so powerful as a universal explanatory framework and that: 'The idea of having a political science specialist for every piece of international real estate may soon be seen as arcane as having a specialist for every planet in the astronomy department' (Emmerson 2009, 203, citing Laitin 1993). It is against such claims – claims to having access to general rules governing all human political behaviour that can be tested in a scientific way – that the Southeast Asia politics specialists must defend themselves in the United States. They have done so in a mere echo of a much large debate, which went under the name of 'Perestroika' in American political science over the last ten years or so, in which adherents of case study and qualitative research tried to launch what one book detailing the debate called a 'raucous rebellion' against the domination of the field by rational choice paradigms and quantitative methods (Monroe 2005). This defence takes place, it should also be added, in a context where our US colleagues have experienced a significant decline of traditional area studies (Fukuyama 2004), and where many experts of Indonesian politics find themselves as lone Southeast Asia experts in political science departments with little interest in the Asian region, and where they have to justify their research choices to strict disciplinarians and comparativists, especially in the context of appointment, tenure and promotions.

Indonesian studies is in many respects an international endeavour, and it is typically written about in this way (see for example Cribb 2005). However, in observing this debate in the American academy, I was struck by how little it has been considered or engaged with by persons in Australia whose professional lives revolve around the study of Indonesian politics. Those of us who work on Indonesian politics in this country rarely feel inclined to justify or defend ourselves in disciplinary or even theoretical terms; we rarely attend general political science conferences or publish in general comparative politics or theoretical journals as opposed to area studies ones. Indeed, I suspect, although I have no concrete data to support it, that most academics who teach and research Indonesian politics in Australia have not had extended postgraduate coursework training – and sometimes not even undergraduate training – in political science.

This is not to say that those who research and teach the politics of Indonesia do not feel the need to justify themselves and what they do in Australia. On the contrary, they frequently do so. However, when they do, they tend to do so by defending the relevance of Indonesia to Australia, and hence justifying the importance of sophisticated study and understanding of Indonesia. This is a debate, in other words, that largely occurs in the public sphere and is pitched in policy and national interest terms, not in strictly academic ones. This difference in turn reflects the very different way that Indonesian studies is carried on in Australia compared to in the United States. One obvious difference is the fact that a significant proportion of Australian specialists of Indonesian politics are located in Asian, Southeast Asian or Indonesian studies centres or departments rather than in political science departments. This is difficult to quantify, but one starting point is a list of 157 Indonesia experts recently compiled by Helen Pausacker (2009: 119–123). Of the 38 persons noted in that list as including 'politics' as one of their fields, just under half (18) are located in Asian, Southeast Asian or Indonesian studies programs, schools or centres. Of the remainder, about half are located in large catch-all units produced by university rationalisation, restructuring and reorganisation over the last two decades (such as schools of arts, of humanities and languages or of international studies). Half again (or about a quarter of the total) are located in departments, programs or schools of politics and international relations (or close cognates). Of that number, my guess is that only about half would view Indonesia as the major focus of their scholarly research, leaving less than 10 Indonesia specialists located in political studies departments around Australia.[1] This initial observation is a starting point for considering what sorts of contexts shape the nature of the Indonesian political studies in Australia. It seems to me that three contexts are the most important.

---

[1] To further complicate matters, some of these individuals are also affiliated with Asian or Southeast Asian studies programs or centres, or their departments are themselves located in over-arching area studies institutions (my own Department of Political and Social Change, located in the College of Asia and Pacific (formerly the Research School of Pacific and Asian Studies) at the Australian National University).

Political context

Several decades ago, Benedict Anderson analysed the dominant thematic concerns and methodologies in American studies of Indonesia in terms of an underlying American 'cultural paradigm', which he said 'assumes a natural and inextricable interconnection between private enterprise and property (capitalism), constitutional democracy, personal liberty and progress' (Anderson 1982, 70). In his view, this paradigm interacted with the changing contours of domestic political dynamics in Indonesia and of America's role in the region to produce two varieties of liberal scholarship on Indonesia, which he labelled 'anti-colonial' and 'imperial' liberalism.

In general terms, the Australian cultural paradigm is similar in its content to the American one identified by Anderson, although we might argue about the margins. Where Australians' perceptions of themselves and their country's place in the world are clearly different from those in the United States is in terms of scope and ambition. Given that for much of the last century the United States has been the major global power, the scope and ambition of the American cultural paradigm has been almost without limit. It has also lent itself to the assumption that American values are – or should be – universal ones, with sometimes disastrous foreign policy results. It is in this context that we see the rise in American political science of attempts to devise universally applicable theories of political behaviour that eschew local cultural context and which are based on the quintessentially capitalist notion that politics is simply the playing out of calculations made by interest-maximising individuals. We might say that global power gives rise to attempts to devise globally applicable theories explaining social and political behaviour.[2]

In Australia, the situation is different. Australia is much more modest and insecure in its global role. It is not a global hegemon but a middle-level power (Cooper et al. 1993). Moreover, the relationship between Australia and Indonesia is rather special and unique (unlike that between the US and Indonesia, which is a relationship simply of imperial centre to one among many subordinates). Australian attitudes to Indonesia share much of the indifference and condescension expressed in advanced countries about underdeveloped ones. Historically, the British origins of Australian society and the White Australia Policy added a dose of paranoia and hostility in

---

[2] See Amadae 2003 for an elaboration of the Cold War origins of the rational choice approach.

attitudes to Indonesia and to Asia more generally (Burke 2008). However, attitudes have changed much over recent decades. In Australian official political discourse, foreign policy calculations and security planning, Indonesia has been seen variously as a pivotal and important country for Australia: the key to greater economic integration into the Asian region, a major source of security threats, and so forth. Moreover, Indonesia plays a role in popular political culture and debate which it can never do in the United States: as a source of invasion fears, exemplar of the foreign 'Other' on our doorstep, brutal oppressor of peoples who as inhabitants of 'our' sphere of influence 'we' should be able to protect, and so on.

One obvious result is that there has been significant support in the government and among education policy-makers for the study of Indonesia in Australia, with it generally being acknowledged that the Australian contribution to the scholarly study of Indonesia is, at the very least, disproportionate to the country's population and to its contribution in most other fields of scholarly endeavour (Graf 2009, 200). But what else does this context impart to the study of Indonesian politics in Australia? No doubt there are many effects, but two seem especially important. First, it provides relevance: a public audience for discussion of Indonesia that is lacking in the United States or other major Western countries, and a need on the part of government for expert advice and especially, training of personnel. Second, it produces specialisation: Australian academics who research Indonesia are generally able to specialise to a degree that is rare elsewhere. These observations lead us back to the shape of the Indonesian studies field in the Australian academy.

The academic political economy

So what is the institutional context of the academy which produces the mixture of professional incentives and constraints that go towards producing specialist knowledge about Indonesian politics in Australia?

The obvious point to make is the one I made at the outset: it is an academic setting based around an Indonesian area studies context that stresses deep and specialised knowledge of the language, culture and history of the country before one can speak authoritatively about its politics. Most Australian academic experts on Indonesia were trained and now teach and research in such a setting. This is not the only setting in which studies of Indonesian politics are conducted in Australia, but it is the dominant one. Moreover, Australian academics of Indonesian politics rarely believe that by studying Indonesia they will be equipped to study other countries, or at least this is rarely their aim. Unlike in the United States, with few exceptions Australian Indonesianists do not go on to conduct detailed or sustained studies of other places.

To be sure, this Indonesian area studies context has been threatened over the last two decades by the increasing dominance of neo-liberal principles in the higher education sector and its reorganisation along market principles. This shift has posed difficulties for Indonesian studies given generally low student numbers in Indonesian and Southeast Asian studies programs. Especially over the last 15 years, Indonesian studies academics in Australia have been increasingly worried about the decline of learning of the Indonesian language in both schools and universities, and gripped by fears about a resulting crisis in Indonesian studies. With universities increasingly organised on the basis of decentralised models in which individual departments and programs are distinct budget units which, in most cases, derive the lion's share of their funding from student income, declining student numbers do indeed pose a major challenge to the survival of Indonesian studies in many campuses. Programs have been closed, especially in regional and smaller universities. In a recent report, it has been noted that the number of universities offering Indonesian language programs has dropped from a high of 28 in 2001 to 15 by 2010 (Hill 2010), although the contraction may in part be seen as a correction after a large increase in the number of such programs between 1988 and 2001 (Hill 2010, 1).

However, the key point is that, unlike in the United States, Indonesia area studies scholars in Australia have been able to mount relatively successful rearguard actions against such pressures, and even take advantage of new opportunities provided by new competitive funding arrangements (notably the expansion of the research grants provided by the Australian Research Council, which have flowed to Australian Indonesia specialists with a relative ease that make us the envy of our American colleagues). The defence of Indonesian studies has largely been carried out by appealing to the larger national interest framework about the importance of Indonesia to Australia. In other words, this has not been a battle waged within university departments expressed in terms of the relative merits of deep country knowledge versus comparative, quantitative or theoretical approaches. Instead, it has largely taken place in formal and informal meetings between senior academics and policy-makers and, when things get tough, in the media. During the years of Prime Minister Paul Keating

(1991–1996), seen at the time as marking a qualitative jump forward in Australia's 'Asian engagement', scholars made these arguments by echoing what was then the government's mantra about greater economic integration into the Asia–Pacific region. During the years of Prime Minister John Howard (1996–2007) and in the aftermath of the collapse of the Suharto regime, the Australian intervention in East Timor and the terrorist bombings in Indonesia, these arguments were often reframed in security terms.[3] The defence of Indonesian studies in these terms – especially after the Bali bombings of 2002 – has been relatively successful, especially in that many language programs have survived despite declining enrolments. One obvious example is the Indonesian studies program at the University of Sydney, which was under threat in the mid-2000s, but was saved after a lobbying and media campaign by staff and sympathisers.[4]

The irony is that many specialists of Indonesian studies are not especially personally committed to arguments that position Indonesia primarily as a source of economic benefit or security threats to Australia and Australians, and might in fact be personally repelled by them. They are not the concerns which motivated them to study Indonesia, they are not the reasons they view the study of Indonesia as important, and they are not the sort of things they believe to be important in the Australia–Indonesia relationship. Before I go on to look at the influence of such personal views in more detail, there are a few more points to make about the effect of this broader political context on the shape of Indonesian studies.

Arguably the most important effect is to generate a certain style of scholarship: practical and easily comprehended by a general and policy-oriented audience, and seeking to lay out in readily comprehensible terms the composition, outlook and internal dynamics of the Indonesian governing elite and the country's political and social dynamics more broadly. Much of the writing on Indonesian politics in Australia is noteworthy for its lucidity and accessibility, rather than for its deep engagement with complex theoretical argumentation or its framing in the stylistic conventions of mainstream political science (although of course there are many exceptions). In the New Order era, Australian policy-makers wanted to know about the key institutions and decision-makers, and how best to understand their

---

[3] For one eloquent example, see Tim Lindsey, 'Learn the lingo to earn from Asia', the *Australian* (Higher Education Supplement) 26 August 2009.

[4] See, in particular, Louise Williams, 'Fading expertise in close neighbour', *Sydney Morning Herald*, 10 September 2004; Bernard Lane, 'Indonesian rescued', the *Australian* (Higher Education Supplement) 17 August 2005.

interests and modes of behaviour. Since the New Order, a sort of practical 'reform orientation' has come to characterise much of the writing about Indonesian politics in Australia, where the main questions asked concern the major obstacles encountered in Indonesia's political reform, and how they are being, or might be, fixed (Crouch 2010 is an excellent example). All of this does not mean that Australian Indonesian politics specialists have a policy audience or wider public consciously in mind when they write their scholarly work. Nevertheless, the possibility of such an audience, and the broader policy context that shapes our institutional homes, shadow their work and exercise a subtle influence on it.

There are particular institutional structures that accelerate these tendencies. For instance, there is the special place of the Australian National University (ANU) in all this. It is not only that the overall weight of the ANU's contribution to the field is so great (according to one recent assessment 'the ISI-indexed output of the Australian National University (ANU) is alone by far bigger than that of any other institution engaged in Indonesian Studies worldwide, and in fact even bigger than that of all institutions in the Netherlands combined' (Graf 2009, 200). Even more relevant are the ANU's physical proximity to the centre of national government, and its status as a site where the interchange between policy and academia is especially intense. Consequently, the various tendencies towards realist, policy-oriented, practical, even elitist studies of Indonesian society are arguably strongest at the ANU. But there are also other institutions that contribute to the impetus for a practical, national interest oriented style of Indonesian studies scholarship, with support for policy-oriented research and research support provided by other products of the Australian–Indonesia relationship, notably the massive AusAID-funded higher degree scholarships scheme and much smaller grant programs such as the (short-lived) Australia–Indonesia Governance Research Partnership and the Australia–Netherlands Research Collaboration (ANRC) scheme, both of which had an explicit policy orientation and an Indonesia or Southeast Asia focus. The Australian Research Council has also taken into account 'national interest' arguments, allowing every Indonesia scholar who applies to stress in their application the central importance of Indonesia for Australia and of the development of robust Indonesia knowledge.

Another important change over the last decade or so is not so much due to the Australian context, but more to do with the broader international attempt to remake Indonesia in the image of a modern liberal democracy. Since the collapse of the Suharto regime, major donors, international agencies and NGOs have poured many millions of dollars into such diverse programs as building democratic institutions, peacebuilding, election monitoring, Islamic civil society programs, and so on (Aspinall 2010). The rise of this 'democracy assistance' industry focused on Indonesia has also generated demand for expert consultants and for staff with Indonesia knowledge and other relevant skills. The new political consultancy opportunities have generated both a source of additional income and new research opportunities for at least a group of Australian academics who specialise on Indonesia, and the democracy assistance industry more generally has emerged as an important alternative career path for Australian graduates of Indonesian studies and former students who have participated in exchange programs in Indonesia (notably in the influential but dwindling program organised by ACICIS, the Australian Consortium for In-Country Indonesian Studies). Bodies like the Asia Foundation and any number of big international NGOs, also certain parts of the World Bank, USAID, the International Crisis Group and similar bodies have recruited many Australian graduates, and employed established academics as consultants.

It is difficult to pronounce definitively on the impact of the development of the democracy assistance world for scholarship, because it is relatively new and may prove to be largely ephemeral, but I think it is having an impact. Consultancy partly counters the trend to extreme specialisation that we see among Australian Indonesia experts, because the agencies seek generalists. Most importantly, it reinforces the tendency to adopt a practical outlook rather than a theoretical position, and a practical outlook that is unquestioningly placed within a normative framework favouring democratisation and the development of liberal institutions. Thus, although on the one hand the general institutional context allows for specialisation on and within Indonesia; on the other, the growing influence of political consultancy and policy-oriented studies imparts a certain reform-oriented practicality to much of the writing generated by Australian specialists on Indonesian politics.

Structures of affect

In addition to political context and academic political economy, a third layer of context is much harder to analyse and articulate: the influence of personal background, proclivities and experiences in motivating research agendas and styles. I would suggest, however, that it is as important as these other factors.

Affect plays a big role in determining who is attracted to the study of Indonesia. Indeed, it is striking for anyone who has taught in Indonesian studies programs just how little calculations about national interest or personal career play in influencing the choices of many students to study Indonesian. Most students are instead motivated by personal experience – a childhood connection with Indonesia, a personal interest in the 'Other', a fascination with crossing cultural borders, the impact of a personal relationship, a church exchange, a boyfriend or a girlfriend, a marriage, often an inspiring high school teacher, more occasionally an inspiring lecturer. As Barbara Hatley (2009) documents in her personal account of her first encounters with Indonesia in the 1960s and 1970s, there are important generational differences here: the experiences of the Indonesianists who were recruited around the time of the late 1960s early 1970s counter-culture were somewhat different from those of my generation who first studied Indonesia in the late 1980s and 1990s, and of undergraduates today. For one thing, it seems to me that whereas that earlier generation's first footholds in Indonesian society were cultural (involvement in a traditional art form, or a theatre group, or a fascination with literature, for example), today they are just as likely to be political (involvement in an NGO, an environmental group, or the like).

Out of this mass of highly varied personal experiences, I think most insiders would be able to identify a certain type who is predominant in the Australian Indonesianist scene: a person with a certain sort of soft left political sensibility, a commitment to pluralism, and a fascination with cultural difference. Again, participants in the field will be able to think of exceptions, but most will probably agree with the generalisation. Perhaps it is not surprising that this should be so: humanities scholars and social scientists are generally on the left in all Western societies (see for example Fosse and Gross 2010), and social scientists working on non-Western societies probably especially so. Such personal backgrounds and inclinations in turn influence the choice of topics to do with Indonesia that are studied and researched. In Australian academe, these often focus on this or that sector of Indonesian progressive life, whether in the arts, social movements, civil society, or the intelligentsia, or on this or that problem, form of oppression or inequality experienced by this or that sector of Indonesian society and the power structures that make such things possible. One could say that the outlook of the typical Australian Indonesia expert roughly conforms with the outlook presented in the magazine, now online, *Inside Indonesia*. This outlet presents itself as aiming to 'provide a deeper image of Indonesia than that painted by mainstream media' and as focusing on 'human rights, environmental, social and political issues' though not being limited to those issues'.[5] It is indeed significant that *Inside Indonesia* is one of the longest-lasting institutions in the Australian Indonesian studies scene, being founded in 1983, and that it survives almost entirely without institutional support, but relies instead on the voluntary labour and financial contributions from Indonesianists (although now increasingly also drawing in persons from beyond Australia). It hence can be seen as being fairly representative of a broadly shared political outlook among Indonesia experts, and it is noteworthy that almost every Australian Indonesian expert of note has written for the magazine at least once.

So by personal outlook, most Australian scholars of Indonesian politics (obviously there are exceptions) are pulled in the opposite direction of the current generated by the dictates of the wider institutional and political context. If the institutional context requires a practical approach and an elite orientation, personal proclivities push towards specialisation and the study of the politics of, if not resistance, at least reform.

Is there a distinctive Australian style of studying Indonesian politics?

Of course, it is still very hard to generalise. This is both because of the overall small numbers of participants involved, and because the work they produce is highly varied. But if we do generalise, some observations can be made. Firstly, in the Australian Indonesian studies scene, including that concerned with the study of politics, high value is placed on specialisation, both in terms of scholarly apprenticeship (the acquisition of high-level language skills and of lengthy fieldwork and in-country immersion) and typically in terms of topic as well. Indonesianists in Australia tend to judge their peers in terms of how they know a particular Islamic group or a region, for example, which they claim as falling within their area of expertise.

---

5   'About us', *Inside Indonesia* website. Accessed 2 February 2011. Available from: http://www.insideindonesia.org/about-us/about-us. In the interests of disclosure, I must note that I am one of the coordinating editors.

Secondly, there is a tendency to empiricism. Emphasis is placed on the collection of facts in the field, especially from personal interviews with key political actors, rather than collection of information from less direct sources; high value is also placed on being 'up to date' (it is no coincidence that one of the key institutions in the field is the annual Indonesia Update conference at the Australian National University).

Thirdly, there is also a tendency – again not a universal one – to avoid theorising and comparison, or at least to limit the range of theoretical exploration to a few core themes or topics (see Philpott 2000, 145–46 for the key themes, although we would now need to add democratisation to his list). There is of course a practical dimension to this: accumulating language expertise, fieldwork skills and connections, and detailed knowledge on one's chosen topic is an all-consuming set of tasks which, when added to all the teaching and other burdens that are part of contemporary academic life, can leave little time for theoretical exploration (the absence of a coursework component in Australian PhD programs probably also contributes). It is not that most Australian scholars working on Indonesian politics are anti-theory; on the contrary most will draw on theoretical literature just enough to frame an argument, book-end an empirical analysis or make observations about its relevance to a wider universe of cases. But I suspect that few would feel that their primary contribution is theoretical innovation.

Three strands of political commentary on Indonesia

Australia is coming to an end of a period of a decade or so of intense media and public interest in Indonesia. This began with the 1998 collapse of the Suharto regime, an event that attracted blanket media coverage in Australia. Australian public interest was then sustained by the East Timor independence referendum and subsequent Australian military intervention, the series of terrorist bombings that targeted Australians among others, several high-profile arrests of Australians for narcotics offences in Indonesia, the 2005 Indian Ocean tsunami and large Australian aid response to that, as well as by a series of others issues such as the passage of Middle Eastern and other asylum seekers to Australia through Indonesia, and by the arrival of a few Papuan asylum seekers on Australian shores. This has been a period of very intense public interest that has in recent years begun to subside, as is made obvious now by the virtual disappearance of coverage of developments in the domestic politics of Indonesia in the Australian media, in contrast to the early years of the post-Suharto transition.

In this context, Australian experts on Indonesian politics have been called upon to provide two overlapping kinds of commentary on Indonesian affairs for the Australian and international media. The first was specialist commentary on Indonesian events that are important for Indonesia and only indirectly so for Australia ('What does this or that outbreak of political violence signify?', 'What is the mood of the Indonesian population regarding the performance of the current president?'). The other is commentary about issues where the key question goes to some Indonesian decision or action that directly impacts upon Australia or Australians, or where it goes to a posture that the Australian government or Australians generally should adopt with regard to Indonesia ('What sort of threat do Indonesian Muslims pose to Australians?', 'Why have the Indonesian authorities treated the latest Australian narcotics detainee so poorly'?, What should the Australian government's policy be towards the latest human rights abuse in Papua?'). It is this second category of questions that tend to generate most interest, and also most heat, in the Australian public debate, unsurprising perhaps given the utilitarian and often narcissistic manner in which Southeast Asia is viewed in public discourse in this country.

Indonesia specialists enter into these second set of debates at our own peril: we do not set the terms of the debates, and they can be a trap. Commentators can either end up trying to defend the indefensible in Indonesia or becoming a plaything of Australian nationalism and xenophobia and risk valorising and reinforcing popular myths about Indonesian alienness, hostility and dysfunction. Overall, on this second category of questions about how issues in Indonesia affect Australia and Australians, it is possible to detect three general postures among Australian Indonesianists.

A Jakarta lobby?

The term 'Jakarta lobby' (sometimes, 'Indonesia lobby') was first coined in the debates of the 1970s and 1980s that followed the Indonesian invasion of East Timor. Put most simply, the idea was that there was a small group of people inside and outside the Australian government who promoted close ties with Jakarta in the interest of Australian elites, especially business elites, at the expense of human rights in Indonesia. As one critic of the supposed lobby described it, the lobby consisted of 'an informal group of bureaucrats, academics and journalists who have tightly controlled Australian foreign policy towards Indonesia and East Timor ... The Jakarta lobby has long regarded Australia's relationship with Indonesia as an exceptional case requiring careful management by "experts" with a proper sympathy for and understanding of Jakarta's difficulties' (Burchill 1999). This accusation is still made in public debate, especially by Papua solidarity activists and their supporters.

It is of course true that Realpolitik views about the importance of Indonesia for Australia and what this should mean about official attitudes to East Timor, human rights, Papua or similar issues have been expressed frequently in Australian political debate down the years. They were especially liable to prompt controversy during the Suharto years, when many Australians felt uncomfortable about their government developing such close ties with an autocratic regime responsible for gross human rights abuses. Typically, the most forceful articulators of such Realpolitik views, however, were not academic specialists on Indonesia, but journalists and former diplomats, such as Paul Kelly and Greg Sheridan of the *Australian* and Richard Woolcott, the former Australian ambassador to Indonesia (each of whom still argues along these lines from time to time: see for example Woolcott 2006). It is questionable, however, whether there is a lobby in the sense of an organised group seeking to exercise influence over Australian government policy from the outside. There is no real need for a lobby of such a sort because all Australian government policy-makers and leaders over the last few decades have held the Realpolitik views ascribed to the lobby. Those people who are accused of being part of the lobby are merely publically articulating the government line.

Has there been significant involvement by academic Indonesia specialists in such a 'lobby' or in arguing the position that is seen as underpinning it? The ANU is generally identified as being a centre of such a tendency, in part because of the significant role played by economists in this institution, and their close connections with Indonesian economists, technocrats and policy-makers during the Suharto years. During his time as head of the Department of Economics (1960–1980) at the Research School of Pacific Studies, and after he retired, Professor Heinz Arndt sometimes wrote in the media to defend Indonesia's record in East Timor, in the face of all the evidence of the human rights record there, as well as to defend Suharto's development record or advocate closer Australia–Indonesia ties. More broadly, as I have indicated above, it must be acknowledged that there is a certain ambience or milieu at the ANU that makes it different from the other major sites of scholarly research on Indonesia in Australia. Indonesia scholars at the ANU – currently a large and diverse group of several dozen persons – are certainly not closely integrated with the Australian government as a group, but many of them have informal and personal ties with serving and retired government officials in bodies like AusAID, the Department of Foreign Affairs and Trade and the Office of National Assessments. Such links provide opportunities (albeit limited and indirect ones) for input into policy-making and evaluation processes and for providing information to government that are generally absent in other places. It is therefore not surprising that the ANU has remained the key centre of Australian academia and from time to time generates argumentative pieces that combine classically realist appraisals of Australia's national interests, cautious analysis of Indonesia's political circumstances and advocacy of close Australia–Indonesia ties (see for example Monfries 2006, McGibbon 2006, Mackie 2007, MacIntyre and Ramage 2008). Even so, the onset of democratisation and East Timor's independence have taken much of the public heat out of debates about Australia's relations with Indonesia, except on a few highly contentious issues such as the status of Papua. Anyone looking for a Jakarta lobby advocating a line of closer ties with Indonesia in defiance of all consideration of human rights and with deep roots in Australian academia will have difficulty finding it.

A critical position or an anti-Indonesia lobby?

Within the community of specialists of Indonesian politics in Australian universities there is now relatively little serious dispute on basic political questions to do with Indonesia. This is very different, say, from the Burma studies field which is deeply divided about questions arising from the sanctions debate (see for example Aung-Thwin 2001–2002), and where personal rancour is sometimes extreme. It is also different from Indonesian studies in the 1960s and 1970s, when both American and Australian scholars were divided by the politics of the Cold War, the increasing radicalism of Indonesian nationalism, the post-1965 rise to power of the military, and the implications of such developments for scholarship. As a consequence of these factors, a radical critique of mainstream approaches to Indonesia arose both in the United States and in Australia during the 1960s and 1970s (see for example Levine 1969; Mortimer 1973; Robison 1981). In Australia, this division was partly institutionalised in the emergence during the 1960s and early 1970s of a purported division between Monash

University, which was seen (rightly or wrongly) as a centre of more critical scholarship on Indonesia, and the ANU, where the dominance of the economists was associated with a more sympathetic posture towards the New Order and its developmentalism.

Now, the left–right axis that once divided Indonesian studies has largely faded. The Cold War has ended. Democratisation has taken away much of the passion about how academics should best position themselves and their work vis-a-vis the Indonesian regime. Equally important, the Marxist project for remaking capitalist societies that underlay many of the radical critiques of mainstream analyses of Indonesian politics has also been eviscerated. In its place has come a post-1960s leftish sensibility that combines celebration of difference, identity and multiplicity with a liberal sympathy for democracy and human rights, which as I have tried to outline above permeates the Indonesian studies field. Evidence of this transformation is found, ironically, in the one place where there has been anything approaching a coherent neo-Marxist school of analysis of Indonesia in Australia – in the work of Richard Robison and that group of scholars he has trained and been associated with, with the chief of the Indonesia scholars among them Vedi R. Hadiz. Robison and Hadiz make use of the tools bequeathed by Marxism to devastating effect whether in portraying the class dynamics at the heart of the New Order regime (Robison 1986) or in portraying the continuities in oligarchic power in post-transition Indonesia (Robison and Hadiz 2004; Hadiz 2010). Yet the gulf between their analysis and those of other scholars of Indonesian politics is much narrower than it might appear, with an emphasis on elite dominance and recalcitrance being a widely accepted theme in studies of post-Suharto democratisation. If anything, they are distinguished chiefly by their pessimism about the prospects of Indonesia's democratic transformation, a pessimism that derives from the absence in their analysis of the belief in revolutionary change and the transformative potential of subordinated groups that once animated left-wing scholarship.

In Australian studies of Indonesian politics, we thus see little fundamental disagreement about the basic dynamics of Indonesian politics, the nature of Indonesian society or the direction in which Indonesia's democratic transformation should proceed.[6] At most, there are occasional

---

6   Arguably, Max Lane is the only Australian author with long-standing Indonesianist credentials who stands outside this broad scholarly consensus (see Lane 2008) but, tellingly, until recently he has had no footing in the institutional structures of Indonesian studies.

disagreements of the glass half-empty or half-full variety about such issues. Overall, there is remarkable normative consensus about such issues, driven by the overpowering resurgence of what Rex Mortimer (1973, 114) once called the 'critical liberalism' that first became obvious in the early post-World War II Australian scholarship on Southeast Asia.

However, there has been over the last decade or so one area that presents a significant exception to this scholarly consensus, and where there has been considerable critical and even vociferous public scholarship about Indonesia in Australia. That area is the secessionist regions of Indonesia: formerly, East Timor, now Papua. Precisely because of the relevance to Australian policy, these topics have attracted great public attention and given rise to a new form of activist scholarship that seeks to influence public opinion and change government policy in the direction of placing greater support for human rights and/or self-determination. This activist scholarship and the associated public debate is not, however, dominated by Indonesian studies scholars. Instead, the chief protagonists have tended to be individuals who have come to their topics directly through an avenue of political solidarity, and who sometimes do not know Indonesia well or lack the language skills or extensive Indonesian fieldwork experience that are so prized among Indonesian studies professionals (representative books by Australian authors on Papua over the last decade include Elmslie 2002; King 2004; Leith 2003; Fernandes 2006). Such works, and even more so, much of the public debate and commentary about human rights and self-determination in Papua (to take only the most recent example) promotes a strong position of solidarity with the people of Papua, in an idiom that is borrowed from earlier anti-imperialist solidarity campaigns (most obviously the anti-Vietnam War movement). They also tend to view the issue through a narrative of 'Australian betrayal' of the Papuan people and their struggle, and to occasionally echo broader fears and suspicions of Indonesia that are deeply embedded in Australian popular culture (Aspinall 2006).

The silent majority

As Freddy Kalidjernih (2008) has suggested, most Indonesia specialists in Australia, with a few exceptions, have shied away from public debate on sensitive issues such as Papua. In the case of Papua, this silence is no doubt partly because most Australian Indonesianists are trained to view specialist knowledge of a topic as a prerequisite to being able to speak authoritatively on it, a belief that constrains few other commentators in public debate on Indonesia in Australia. Perhaps the fear of being banned from Indonesia, or of otherwise suffering adverse consequences for one's own research, is a constraining factor. However, the deeper and more fundamental problem is the moral ambivalence or conflict that arises from the contradictions between Australian Indonesianists' political attitudes and their desire to promote public sympathy for and interest in Indonesia. Exponents of critical liberalism, Australian Indonesian specialists are often personally highly committed to issues to do with human rights, such as those afflicting Papua and, previously, East Timor. Yet the driving rationale of the Australian Indonesian studies scene remains a determination to combat Australian fears, misperceptions and stereotypes about Indonesia (and in so doing to contribute to an Australian polity and society that is itself more plural and multicultural). At the very least, this combination of motives can give rise to a degree of nuance, complexity and qualification that does not equip one well to be a commentator in the media, where quick and clear judgements are generally expected. And although the Papua case is a particularly difficult topic, similar problems arise in commentary on almost any issue where Australian interests are involved and public opinion is aroused. As a result, it is not surprising that much of the public debate and commentary about Indonesia in Australia tends to be dominated by people who do not know the country well. The low quality of much public debate about Indonesian affairs in Australia frustrates many of the country's Indonesia specialists, but perhaps we are ourselves partly to blame for it.

Conclusion

I have tried here to explore some ways in which political and institutional contexts have shaped the way that the study of Indonesian politics is carried on in Australia, and their implications for how Indonesian studies scholars participate in public debate. Compared to the relationships that most Western advanced capitalist countries have with developing countries, the relationship of Australia to Indonesia is unusual. Australia's position vis-a-vis Indonesia is not that of a former colonial metropole to post-colony or of a contemporary global power to a marginal player in the world economic order. To be sure, Australia's relationship with Indonesia was marked, especially in the early decades of Indonesia's independence, by considerable indifference and ignorance on the part of the Australian public and policy-makers. Indonesia studies scholars in Australia consequently viewed themselves as blazing a trail that would enlighten Australians to the implications of their geographic location on the periphery of Asia, and to begin the long task of making Australians, as the current buzz phrase puts it, 'Asia literate'. As Indonesia has evolved politically and economically, and as trade, tourism, migration and other flows between the two countries have expanded, the country has come to play an increasingly large role in Australian public imagination and policy debate, whether as threatening danger, source of promise, or both.

Not surprisingly, this unusual relationship has produced opportunities for the development of a field of study of Indonesian politics in Australia that is disproportionate to the size of Australia's population and its academy. But it has also left its mark on aspects of the study pursued in this country in the form of, among other things, considerable specialisation, an area studies approach and an emphasis on detailed empirics rather than global theories. At the same time, Indonesian studies scholars have viewed themselves as interpreters of Indonesian political events for a wider Australian public and for government, and as advocates of closer Australian engagement with Indonesia, even if they are not always well suited to playing those interpretative and advocacy roles on the issues that most excite public controversy in Australia.

It is difficult to foresee any of this changing much in the near future while Australia's relationship with Indonesia continues to be widely viewed in Australia as both important and problematic, and with the important proviso that considerations of national interest continue to at least partially inoculate the Indonesian studies scene from the market pressures that might otherwise lay waste to it. Over time, however, it might be that economic and other changes in both countries, and greater integration and exchange between them will have transformative effects. To be sure, it is still hard to imagine an Australian society that achieves the degree of social and cultural integration with Indonesia, and the sophisticated knowledge of the Asian neighbourhood, to which many Australian specialists of Indonesia aspire. Nor is it yet easy to imagine Indonesia experiencing such a seamless integration into a liberal–democratic order that its politics are seen as so normalised that they no longer give rise to a perceived need for specialist knowledge and area studies skills. Even so, economic and social changes in Indonesia, and their attendant effects on intellectual life there, might still affect the way the country is viewed and studied in Australia. Already, Indonesian studies in Australian universities is increasingly populated by scholars from Indonesia, whose contributions have included not merely bringing their own form of specialised knowledge about Indonesia but also of injecting a new level of theoretical sophistication.[7] One can only speculate on what the growth of Indonesia's own intellectual life and the increasing participation by Indonesia-based scholars in international scholarly debate and publishing on their country's politics, will have on transforming the international study of Indonesian politics, including in Australia.

References

Amadae, S M. 2003. *Rationalizing Capitalist Democracy: The Cold War Origins of Rational Choice Liberalism*. Chicago: University of Chicago Press.

Anderson, Benedict. 1982. 'Perspective and method in American research on Indonesia', In *Interpreting Indonesian Politics: Thirteen Contributions to the Debate*, edited by Anderson; Benedict; Kahin, Audrey. Ithaca, NY: Cornell Modern Indonesia Project, Southeast Asia Program, Cornell University: 69–83.

Aspinall, Edward. 2006. 'Re-thinking Papua, Indonesia and Australia'. *Policy and Society* 25 (4): 121–130.

Aspinall, Edward. 2010. *Assessing Democracy Assistance: Indonesia*. Madrid: FRIDE (Fundación para las Relaciones Internacionales y el Diálogo Exterior).

Aung-Thwin, Michael. 2001–2002. 'Parochial universalism, democracy *jihad* and the Orientalist image of Burma: The new evangelism'. *Pacific Affairs* 74 (4): 483–505.

Burchill, Scott. 1999. 'The Jakarta Lobby: mea culpa?'. *Age* (4 March).

Burke, Anthony. 2008. *Fear of Security: Australia's Invasion Anxiety*. Cambridge: Cambridge University.

Cook, Ivan. 2006. *The Lowy Institute Poll 2006. Australia, Indonesia and the World: Public Opinion and Foreign Policy*. Sydney: Lowy Institute for International Policy.

Cooper, Andrew F; Higgott, Richard A; Nossal, Kim Richard. 1993. *Relocating Middle Powers: Australia and Canada in a Changing World Order*. Melbourne University Press, Melbourne.

Cribb, Robert. 2005. 'Circles of esteem, standard works and euphoric couplets: Dynamics of academic life in Indonesian studies'. *Critical Asian Studies*. 37 (2): 289–304.

Crouch, Harold. 2010. *Political Reform in Indonesia after Soeharto*. Singapore: Institute of Southeast Asian Studies.

Elmslie, Jim. 2002. *Irian Jaya Under the Gun: Indonesian Economic Development versus West Papuan Nationalism*. Honolulu: University of Hawai'i Press.

---

[7] In the political studies field, obvious examples are Vedi R. Hadiz and Ariel Heryanto.

Emmerson, Donald K. 2008. 'Southeast Asia in political science: Terms of enlistment.' In *Southeast Asia in Political Science: Theory, Region, and Qualitative Analysis*, edited by Kuhonta, Erik Martinez; Slater, Dan; Vu, Tuong. Stanford: Stanford University Press: 302–324.

Fernandes, Clinton. 2006. *Reluctant Indonesians: Australia, Indonesia and the Future of West Papua*. Melbourne: Scribe.

Fosse, Ethan; Gross, Neil. 2010. *Why Are Professors Liberal?* Working Paper, Department of Sociology, University of British Columbia.

Fukuyama, Francis. 2004. 'How academia failed the nation: The decline of regional studies'. *Saisphere* (Winter).

Graf, Arndt. 2009. 'Indexing a field: The case of Indonesian and Malaysian studies'. *Review of Indonesian and Malaysian Affairs* 43 (2): 191–221.

Hadiz, Vedi R. 2010. *Localising Power in Post-Authoritarian Indonesia: A Southeast Asia Perspective*. Stanford: Stanford University Press.

Hanson, Fergus. 2010. *The Lowy Institute Poll 2010: Australia and the World, Public Opinion and Foreign Policy* Sydney: The Lowy Institute for International Policy.

Hatley, Barbara. 2009. 'Encountering Indonesia as a student, then and now'. *Review of Indonesian and Malaysian Affairs* 43 (1): 95–103.

Hill, David T. 2010. *Indonesian in Australian Universities: A Discussion Paper*. Murdoch University.

Kalidjernih, Freddy K. 2008. 'Australian Indonesia-specialists and debates on West Papua: Implications for Australia–Indonesia relations'. *Australian Journal of International Affairs* 62 (1): 72–93.

King, Peter. 2004. *West Papua and Indonesia Since Suharto: Independence, Autonomy or Chaos?* Sydney: UNSW Press.

Kuhonta, Erik Martinez; Dan Slater; Vu, Tuong (eds). 2008. *Southeast Asia in Political Science: Theory, Region, and Qualitative Analysis*, Stanford: Stanford University Press.

Laitin, David. 1993. 'Letter from the incoming president', APSA – CP (Newsletter of the American Political Science Association's Organised Section in Comparative Politics), 4 (2): 2, 18.

Lane, Max. 2008. *Unfinished Nation. Indonesia Before and after Suharto*. London: Verso.

Leith, Denise. 2003. *The Politics of Power: Freeport in Suharto's Indonesia*. Honolulu: University of Hawai'i Press.

Levine, David. 1969. 'History and social structure in the study of contemporary Indonesia'. *Indonesia* 7: 5–19.

McGibbon, Rodd. 2006. *Pitfalls of Papua: Understanding the Conflict and its Place in Australia–Indonesia Relations*. Sydney: Lowy Institute for International Policy.

MacIntyre, Andrew; Douglas E. Ramage. 2008. *Seeing Indonesia as a Normal Country:*

Implications for Australia. Canberra: Australian Strategic Policy Institute.

Mackie, Jamie. 2007. *Australia and Indonesia: Current Problems, Future Prospects*. Sydney: Lowy Institute for International Policy.

Monfries, John, editor. 2006. *Different Societies, Shared Futures: Australia, Indonesia and the Region*. Singapore: Institute of Southeast Asian Studies.

Monroe, Kristen Renwick, editor. 2005. *Perestroika!: The Raucous Rebellion in Political Science*. New Haven: Yale University Press.

Mortimer, Rex. 1973. 'From Ball to Arndt: the Liberal impasse in Australian scholarship on Southeast Asia'. In *Showcase State: The Illusion of Indonesia's 'Accelerated Modernisation'*, edited by Mortimer, Rex. Sydney: Angus & Robertson: 101–158.

Pausacker, Helen. 2009. 'Is gender still off the agenda? Involvement and visibility of women at Indonesian studies conferences in Australia'. *Review of Indonesian and Malaysian Affairs* 43 (1): 105–127.

Philpott, Simon. 2000. *Rethinking Indonesia: Postcolonial Theory, Authoritarianism and Identity*. Basingstoke: Macmillan.

Robison, Richard. 1981. 'Culture, politics and economy in the political history of the New Order'. *Indonesia* 31: 1–29.

Robison, Richard. 1986. *Indonesia: The Rise of Capital*. Sydney: Allen & Unwin

Robison, Richard; Hadiz, Vedi R. 2004, *Reorganising Power in Indonesia: the Politics of Oligarchy in an Age of Markets*. London: Routledge Curzon.

Woolcott, Richard. 2010. 'John Howard is right to placate Indonesia: Australia's relations with Jakarta should not be hostage to our sympathy for Papuan refugees', *Australian* (21 April).

Chapter 5

Contending Perspectives in the Australian Academy

A View from Indonesia

Bob S. Hadiwinata

This chapter discusses the changing dynamics of Australian scholarly debates on Indonesia as seen from the Indonesian academy. Following on from Aspinall in this volume, it argues that different perspectives in the debate reflect the dynamics of Australian political scientists. While the older generations carried out their debates within what David Goldsworthy termed an Australian intellectual tradition of being impartial, non-partisan, politically detached, and avoiding prescriptive stances on contested public issues (Goldsworthy 1990, 39), the younger generation of Australian political scientists engage in debates that move beyond the tradition set by their predecessors. They became involved in political debates to the extent that they accuse one another. On the issues concerning Papua, for example, while the pro-Papuan camp accused their counterparts of being insensitive to Papuans' sufferings, mute towards Indonesian military atrocities, and clearly pro-Jakarta; the pro-Indonesia camp, on the other hand, accused their opponents of being overzealous, ethnic chauvinists, and imbued with expansionist phobia. This generation represents what Goldsworthy called in the 1980s the new generation who showed an increasing detachment from the Australian intellectual tradition.

Australian scholars, particularly those with history, anthropology and political science backgrounds, offer different perspectives in their understanding of political situations in Indonesia. The discussions on

Indonesia were initially confined to a group of so-called Indonesianists (scholars who show great interest in developing Indonesian studies in Australia). Recently discussions on Indonesia have also included those who have no specific formal training and qualification of Indonesian studies. Kalidjernih has argued that Indonesia's political dynamics post-Suharto, has seen an increased engagement in discussion about Indonesia, especially on issues such as separatist struggles and human rights violations in areas such as Aceh and Papua, by Australian scholars trained in international relations, government, politics, and strategic and defence studies, but with no specialisation on Indonesia (Kalidjernih 2008, 87).

The contribution of this new group of scholars has significantly changed the perspectives of the debates. While Indonesianists have focused on truth finding, empirical testing of theories, and being non-partisan and maintaining some degree of sensitivity not to offend the Indonesian government despite their critical views on Indonesia, some scholars in this new group (with no formal training on Indonesian studies) tend to understand Indonesia in different ways. In critiquing the analysis of this group of scholars – whom he calls pro-independence romanticists – Ed Aspinall argues that their analysis on Indonesia (Papua in particular) has been imbued with ethno-nationalist mythology, expansionist phobia, denying Indonesia's capacity to run a pluralistic society and demonisation of Indonesia (Aspinall 2006b, 141).

In order to be more focused, this chapter is limited to discussion of the exchange of views on Indonesia between scholars from within the disciplines of political science and history. To illustrate the changing perspectives on the way in which Australian scholars view Indonesia it will discuss two intensive exchanges – one among Indonesianists on the failure of parliamentary democracy in the 1950s, and another on the contemporary Papua issue between non-Indonesia specialist political scientists and Indonesianists. This is by no means a comparative study; rather it will try to show how changes in Australian political science in the past few decades have affected the ways in which particular political issues are viewed in Indonesia.

The discussion will be divided into three parts. The first part will look at different generations of Australian political scientists who subscribe to different perspectives. The second part will discuss different views on the failure of parliamentary democracy in Indonesia during the 1950s of Australian Indonesianists such as Herb Feith, John Legge and Jamie Mackie and some other Indonesianists. The third part will examine how the Papua issue is debated by political scientists with no formal training on Indonesian studies: Peter King and Clinton Fernandes on one side, and those with an Indonesian studies background represented by Edward Aspinall and Rodd McGibbon on the other.

Perspectives of Australian political scientists

Like other branches of social science, politics has experienced significant changes in terms of perspectives and methods. In the United States, Gabriel Almond (1990, 13) argued that the political science profession encompasses various schools and sects, each with its own conception of proper political science, but each protecting some 'secret island' of vulnerability.

Almond tried to make distinctions between different schools and sects in American political science along methodological and ideological lines. He divided political science into four separate schools or sects: (1) the 'soft left', who are critical of the value-free and objectivity proposed by the positivists. Associated with the Critical Theory of the Frankfurt School, this group maintains that positivists fail to comprehend that the process of knowing cannot be severed from historical struggle between humans and the world. For this group, knowledge should be freed from simplification and reductionism, and historical materialism should be adopted in order to appreciate the relationship between theory and 'praxis'; (2) the 'hard right', who regard historical, descriptive and unsophisticated analysis as the inferior breeds of political science. They instead propose the use of experimentation and mathematical models in capturing human reality; (3) the 'soft right', who believe that value-free and ethically neutral political science is absurd. Associated with American sociologist, Leo Strauss, this group proposes that ethics, morality and norms should be taken into account in understanding human reality; and (4) the 'hard left', who have faith in class analysis but at the same put emphasis on the necessity of hypothesis testing and empirical verification in generating knowledge. The work of Christopher Chase-Dunn in quantifying the world system approach is an exemplary of this group (Almond 1990).

In Australia, ideological cleavages in political science appear to be less salient. David Goldsworthy argued that, amid the growing number of political science department or schools throughout the country during the 1960s and 1970s, Australian academics began to think strategically about exploring their various strengths and tactically about ways of improving their positions in performance tables in order to boost publication rates and external funding (Goldsworthy 1990, 28). This allowed new schools and perspectives to swell.

Portraying Australian political scientists in different generations, Goldsworthy posited that while the recruits of the 1960s and early 1970s were shaped by the mainstream style of Australian political science which is individualist, analytical and generally non-prescriptive in character, generations who came to the fore one or two decades later – many of whom were consultants to politicians, policy advisers to government and non-government agencies, and public educators through various television, radio and newspaper commentaries – try to detach themselves from the mainstream by producing policy-prescriptive, highly subjective, partisan, and morally bound essays and commentaries (Goldsworthy 1990, 39). It should be noted, however, that not all Australian political scientists of older generations are absolutely value-free. As their analysis has to some extent been influenced by their ideological purports, including liberalism, socialism and Marxism, as reflected in debates between Herb Feith (1965) and Harry Benda (1964) on the failure of Indonesia's parliamentary democracy of the 1950s in the 1980s, which will be discussed later in this chapter. But, it can be said that different ideological orientations seemed to be outshone by their methodological argumentations that made the academic debates flow and cleverly avoided mutual accusations.

This is not to suggest that subjectivity, partisan, moral enclosure and policy prescription are necessarily bad; rather, it indicates that scholars (whose main duties, among others, are finding truth and getting better understanding of complex reality of human life) may be deceived by a political agenda that could disrupt their understanding of the social phenomena they are studying. Goldsworthy argued that there has always been a risk that the pursuit of 'policy relevance' and preconceived values in political science exercises, if taken too far, may undermine an understanding of the complexity of the social world as the main countenance of the discipline (1990, 40).

Hugh Emy and Andrew Linklater (1990) depicted the trends in Australian political science by using four broad categories of perspectives of Australian political scholars: (1) the 'scientific empiricists', who put emphasis on accumulating a body of reliable (empirically tested) propositions about political phenomena from which they can develop a systematic and empirical theory. To achieve this goal, they commit to a 'scientific method', the importance of empirical testing and verification, and to maintain categorical distinction between facts and values; (2) the 'modified empiricists', who believe that intellectual progress is measured by the ability to devise (empirical) theories which not only explain the causal relationship between key variables but also predict how such variables may behave in different circumstances. This group, however, no longer affirms the ideal of 'value-free' social science, as they believe that it is extraordinarily hard to exclude values from empirical testing. They also maintain that political research must have some degree of policy-relevant and problem-solving capacity; (3) the 'normative post-positivists', who stress the special significance of culture and identity in understanding socio-political phenomena. They believe that culture and identity could reveal the complexity of the cultural patterning that helps sustain social life. For this purpose they argue that political science requires the use of hermeneutic approaches designed to interpret, deduce and reconstruct the web of meanings embodied in a given context or event. For them, developing a more sophisticated understanding of the symbiotic link between humankind and culture can contribute to building more desirable institutions or societies; and (4) the 'ethical-normative moralists', who try to revive moral and ethical dimension in the study of politics. They are more interested in Socratic and classical questions such as: How should human beings seek to live? What is 'just society'? And how it might be achieved? They strongly believe that politics is much more concerned with elucidating better or ideal forms of human association, rather than separating knowledge and reality as prescribed by the empiricists (Emy and Linklater 1990, 5–14).

Although these categories do not accommodate all Australian political scientists, as Emy and Linklater admitted (1990, 5), the four categories nevertheless portray the dynamic perspectives in Australian views of social and political phenomena in which departure from the tradition of 'value-free' objectivism, moral obtuseness and non-partisanship seems to be underway. On the general trend of Australian political science, Goldsworthy commented:

> ... it has to be said that Australian political science has so far maintained a fairly high degree of professional chastity in relation to divisive political issues. Nevertheless, a minor but honourable tradition of critical partisan engagement does exist within the ranks; and it deserves to be nurtured as we collectively find our way into the new world (1990, 26).

The rise of a new breed of political scientists can be linked with developments within political science itself as well as the changes in career progression of Australian political scholars. More attention on new humanitarian issues such as environmental issues, women's issues, human rights, world poverty, global injustice, and so forth has prompted scholars to engage in more partisan, morally bound and policy-prescriptive exercises. With respect to career progression, new generations of Australian political scientists no longer confine themselves to teaching and academic research activities as they predecessors did. They instead serve many non-academic activities, such as becoming advisers to politicians or state officials, consultants to government agencies and non-government organisations (NGOs), and media commentators in their capacity as public educators.

A past debate: the failure of Indonesia's parliamentary democracy of the 1950s

In the 1960s and 1970s, foreign scholars were enticed by the political dynamics of the post-colonial Indonesia, especially with regard to how revolutionary ideas were manifested in daily politics, how leaders set up the political framework in managing a highly pluralistic society, what kind of ideologies shape national politics, and how the newborn republic dealt with political institutions adopted from the West. Examples of influential scholarly works on Indonesia at that time include George Kahin's *Nationalism and Revolution in Indonesia* (1958), Herb Feith's *The Decline of Constitutional Democracy in Indonesia* (1962), Ruth McVey's *The Rise of Indonesian Communism* (1964), Daniel Lev's *Transition to guided Democracy: Indonesian Politics 1957–1959* (1964), R. William Liddle's *Ethnicity, Party, and National Integration: an Indonesian Case Study* (1970) and Herb Feith and Lance Castles (eds) *Indonesian Political Thinking 1945–1965* (1970).

Writing in the early 1980s, Benedict Anderson (1982) divided foreign scholars studying Indonesian post-colonial politics into two groups. The first group, which he termed 'anti-colonial liberalism and historical method' can be associated with scholars, particularly George Kahin, a professor at Cornell University, who used historical method with strong emphasis on the uniqueness and intrinsic dynamic of historical experience. Kahin's *Nationalism and Revolution* contained detailed accounts on how colonialism had severe impacts on Indonesian society: population disequilibrium, indigenous elites co-opted into the bureaucracy, political repression, economic exploitation, and so on. The liberal-democratic nuance in Kahin's analysis was the pronounced focus on constitutional politics and parliamentary institutions at work in the post-colonial Indonesia, at least in the 1950s. Kahin's approach and method was subsequently followed by his students at Cornell such as Harry Benda, Daniel Lev, Ruth McVey, and some others (Anderson 1982, 72).

The second group, which Anderson termed 'imperial-liberalism and comparative method', refers to Indonesianists who were under strong influence of comparative analysis and theory developed in the United States during the 1950s and 1960s, pioneered by scholars like Gabriel Almond, Lucian Pye, David Apter and Leonard Binder. This group was also influenced by 'modernisation theory'. This approach argues that for post-colonial states to move away from their traditional 'backward' situation to a more 'advanced' and modern status they should replicate economic liberalism and Western-style democracy. Anderson cautiously associated this group with Herb Feith, particularly his publication *The Decline of Constitutional Democracy* (1962; Anderson 1982, 75). Other scholars in this group include Karl D. Jackson, R. William Liddle and Dwight King.

Another category may be added to Anderson's groupings: that is, 'cultural–ecological or hermeneutic method', which can be associated with the works of American anthropologist, Clifford Geertz and his followers. In his seminal work *The Religion of Java* (1960), Geertz employed an ecological approach focusing on material interdependence of small organisms that subsequently shape the characteristics of a community. With this concept, Geertz was able to portray the internal dynamics of a community by looking at physical and psychological characters of its members. While criticising Western scholars, especially Bronislaw Manilowski, for encapsulating themselves with 'scientific arrogance' in analysing socio-cultural phenomena in non-Western societies, Geertz proposed the use of the hermeneutic method to understand a community by looking at meanings in local languages and in other linguistic symbols practised in that community (Geertz 1984, 132–36). Geertz' path-breaking work enticed other Indonesianists, including Feith, who together with Lance Castles compiled political writings and commentaries written by Indonesians, which was published as a book titled *Indonesian Political Thinking 1945–1965* in 1970.

Feith is a prominent Australian pundit who contributed much to the expansion of Indonesian studies in the country and beyond. In the early 1960s, he produced his first masterpiece on Indonesian politics titled *The*

Decline of Constitutional Democracy in Indonesia (1962). The book – originally a doctoral thesis at Cornell University – offered a comprehensive explanation on the failure of parliamentary democracy in Indonesia during the 1950s. Using data collected from extensive fieldwork and historiography on Indonesia, Feith tried to provide a comprehensive answer to the perplexing question: why did the parliamentary democracy established following the 1955 general election began to founder in the late 1950s?

Using his Indonesian language skills combined with good personal acquaintance with prominent figures in Indonesian politics during that period, Feith linked the collapse of parliamentary democracy with at least two factors. The first was related to disappointment about the post-independence regime, which generated pressures on the democratic institutions. Feith identified three types of unmet demands that led to popular dissatisfactions: (1) material expectations, in which the new government faced difficulties in increasing the national economy's productivity and distribution due to the lack of infrastructure, population growth and weak bureaucracy; (2) demand for the escalation of social status in which many Indonesians pressed the government to provide more white-collar jobs; and (3) rapid social change which generated confusion among younger generations who were caught between their traditional orientations and modern values (1962, 598–99). These demands had substantially weakened the newly elected government.

Second, leadership conflicts, which involved what Feith termed 'solidarity makers' versus 'administrators'. Solidarity makers, in Feith's view, refer to politicians whose claim to political power lay in their ability to use symbolic rhetoric in their attempt to integrate the nation and mobilise supports. This type of leadership can be associated with Sukarno, political propagandists, local military leaders, ex-guerilla fighters, religious leaders and some militant Muslims. Administrators include those who retain their political positions due to their modern-type skills, education, and commitment to problem-solving. Because of their skills, this group contributed much in the diplomatic battles against the Japanese and the Dutch, which led to Indonesia's independence. Leaders such as Mohammad Hatta, Mohammad Natsir, Sutan Sjahrir and Mohammad Roem are certainly representatives of the administrators. For Feith, it was the domination of the solidarity makers (at the expense of the administrators) within the cabinet and the parliament since 1950, which subsequently led to the collapse of the parliamentary democracy (1962, 111–14). During that critical period political leaders were interested in mobilising people to support national unity rather than maintaining democracy. Unable to face these challenges, the Indonesian government was facing serious problems which included a crisis of governance due to short-lived cabinet ministers, a series of rebellions, and ongoing political wrangles among elites, which made the elected government finally crumble.

Upon publication Feith's book invited praise as well as criticism. Understandably, compliments came from Feith's supervisor and mentor George Kahin, who wrote in his preface to the book:

> In the course of four years work in Indonesia, Herb Feith gathered an impressive body of new data, which in itself constitutes an important contribution. The richness of his findings attests to his full fluency in the Indonesian language, his sensitive understanding of Indonesian culture, and the friendship and respect with which he has been regarded by Indonesians – qualities which made it possible for him to talk candidly to so many of them … I believe his study constitutes a good example of the maxim that a scholar best serves such friendship through frankness of exposition and objectivity of appraisal (Kahin 1962, viii).

Generations of scholars have expressed their admiration of Feith's book. His biographer Jemma Purdey concludes that *The Decline of Constitutional Democracy* is considered a 'magnum opus, a formidable and lasting analysis and narrative of the period of parliamentary democracy in Indonesia from 1950–1957' (Purdey 2008, 71). The inclusion of this book in the reading lists of Indonesian studies courses around the world attest international recognition of Herb Feith's scholarship.

Other scholars, however, evaluated Feith's work in more critical ways. Most direct critics are two non-Australian scholars. While consciously expressing his admiration of the scholarship quality of Feith and his humane approach to the work, Benedict Anderson could not help to say that Feith had moved away from 'anti-colonial liberalism and historical method'[1] set up by his mentor at Cornell University by his affection to comparative method, which carries with it Western ethnocentrism. While criticising Feith for epitomising democratic liberalism by focusing on 'the decline of constitutional democracy' rather than on 'the rise of radical

---

1   Feith termed this type of analysis as 'Kahinian' school of Indonesia specialists. See Feith 1965 305–312.

autonomism' in analysing Indonesian politics in the 1950s, Anderson maintained that Feith did not deliberately aim at discrediting Indonesian local dynamics. Thus, his emasculation of Indonesian nationalism was only an effect of his approach (Anderson 1982, 78).

Stronger critique came from Harry Benda, a New Zealander of Czech origin, who also studied Indonesian politics at Cornell. There are at least three points in Benda's criticism (1964). First, he blamed Feith for looking at Indonesian politics through the Western lenses, which resulted in a value-laden analysis of Indonesia. He accused Feith of asking an irrelevant question: 'What's wrong with Indonesia?', which for Benda attests to the naïve character of Western scholars of historical parallelism and of methodological Europocentrism. Second, Benda also attacked Feith's categorisation of Indonesian elites – 'solidarity makers' and 'administrators' – for oversimplifying and overlooking cultural tensions, especially between Javanese and non-Javanese. He objected to Feith's association of 'administrators' with problem-solvers. Third, Benda accused Feith's analysis of being unhistoric for looking at post-war Indonesia primarily as a continuation of the country's most recent history and largely ignoring what had happened before. This omission can lead to significant interpretational errors (Benda 1964, 449–456).

Some Australian scholars developed different views in interpreting political events in the 1950s that led to the collapse of parliamentary democracy. Avoiding direct attacks on Feith's analysis, historian John Legge pointed to a number of factors as the major cause of the collapse of the democratic government. First, the rise of 'extra-parliamentary' political forces which included local military officers and political bosses resenting central government manifested in a series of insurgencies throughout the country. Second, the poor discipline of party functionaries – resulting from poor cadre development – which subsequently led to problems in decision-making and the long wrangles in the parliament, especially on controversial issues. Third, problems of unity within the military that weakened government control of the military, especially when local military commanders were preoccupied with regionalism and resentment against central commanders. Fourth, the growing political rivalry between civilian politicians and the military, as manifested in the aborted coup attempt in 1956 led by Colonel Zulkifli Lubis (Legge 1964, 140–44).

Writing much later, Jamie Mackie, an Australian political scientist, did not attack Feith's analysis of Indonesia. He instead tried to defend Feith's position by saying it was neither determinist nor reductionist (1994). With this point in mind, Jamie Mackie provided supplementary explanations of the political events in Indonesia during the 1950s that led to the collapse of the parliamentary democracy. He referred to several factors. First, strong resentment against liberal democracy among several political forces, especially within the army and President Sukarno himself, as they believed that liberal democracy was not suited to Indonesia's national identity (*kepribadian nasional*). They made every attempt to weaken the parliament and opted for 'guided democracy'. Second, a regime crisis that could be linked to the failure of the parliament, parties and cabinet to resolve the challenge from regional dissidents whose aim was to overthrow the government. Third, a combination of political, economic and geographical factors marked by high inflation rates, undervalued exchange rates, and economic takeover of Dutch companies operating in Indonesia. All these factors generated conflict between Java and the outer islands, and between Masyumi (the Islamic party) and other parties (Mackie 1994, 32–36).

The exchange of views on Indonesia during the 1970s and 1980s seems to reflect the dynamic views within Goldsworthy's category of mainstream political science, where scholars debated for the sake of truth finding, objective analysis, and accuracy. It is clear in the discussions that those scholars debated on how certain methodology affected political research, how norms and values should be treated in political research, and how appropriate paradigm can ensure accuracy. None intentionally tried to suggest that Indonesia should follow a particular path of political development. In his defence of Herb Feith against Benda's critique of oversimplification, Jamie Mackie, for example, argued that Feith 'was just trying to single out what he saw as the most deeply rooted set of factors relevant to the explanation, even though he would have admitted that a multifactoral explanation had to be given' (Mackie 1994, 29).

In their debates on the failure of liberal democracy experiment in Indonesia during the 1950s, unlike non-Australian scholars – especially Benedict Anderson and Harry Benda – who were somewhat disturbed by Feith's defence of liberal democracy, Australian scholars were too careful in not questioning Feith's ideological stand point. This seems to corroborate Goldworthy's 'political detachment' of Australian scholars of the older generation. However, Feith himself could not conceal his ideological stance. Writing in the 1990s, he explained:

> I first arrived in Indonesia in July 1951 and spent over four of the next six years there. I had wonderful time in those years and so I loved the

Indonesia of the liberal period. Those feelings continue to shape my perceptions of that time, and so affect my preferences of the kind of country I would like Indonesia to become (Feith 1994, 17).

Compared with his 1960s strong denial of Benda's accusation of his value-laden analysis on Indonesia, this indicates a shift in Feith's ideological point of view (Feith 1982a, 23). Feith's ideological stance appeared even more confusing given that since the 1970s, as his biographer Jemma Purdey has learned, Feith began to search for a new way to better understand Indonesia by engaging in radical theories of Third World, anti-establishment and peace paradigms. This change somewhat disturbed Feith's reputation, as many fellow Indonesianists felt they could no longer count on him for objective insight and knowledge (Purdey 2008, 72).

A contemporary debate: Papua

West Papua has drawn interest from Australian scholars for some time. A small number of them conducted studies on various aspects of West Papua. Peter Worsley (1968), for example, studied revolutionary struggles of West Papuan people against Dutch colonialism. Ross Garnaut and Chris Manning (1974) studied economic transformation in West Papua. Robin Osborne (1985) wrote about the guerilla struggle in West Papua. In the post-Suharto era, Australian scholars' focus on Papua grew significantly amid the revival of Papua nationalism, growing separatist sentiments among West Papuan people, the central government's plan to split the province into three, the enactment of autonomy law, and continuing human rights violations by Indonesian security apparatus. The new interest on Papua attracts not only those with training on Indonesian studies, but also political scientists and international relations specialists in general.

The debate is much more heated and goes beyond the Australian academic tradition of political detachment and impartiality. Freddy Kalidjernih (2008) categorised Australian scholarly works on Papua into two clusters. While I have a semantic problem with Kalidjernih's categories, I agree with his differentiation between the pro-Papua and the pro-Indonesia elements in recent Australian scholarly works on Papua.

The first group is what he terms 'skeptical reformists' whose views on Papua signal a strong anti-Indonesian sentiment with blatant support for West Papua's independence. Scholars including Peter King (professor at Sydney University) and Clinton Fernandes (senior lecturer at the University of New South Wales) belong to this group. In his book-length account of the situation in West Papua, Peter King (2004) argues that Papuan people are distinctively different from other Indonesians in terms of ethnicity, culture and religion. He went on to argue that the growing nationalism among Papuans, problematic integration with Indonesia, violence against West Papuans committed by Indonesian military, economic marginalisation, and genocide justify the West Papuan appeal for independence. In his view, Papua's partition from Indonesia is the only solution to the problem. He also calls on the Australian government to adopt a more aggressive foreign policy in the region with emphasis on 'peaceful self-determination' for Papua by pressuring the Indonesian government to negotiate with the independence movement in Papua. In a similar vein, Clinton Fernandes (2006) argues that West Papuans' struggle for independence is a rational choice. He believes the Indonesian government has intentionally developed racial discrimination and antagonism towards the Papuans. Strongly opposing continuous military repression in West Papua, he indicates that human rights abuses in West Papua take place in various areas of society, including the health sector (high indication of HIV-positive among Papuans), education (low rates of educated Papuans), population (the growing number of non-Papuan settlers), economy (economic dominance of non-Papuan settlers), and with regard to the environment (environmental degradation and deforestation).

The second group, which Kalidjernih calls 'affirmative revisionists', includes those who view Indonesia in a more positive way, although they express concern about ongoing human rights violation and economic backwardness in West Papua. Understandably, they maintain that West Papua's independence is not the best option; they instead believe that full autonomy is the most plausible solution for West Papua. Scholars including Edward Aspinall (fellow at the Australian National University) and Rodd McGibbon (researcher at Office of National Assessments) are members of this group (Kalidjernih 2008, 77–78).

This group – who have Indonesian studies training – have expressed views critical of their fellow observers. Edward Aspinall (2006a) argues that the Australian public, especially activists of the left and the Christian social justice lobby, tend to treat the West Papua issue on the basis of unexamined fears and prejudices towards Indonesia. Consequently, their views on human rights abuses and other wrongdoings in Indonesia tend to be biased, as they narrowly focus on West Papua and fail to show interest on human rights issues elsewhere in Indonesia. Aspinall euphemistically rejects the idea of self-determination as the solution for West Papua. He argues that romanticising self-determination is inappropriate given that independence could cause considerable suffering and disenfranchisement for West Papuans, already facing rampant corruption and embezzlement committed by West Papuan local officials (Aspinall 2006a, 122–23). Moreover, he argues, it seems somewhat awkward for Australians to excoriate Indonesia's unwillingness to allow self-determination, while Australia's own constitution calls the Australian federation indissoluble. Aspinall is critical of King and Fernandes for arguing that Papuans should be independent simply because they are so ethnically and racially different from other Indonesians. This view, he argues, emanates from their underestimation of Indonesia's capacity to run a pluralist society; and Papua is just one of hundreds of separate language and cultural groups in Indonesia. In his reply to Peter King's criticisms on his position, Aspinall (2006b) refutes the accusation of genocide on West Papuans by Indonesian security apparatus, criticising King for treating all abuses in Papua as ipso facto evidence of genocide. In his view, King's conclusion is framed by his preconceived belief that Papuans and Indonesians are distinct and incompatible groups (2006b, 140).

Aspinall's critique of the pro-Papuan scholars is shared by another Indonesianist, Rodd McGibbon (2006) who challenges his 'pro-Papuan' colleagues by arguing that their determination to contest Indonesia's sovereignty over Papua tends to create more problems rather than moving towards a solution (2006, vii). McGibbon posits that the analysis and policy prescriptions made by the pro-Papuan camp face three basic errors. First, an exaggerated sense of Australia's foreign policy influence. For McGibbon, King seems to be over-confident on Australia's foreign policy influence in the region, as he suggests the Australian government should serve as a sub-regional hegemon and develop 'its own initiative' within the framework of 'Australian peace-making role'. Such a role, McGibbon argues, will raise the perception among Indonesian nationalists of Australia's intervention. This can potentially disrupt Australia–Indonesia bilateral relations, which may lead to a serious conflict.

Second, McGibbon argues that these arguments demonstrate the lack of a serious appreciation of the rise of new forces that drive contemporary Indonesian politics. Indonesia's fledgling democracy has created potential openings for new initiative on Papua, including the drafting of a special autonomy law that grants Papua full autonomy. Despite its troubled implementation, in McGibbon's view, this law remains the most promising framework for resolving the conflict and ensuring the peaceful integration of Papua into Indonesia.

Third, while acknowledging continual rights abuse and economic marginalisation of the Papuans, like Aspinall, McGibbon casts doubt that ethnic and cultural distinction is enough to justify Australian support for West Papuan independence. He recommends the Australian government engage more vigorously in the public debate in Australia on Papua through promoting of greater knowledge about West Papua and countering inaccurate information, building a better understanding of the importance of Indonesia to Australian security interests, and educating the public on Indonesia's new democracy (2006, viii–xiv).

In his response to critiques from the pro-Indonesia camp, Peter King restates his argument that West Papua's partition from Indonesia is justified, given that Papuans, as Melanesian Christians, are essentially different from Indonesians (2008, 5). Elsewhere he reiterates his accusation of genocide committed by Indonesian government (King 2006). He identifies several factors as indications for genocide: transmigration of hundreds of thousands of settlers from Java, Sulawesi and elsewhere, which caused Papuans' marginalisation; an HIV/AIDS epidemic related to TNI's prostitution rackets; recurring large-scale killings committed by security agents; and aggressively promoted family planning (King 2006, 132–33). King restates his call for Australia's intervention on the basis that it is as a sub-regional hegemon and should protect West Papuans as it did the East Timorese in 1999. He argues that Australia's triumph in an arm wrestle with TNI and the Jakarta elite over East Timor should be considered a precedent for such policy on Papua (King 2006, 135). Agitated by his pro-Indonesian fellows, King launches an attack on those he labels as belonging to the 'Jakarta lobby' (see Aspinall, this volume). For him, in their attempt to appease Indonesia, those people – whom he sometimes refers to as the hegemonic coterie of Australian National University Indonesianists – are guilty, as they have for many years borne the burden of covering up, or apologising for the Jakarta-led oppression of the Papuans (King 2008, 1).

King's association with pro-Papuan activists, which include the AWPA (Australia West Papua Association), networks within various Christian denominations, Green and Australian Democrat parliamentarians, a small number of academics and journalists may explain his biased and partisan analysis on the Papua issue.

This seems to corroborate Goldsworthy's argument that many Australian political scholars have moved beyond their traditional academic role. The call for new duties to consult politicians, provide policy advice to various agencies and serve as public educators has, Goldsworthy argues, driven some Australian political scientists to engage in partisan public activism (1990, 41). The involvement of scholar-activists – such as Peter King and some others clearly turns the discussions into endless political debates that may jeopardise the reputation of Australian academia embodying political neutrality, balanced view, political detachment, and objective analysis. Exchanges between Aspinall and King put them in mutual accusations: while Aspinall labels King as ethnic enthusiast (2006b), King regards Aspinall as and Indonesia lobbyist insensitive to West Papuans' sufferings (2006).

Debates on the Papua issue clearly shifted Australian political science away from its tradition. According to Goldsworthy:

> Australian political science has a strong tradition of seeking to avoid overtly prescriptive stances on contested public issues. Typically it aims to elucidate and expound 'all sides' of a problem to its various public rather than espouse controversial views' (1990, 39).

Peter King's continuous insistence of Papuan independence and McGibbon's defence of Papua integration to Indonesia clearly indicate such a shift.

Conclusion

This chapter discusses the changing perspectives of Australian political science where demands for more policy-relevant studies, critical theory's suggestion of science serving human interests, and activists' claim of 'indigenous rights' have entered political debates. No longer avoiding sensitive public issues, political scholars – many of them serving as advisers and consultants to politicians and various government and non-government agencies – engage in more heated political debates avoided by their predecessors.

This new trend has changed substantially the characteristics of Australian political science scholarship on Indonesia. If debates on the failure of parliamentary democracy of the 1950s pitted what Benedict Anderson (1982) terms 'anti-colonial liberalism and historical method' against 'liberal-imperialism and comparative' approaches; recent debates on Papua reflect the opposition between what Emy and Linklater (1990) call 'normative post-positivists' and the overzealous version of 'ethical-normative moralists' perspectives discussed earlier.

Debates on Papua remind us of the potential contamination within academic discussions, of ethnic and religious zealotry. Writing in the context of American academic freedom, Neil Hamilton argues that academic freedom has been assaulted repeatedly by waves of zealotry, which includes religious fundamentalism, unfettered capitalism, leftist radicalism, stringent anti-communism, and so forth. On many occasions defence of academic freedom has fallen short (Hamilton 1995, 4). Edward Aspinall's fear of the influence of ethnic and religious zealotry brought by his pro-Papuan fellows in analysing the Papua issue indicates his concern for the tendency of some Australian academics to cross the line by suggesting the ultimate solution for Papua. He therefore feels it is necessary to remind his fellow Australians not to engage in problem-solving exercises, especially on sensitive issue such as Papua. In his reply to Peter King, he posits:

> While I do not have a view on whether in the long run Papua should or should not remain part of Indonesia (who are we to say?), I do indeed believe that the most desirable long-term outcome would be for Indonesia to become a country in which democratic values and social equality prevail (such that groups like the Papuans do not feel they need to secede) ... (Aspinall 2006b, 141).

What practical impact did those two debates make? Debates on the collapse of Indonesian democracy articulated in Western academies in the 1960s had no practical impact given that those scholars made no clear message on Indonesia's political directions. For the next four decades or so, Indonesia endured non-democratic governments under Sukarno's 'guided democracy' from 1959 to 1965 and followed by Suharto's authoritarianism from 1966 to 1998. On the other hand, I would argue that debates on Papua have potential practical impact. Indonesia has a lot to learn from those scholars who, despite their differences, agree on the need for Indonesian government to end the ongoing human rights violations and provide better living conditions for West Papuans. Debates on the Papua issue also affect Australia–Indonesia bilateral relations. In his article, Kalidjernih concludes that the writings and commentaries of pro-Papuan scholars – whom he labelled 'skeptical reformists' – tend to jeopardise Australia–Indonesia relations (Kalidjernih 2008, 89). In February 2003, Indonesia derailed RMIT's bid to host an international conference on Papua. RMIT's Globalism Institute had planned to host a two-day conference on the future of Papua. A few days before its commencement, the university's management – pressured by Indonesian government – intervened. It contributed some funding, but it did not want the conference carry the university's imprimatur (Faroque, 2003). As a result, the conference was held at a location outside the university campus, and in May 2006 the Indonesian government blacklisted two Australian academics on the basis that they had been promoting separatism in West Papua. The academic arguments aside, the consequences for such activities as handed out by the Indonesian government would already appear to be clear.

References

Almond, Gabriel. 1990. *A Discipline Divided: Schools and Sects in Political Science.* Newbury Park and London: SAGE.

Anderson, Benedict. 1982. 'Perspective and method in American research on Indonesia'. In *Interpreting Indonesian Politics: Thirteen Contributions to the Debate*, edited by Anderson, Benedict; Kahin, Audrey. Ithaca, NY: Cornell Modern Indonesia Project, Southeast Asia Program, Cornell University: 69–91.

Aspinall, Edward. 2006a. 'Selective outrage and unacknowledged fantasies: Rethinking Papua, Indonesia and Australia'. *Policy and Society* 25 (4): 121–130.

Aspinall, Edward. 2006b. 'A reply to King'. *Policy and Society*. 25 (4): 139–141.

Benda, Harry J. 1964. Review of *The Decline of Constitutional Democracy in Indonesia*, 'Democracy in Indonesia' in *Journal of Asian Studies* (May): 449–456.

Emy, Hugh; Linklater, Andrew. 1990. 'Introduction: Departures and reappraisals in politics'. In *New Horizons in Politics: Essays with Australian Focus*, edited by Emy, Hugh; Linklater, Andrew. Sydney: Allen & Unwin: 1–22.

Faroque, Farah. 2003. 'Indonesia derails RMIT bid to host conference'. *The Age* (25 September).

Feith, Herbert. 1962. *The Decline of Constitutional Democracy in Indonesia.* Ithaca, NY: Cornell University Press.

Feith, Herbert. 1965. 'History, theory and Indonesian politics: A reply to Harry J. Benda', *Journal of Asian Studies* 24 (2) (February): 305–312.

Feith, Herbert. 1994. 'Constitutional democracy: How well did it function?'. In *Democracy in Indonesia 1950s and 1990s*, edited by Bourchier, David; Legge, John. Clayton: Centre for Southeast Asian Studies: 16–25.

Fernandes, Clinton. 2006. *Reluctant Indonesians: Australia, Indonesia, and the Future of West Papua.* Melbourne: Scribe.

Garnaut, Ross; Chris Manning. 1974. *Irian Jaya: the transformation of a Melanesian economy.* Canberra: Australian National University Press.

Geertz, Clifford. 1984. 'From the native's point of view: On the nature of anthropological understanding'. In *Culture Theory: Essays on Mind, Self and Emotion*, edited by Shweder, R A; LeVine, R. New York: Cambridge University Press: 123–136.

Goldsworthy, David. 1990. 'Australian political science in the age of accountability'. In *New Horizons in Politics: Essays with Australian Focus*, edited by Emy, Hugh; Linklater, Andrew. Sydney: Allen & Unwin: 23–42.

Hamilton, Neil. 1995. *Zealotry and Academic Freedom: A Legal and Historical Perspective*. New Brunswick, NJ: Transaction Publishers.

Kahin, George McT. 1962. 'Foreword'. In Feith, Herb, *The Decline of Constitutional Democracy in Indonesia*. Ithaca, NY: Cornell University Press.

Kalidjernih, Freddy K. 2008. 'Australian Indonesia specialists and debates on West Papua: Implications for Australia–Indonesia Relations'. *Australian Journal of International Affairs* 62 (1) (March): 72–93.

King, Peter. 2004. *West Papua Since Suharto: Independence, Autonomy or Chaos?* Sydney: UNSW Press.

King, Peter. 2006.'In defence of the Papua sympathisers: A rejoinder to Ed Aspinall', *Policy and Society* 25 (4): 131–137.

King, Peter. 2008. *Lowying the Boom on West Papua: Self-determination Unthinkable for Australia's Foreign Policy Think Tank*. West Papua Project, Centre for Peace and Conflict Studies, University of Sydney.

Legge, J D. 1964. *Indonesia*. Englewood Cliffs: Prentice-Hall.

Mackie, J A C. 1994. 'Inevitable or avoidable? Interpretations of the collapse of parliamentary democracy'. In *Democracy in Indonesia 1950s and 1990s*, edited by Bourchier, David; Legge, J D. Clayton: Centre for Southeast Asian Studies.

McGibbon, Rodd. 2006. *Pitfalls of Papua: Understanding the Conflict and Its Place in Australia–Indonesia Relations*. Sydney: Lowy Institute for International Policy.

Purdey, Jemma. 2008. 'Many voices, one life: Dealing with memory and "telling" in the biography of Herb Feith'. *Journal of Historical Biography* 3, Spring 2008: 56–86.

Worsley, Peter. 1968. *The trumpet shall sound: A study of cargo cults in Melanesia*. N.Y.: Schocken Books.

Chapter 6

Finding a Middle Way

The Future of Indonesian Studies in the Western Academy

Heather Sutherland

When I was in my second year at the Australian National University, in 1961, I was the only student entering the Indonesian and Malay branch of the new Oriental studies faculty.[1] The courses I followed were based on traditional European colonial approaches. While the aim was not to train officials for overseas service – as had been the case in Leiden, one of the models for the curriculum (Fasseur 1983) – government funding was nonetheless intended to create a cadre of useful specialists knowledgeable about Australia's Asian neighbours. This was deemed to require a geographically focused and exotic education, combining languages and a knowledge of Oriental cultures with a straightforward view of their history, framed in accounts of states and dynasties, colonialism and nationalism. Looking back, this program seems to have been both sophisticated and naïve. There was a serious effort to understand societies 'in their own terms', but without questioning how these were framed, or the epistemological and political context that shaped their 'knowing'. Some decades later, shifts in global and national politics in the priorities of academic institutions and in intellectual fashion would all combine to challenge the assumptions sustaining this approach.[2] This

---

[1] I am grateful to Leo Douw, Thomas Lindblad and Ot van den Muijzenberg for their suggestions and advice; as always, the faults are my own.

[2] In the 1990s Simon Philpott decided, correctly that 'it was time to consider the culture, traditions and sources of authority in the discourse of Indonesian politics'; 'Indonesian politics studies is as legitimate a field of study as Indonesian politics itself'.(Philpott 2000, xiv). Philpott emphasises Orientalist discourse; my approach here is more institutional and financial: 'follow the money'.

chapter seeks to outline some points concerning the relationship between area studies and the disciplines, to sketch recent Dutch experience, and, finally, to consider several recurring fundamental problems in the intellectual and institutional organisation of Indonesian (and area) studies.

Area studies

If the content of the initial ANU program (and most of the staff) were of European origin, the area studies model, as it evolved in the post-war United States, soon became a powerful influence, introducing – but effectively after my time – more attention to anthropological and political studies. As in Australia, concern about the stability of 'developing nations' was a priority, but, as befits a world power, in the US the new centres were politically justified by their potential contribution to America's global competition with the USSR for the allegiance of post-colonial regimes. Some of the staff of the new centres had laid the basis for their careers during the Second World War, when military language programs and deployments had created opportunities for contact with other cultures. Despite this background and the strategic context, the scholars themselves did not necessarily share their governments' Cold War perspective.

Intellectual traditions often combined uneasily with politicians' plans.[3] European colonial training curriculums were strongly shaped by philology (rooted ultimately in biblical hermeneutics), but were also intended to produce young men capable of administering tens of thousands of natives. In a similar paradoxical fashion, Cold Warriors sought tactical insights through anthropology and history as much as, if not more than, political science as such. These combinations had their own liabilities: if the former led to an emphasis on classical cultures and 'pure' traditions (on correct grammar rather than on spoken language, with all that that implies),[4] the latter could drift towards cultural determinism. Both dimensions in these somewhat strange interactions of scholarly fashions and pragmatic social functions were subject to change.

Decolonisation also encouraged an emerging generation of imperial historians to reframe their research, while the Cold War funding boom of the 1950s gave them new opportunities. US Government money was

---

[3] It is not the intention in this article to look at historiography as such; for a summary see (Legge 1999, 25–26).

[4] I am grateful to Ot van den Muijzenberg for this point.

channelled through the National Defense Education and National Defense Foreign Languages Acts, while the Ford and Carnegie Foundations strongly supported interdisciplinary efforts in area studies. The Social Science Research Council and the American Council of Learned Societies helped shape the intellectual agendas of the new university centres; the resulting research and teaching were expressed and organised in new journals and associations (Manning 2003).[5] For Indonesianists Cornell emerged as the main point of reference. There the Modern Indonesia Project (established in 1956) sought to create a basic body of knowledge through translations of essential material. Cornell's role was confirmed by path-breaking (if not hegemonic (Cribb 2005)) monographs produced by George Kahin, Ruth McVey and Benedict Anderson, as well as the sense of community created by their journal *Indonesia*, first published in April 1966. Harry Benda at Yale also played a prominent role, both because of his personal charisma (enhanced by his passionate opposition to the war in Vietnam) and his success in bridging European and American intellectual traditions.

The major contributions of area studies scholars resulted from their tight focus on specific societies; they usually drew on an extensive personal experience of their field, examining it through the analytic lenses of several disciplines. The typical package of skills included knowledge of at least one local language and a familiarity with the relevant historical, anthropological and political literature. New combinations of methodologies also became standard; archive and field work, life histories and oral traditions all became familiar tools. But if the permeability of disciplinary boundaries had always been one of the most dynamic assets of area studies, geographical borders seemed much harder to breach. This reflected both the heavy investment in region-specific language skills and knowledge by researchers, and also the institutionalisation of territoriality in university departments and academic infrastructure.

The tendency simply to accept established geopolitical boundaries and to see regional events in isolation is identified by Patrick Manning as a central weakness in the area studies tradition (Manning 2003, 155; 170). There has been considerable recent interest in this theme of demarcation, for example the collections *Knowing Southeast Asian Subjects* (Sears et al. 2007) and *Locating Southeast Asia* (Kratoska et al. 2005; Sutherland 2003), but movement has been slow. Manning (himself a historian of Africa)

---

[5] See Philpott, 2000: 46–51, 102–120, on the Cold War and capitalism as determining forces in the development of Southeast Asian studies.

emphasises that area studies tended to allow regional solidarity to develop into a restrictive emphasis on parochialism and exceptionalism. He explains: 'Parochialism in that Africanists know about Africa but not other regions, and in that Africanists who know their own corner of Africa tend to assume it is representative of the continent' (Manning 2003, 155). But exceptionalism is even more pernicious, notes Manning, 'particularly when an area of study finds itself on the defensive', as in the case of post-Cold War Russian studies (Manning 2003, 155). Then specialists often try to justify their work (and funding) by claiming that their area is unique, rather than run the risk of weakening their case by opening a debate with other scholars. It is as if the area experts feared that engaging with academics from the disciplines as a whole might suggest that that impressive (and expensively acquired) local knowledge was not actually essential, and that even those without the languages and interdisciplinary background were nonetheless qualified to express an opinion.

This limitation in intellectual reach is all the more surprising, given the pronounced international character of the area studies experts themselves. It is completely usual for a Southeast Asian studies conference to bring together scholars from Europe, Australia, Japan, the US, and the region itself. As Manning (2003) observes, this transnational and interdisciplinary openness of area studies was central to the comparative and methodological advances that have proved to be their greatest contributions. Moreover, some grand themes did cross the boundaries between regions, uniting Africanists, Latin Americanists and Southeast Asianists. An early example is the criticism of teleological notions of modernisation, while more recently, emphasis on such topics as diaspora, creolisation or the role of specific crops or commodities have encouraged a wider focus.

From the late 1980s onward, interest in area studies declined. This can partly be ascribed to the reduced interest in nation states and cultural difference which attended the 'ending of history' (Fukuyama 1992) with the fall of the Berlin Wall in 1989. The subsequent obsession with 'globalisation' fuelled the notion that the serious study of regional societies was irrelevant, perhaps self-indulgent, or, even worse, 'politically correct'. Later, the 'War on Terror', concerns about immigration and the rediscovery of national identities generated new attention and funding in the first decade of the twenty-first century. But this was very unevenly distributed: Southeast Asia and non-Muslim Africa were marginalised. In 2004, the US Social Science Research Council (SSRC), which had always been a major sponsor of area research, identified three important challenges facing such studies. The first was a trend affecting all: 'the emphasis on global processes and de-emphasis of local contextual and linguistic knowledge', but the second reflected the major shift in US priorities after 9/11. This was 'the public challenge ... which has increased the workload of some of these centres in terms of student demand and public outreach' – a problem that many of their colleagues would gladly embrace. The third issue reflected the recognition that some regions of interest, such as Central Asia, were traditionally fragmented between various institutions. In 2004, the SSRC initiated a project on 'the production of knowledge on world regions', which is intended to assess the situation of Middle Eastern, South Asian and Eurasian studies in the USA.[6]

Southeast Asianists were early beneficiaries of geopolitical interests, given the region's central role in the struggle between the 'Free World' and the 'Soviet Bloc' in the 1960s and 70s. As potential dominos, doomed to become communist if Vietnam was lost, countries such as Indonesia benefited from official attention. After the fall of Saigon in April 1975, however, a collective political hangover weakened official enthusiasm for Southeast Asian studies in the United States, although local circumstances in the Netherlands and Australia helped maintain attention to Indonesia. In the former case this was because of the interest generated by the renewal of bilateral contacts after the investment-oriented Suharto replaced the old anti-colonial Sukarno, while in the latter it reflected the pro-Asia policies of the Labor prime ministers Bob Hawke (1983–1991) and Paul Keating (1991–1996). However, a combination of financial retrenchment and a certain disenchantment blunted this concern. While political factors, such as the end of the Cold War and the rise of global rather than national perspectives (Cummings 1997; Kassimir 1997) did weaken the appeal of area studies, another potent cause was the shifts in intellectual perspectives after the 1960s, notably the rise of the various 'posts' – postmodernism, post-structuralism and post-colonialism – and the related role of cultural studies.

The area experts' strength was their knowledge of how things worked in a highly specific setting. Their holistic integration of insights was grounded in a direct knowledge of local languages and life, so they felt that could speak of why the Japanese or the Javanese did things the way they did.

---

[6] The title of the project is 'Producing Knowledge on World Regions'. Accessed February 2012. Available from: http://www.ssrc.org/programs/producing-knowledge-on-world-regions.

Many felt a strong personal identification with their subjects and felt both able and obliged to represent them to the West. After Said's *Orientalism* (1978) this pretension began to seem ambitious at best, and suspect at worst. Later, as post-modernism and cultural studies emphasised the contingency and subjectivity of knowledge, and post-colonial critiques (such as those of the Subaltern Studies Group (Chaturvedi 2000; Chakrabarty 2002; Ludden 2002)) underlined the necessity of 'provincialising Europe' and deconstructing the mechanisms of intellectual colonisation, Western expertise lost its self-evident legitimacy (Sutherland 2007). Increasingly, it seemed, assumptions of 'knowing' became precarious, particularly when applied to post-colonial societies. Some regional fields (like Pacific studies (Tobin 1994; Campbell 1997; Matsuda 2006)) soon became embroiled in these debates while others, like Southeast Asia, remained relatively insulated. A relatively lonely voice, Ariel Heryanto refers to the 'deep anxiety over profound political and ethical questions about the perennial discrepancies of power relationships between the scholars and those they study', adding, however:

> Thanks to post-structuralist thoughts we can see better than before that Southeast Asian Studies, or any area studies for that matter, cannot possibly represent or incorporate the authentic voices of those they study. Neither can Southeast Asian studies possibly establish authentic or autonomous scholarships on their own societies (Heryanto 1996).

In any case, the established certainties of the traditional area studies specialist seemed somewhat out of step with the major arguments in the disciplines. Although today there are still an impressive number of Southeast Asian Studies centres,[7] closer inspection would reveal considerable variety in actual strength. Some are small coalitions of dispersed specialists, while others are superficially impressive lists of scholars, many of whom have only a marginal interest in the region.

Within academe as a whole, increasing numbers of theoretically inclined scholars began to share the interdisciplinary interests which had once been uniquely strong in region-focused programs. The linguistic and historical

---

[7] A partial list produces more than 20 significant centres: in the US: Cornell, Northern Illinois, Ohio, Stanford, Berkeley, UCLA, Hawaii, Michigan, Washington, Yale; in Australia: ANU, Monash, Murdoch, Sydney; in Europe: Amsterdam, Hull, NIAS, London, Leiden; in Asia: Kyoto, NUS Singapore.

'turns' were driven by an awareness that insights and models from different methodologies could transform the way specialists understood their own disciplines (Bonnell and Hunt 1999; Suny 2002). On the whole, historians recoiled from the more rigorous conceptualisations of language, texts and symbols as applied by Foucault, Derrida, Hayden White or Clifford Geertz, but over time such views did filter through and shape general intellectual predispositions. Eventually, many could express sympathy with aspirations such as those expressed by William Sewell or Joan Scott. The former, for example, commented 'although we obviously cannot hope to experience what nineteenth century workers experienced … we can, with a little ingenuity, search out in the surviving records the symbolic forms through which they experienced their world' (in Iggers 2005, 129). The latter explained, 'My argument is not that reality is "merely" a text, but rather that reality can only be attained through language. So social and political structures aren't denied, but … they must be studied through their linguistic articulation' (in Iggers 2005, 132). But sympathising with an aspiration does not necessarily entail trying to realise it in personal practice or even accepting the validity of the results. In general, historians, unlike anthropologists, linguists, political scientists, archaeologists – or indeed most professional intellectuals – seem very averse to theory. Indeed, Terrence McDonald, in his introduction to *The Historic Turn in the Human Sciences* (1996) argued that a rejection of theory is central to the character and separation of the disciplines:

> Having been born in history the social sciences would increasingly attempt to distinguish themselves from it by emphasizing theory and method in the years after the 1930s. But this separation was a two way street. Historians in the 1950s turned to the social sciences … constructing their theoretically subordinate role vis-à-vis social science so as not to have their enterprise destabilised … by the responsibility of producing 'theory'. At the same time, by maintaining an image of history as merely a source of 'facts' … social scientists protected themselves from the potentially corrosive effects of historical self-consciousness (1996, 8).

McDonald suggests that practitioners in both disciplines reinforced their claims to separate identities and institutions by staking claims to either 'facts' or 'theories', with each being somewhat dismissive of the intellectual legitimacy of the other. Historians emphasised the painstaking modesty of their work, contrasting their exhaustive perusal of archives with the casual illustrative story-plucking of historically inclined social scientists. Anthropologists and sociologists deplored the failure of historians to generate comparative or general models, and their reluctance to rise above the level of the detailed, specific case study. According to McDonald, proponents of the 'historic turn' sought to become 'historically self-conscious analysts reconstructing fully contextualised historical actors and representing them in a theoretically sophisticated narrative that takes account of multiple causes and effects' (McDonald 1996, 10). But he also recognises the ambivalence even among committed scholars as to how far and fast such goals can be achieved, noting Margaret Somers' (1996) emphasis on the different 'knowledge culture' within each discipline (McDonald 1996, 11).

The relationship between area studies and the historians working within the discipline shows some parallels with the mutually wary attitudes of old-school historians and social scientists. Like historians, traditional area studies scholars had a defined comfort zone (in their case, the region) and preferred to remain within it.[8] Those (few) historians of Europe with an interest in culturally different societies were inclined either to view them as rather passive objects of Western activities, or to see them as essentially exotic. When either specialist did venture forth onto new terrain, they sometimes burnt their fingers. As Manning comments, although such undertakings could lead to more sophisticated work, '[a]t other times, the links to other disciplines caused historians simply to become more audacious, and willing to speculate in areas beyond political history without training themselves in those fields' (2003, 153). Here he is referring specifically to amateur excursions into economic history, but many an area specialist would justifiably retort that facile generalisations about non-Europeans by unqualified commentators are much more frequent.

Since the formation of the first region-focused programs, there had been a recurring debate about the relationship between area studies, with their multidisciplinary focus on a specific place, and the established disciplines as defined by methodology and institutionalised into secure departments. The concern has always been to seek the best way of organising education and research. The choice has typically been seen as being between creating small bridging units connecting specialists located within traditional departments,

---

[8] Anthropologists also worked within specific traditions; see Fardon 1990.

such as history or political science, or establishing wholly new centres or faculties focusing on, for example, African, Asian or Latin American studies. Neither option seemed to guarantee survival in hard times, when the entrenched and 'natural' subjects, such as the study of the home nation, or of Europe or America, always managed to drain funding away from those seen as a mere exotic fringe.

While the academic and political shifts of the 1960s and 1980s did produce some faltering in intellectual self-confidence and a decrease in political willingness to pay for strategic knowledge, they only became truly threatening to the survival of programs when university funding came under pressure and was more tightly linked to enrolments. Sometimes this coincided with declining student interest. This negative trend was far from universal. While some regions have enjoyed continued or growing interest, such as China, others, including Indonesia, have experienced difficulties, even in those countries that once seemed so naturally committed to its study, such as the Netherlands and Australia.

Indonesian studies in the Netherlands

In 1778 intellectually inclined Dutchmen in Batavia brought the first colonial scientific body into being, the Batavian Society for Arts and Sciences (*Bataviaasch Genootschap voor Kunsten en Wetenschappen*).[9] Further institutes were created in the mid-nineteenth century Netherlands: the still vital KITLV[10] (now the Royal Netherlands Institute for Southeast Asian and Caribbean Studies) in 1851 and the *Koninklijk Instituut voor de Tropen* or KIT (Royal Tropical Institute), the forerunner of which dates from 1864.[11] The collections and libraries of the KITLV and KIT became internationally recognised resources, and although the latter has increasingly specialised in the broader field of development studies, both remain essential sources of books, maps, photographs and documents. Numerous other specialist organisations were also established, ranging from the technical to the religious; all left their paper legacies. The Netherlands' National Archives and other documentation centres, such as those of the NIOD, IISG (or

---

[9] From 1910 this was the Royal or Koninklijke (Royal) Society; it finally closed in 1962.
[10] Koninklijk Instituut voor Taal-, Land- en Volkenkunde (Royal Institute for Linguistic, Geographical and Ethnographic Studies) For a history, see Kuitenbrouwer 2001.
[11] The Koloniaal Museum was founded in Haarlem in 1864. It then moved to Amsterdam as the Koloniaal Instituut in 1926 and became the KIT in 1950.

IISH) and the missions,[12] and many museums[13] have also contributed to a scholarly infrastructure that remains indispensable to research on Indonesia. Unfortunately Dutch governments are increasingly reluctant to fund these institutions, and in late 2011 both the KITLV and the KIT faced such rigorous cuts in their subsidies that their very survival is doubtful.[14] Some of these bodies were founded because of a commitment to scholarship; others were based in practical needs. The combination formed the basis of the Netherlands tradition in Indonesian studies.

The origins of the teaching of Indonesian languages, ethnography and law at university level were pragmatic, driven by the need for more professionally qualified colonial officials (Fasseur 1983). Their training was initially given in a two-year and intermittently three-year practical course in Delft from 1843 and, after 1864, in Leiden. The latter gained full university status in 1921. However, some colonial politicians and businessmen found the staff unacceptably progressive, and in 1925 a new 'Indology' course was established in Utrecht, nicknamed the 'oil and sugar faculty'. A number of academics played an important policy role, such as Christiaan Snouck Hurgronje[15] and C. van Vollenhoven,[16] while others are remembered as the founders of specific school or approaches, examples being J. P. B. de Josselin de Jong[17] and C. C. Berg. After the war, the Indonesian revolution and decolonisation ended the possibilities of a career in the Indies, and the pool of talent began to shrink. The collapse of the Sukarno regime (1965)

---

[12] The NIOD (Netherlands Institute for War Documentation) contains newspapers, documents and objects from the Indies in the period 1940–1950, while the IISG (in English ISSH) or International Institute for Social History, established in 1935, now combines its long interest in economic history, labour and social movements with a commitment to Asia. Both are located in Amsterdam.

[13] Illustrative material from various collections is to be found on line in the excellent *Atlas of Mutual Heritage*.

[14] On 7 October 2011, the state secretary for overseas development announced that the KIT would no longer receive its subsidy of some €20 million, virtually the entire operating budget for the museum and library. The Dutch Royal Academy of Sciences, which manages various institutes, including the KITLV, wishes to cut that institute's budget by 70 per cent. The KITLV may survive in some truncated form, of may be absorbed into Leiden University's area-studies program. The continuation of their Jakarta acquisitions office, a prerequisite for maintaining the library's international role, is uncertain.

[15] His classic book on Mekka, including descriptions of the 'Jawa' community, has recently been translated from, the German (Hurgronje 2007).

[16] See Swellengrebel, J L. (1974; 1978); Maier, H J M. & Teeuw, A. 1976; Wills 1991; Burns 2004.

[17] De Josselin de Jong's concept of the 'ethnologisch studieveld', launched in 1935, shaped structural anthropology in the in Netherlands; see Ridder and Karremans 1987.

reopened the country's doors to Dutch scholarship, and attempts were made to revive the old intellectual traditions (and funding) by referring to the glories of the past. But the raison d'etre for that past had vanished, and the final decades of the twentieth century were characterised by a faltering sense of direction.

The 1970s were years of readily available finance and university expansion, so there was little need for academic reflection, but by the mid-1980s the Ministry of Education was exerting considerable pressure on the universities to cut costs and to create an efficient division of labour. This was reflected in the demand that those working in 'Indonesian Studies' define its role and justify its expense. Scholars had to repeatedly make their case in an effort to sustain access to funding in the face of dwindling student interest and continual budget cuts. The ministry had some success in centralising Asian studies in general, and Indonesian in particular, so confirming the leading roles of Leiden and Amsterdam (and perhaps sharpening their traditional rivalry).[18] But the net effect was to limit the range of institutions engaged in Indonesia-related topics[19] without producing any extra investment for the two centres. But continuing anxiety over declining traditions led to yet another committee being appointed to advise the Ministry of Education on the preservation of the 'small humanities', particularly the more exotic Asian topics. This report, known as 'Baby Krishna' or the Staal report (after its chairman, the Sanskritist Frits Staal), and the parallel document on the social sciences, 'Krishna in the Delta', both appeared in 1991.

Leiden received €2.9 million from the ministry. These funds, the 'Staalgelden', provided a temporary reprieve for a number of specialised courses that were never going to be able to justify their existence in terms of student numbers, but which were rightly deemed to be a rare international intellectual resource. The study of old Javanese, Bugis or Hindu–Javanese archaeology was always going to appeal to minority tastes, but if they were going to be taught anywhere outside Indonesia, then the Netherlands was the obvious place. The expectation was that Leiden would use the time so

---

[18] According to the stereotypes, Leiden was either the centre of solid language, history and archaeological studies or a conservative bulwark of colonial apologists, while Amsterdam was either committed to the professionally advanced and politically engaged social sciences, or a left-wing cabal of superficial theorists. Politically, Leiden was seen as pro-establishment and Amsterdam as progressive.

[19] The Comparative Asian Studies Program at the Erasmus University Rotterdam was disbanded in 1987. Indonesia specialists also disappeared in whole or in part from the Universities of Amsterdam, Groningen, Utrecht, Nijmegen and the Vrije Universiteit Amsterdam.

purchased to reorganise the curriculum to make it more attractive. However, little changed, and within a few years this money was no longer specifically earmarked for the 'non-Western' subjects but was increasingly being used for general faculty expenses. The esoteric but (almost) unique Asian courses were then evaluated according to the same calculations of profitability as other subjects in the humanities, and their staff–student ratios made them inevitable targets for further reductions in support (van den Muijzenberg 1991; Weijts 2004).

In a story familiar in, *inter alia*, the United Kingdom and Australia, the only constant in Dutch government policy was an emphasis on 'efficiency', which translated as more work and higher standards for less money. This was not seen as in any way in conflict with the constant harping on quality. The ministry regularly launched plans to create centres of excellence, or institutes, or research schools; the main results of these initiatives were a great expense of staff time and tightened bureaucratic control over research funding and hence over priorities. These were increasingly determined by government wishes, while money was channelled through national bodies such as NWO (the Netherlands Organization for Scientific Research) or the KNAW (Royal Netherlands Academy of Sciences). Only large projects, typically involving three or four PhD students and a couple of post-docs, could justify the expense of their administration; the increasingly scarce grants for individual researchers could only be subsidised from the universities own shrinking budgets. The universities themselves, locked in competition for money and students, simultaneously claimed distinctive profiles and unique strengths, together with an all-round ability to provide a broad general education. Government policy was consistently inconsistent, as each generation of officials sought to make their mark and move on before the consequences of their decisions became apparent. One year the stress would be on national (and international) cooperation and complementarity, the next, on self-sufficiency.[20] But, in a parody of a 'business model', productivity was the measure of all things; although all united to decry the very idea of a diploma mill, student numbers became the key to survival.

This had profound effects, particularly in Leiden, where philological traditions still ensured that a solid knowledge of the language remained

---

[20] The International Institute for the Study of Islam in the Modern World (ISIM) was established in 1998 by the Universities of Amsterdam, Leiden, Utrecht and the Radboud University Nijmegen. Despite its excellent work, in accordance with the swing against cooperation, it lost its funding in late 2008.

the core element in separate departments for South, East and Southeast Asian area studies. Each of these units was potentially vulnerable, and while Chinese and Japanese were eventually able to consolidate a defensible position, South and Southeast Asian studies experienced dramatic reductions. Leiden Asian studies were in worse shape than those in Amsterdam, which were traditionally based in the disciplines and had a stronger contemporary focus. Staff from both Amsterdam universities, the UvA (University of Amsterdam) and the VUA (Vrije Universiteit Amsterdam), had combined in the Centre for Asian Studies Amsterdam (CASA), which was established in 1987, but this was subsequently absorbed by the Amsterdam School for Social Science Research (ASSR). However, the ASiA (Asian Studies in Amsterdam) network, established in 2001, maintained a high profile, organising an MA in Contemporary Asian Studies as well as a range of cultural and outreach activities.

Forced into following ministry guidelines, in late 2008 Leiden introduced LIAS, the Leiden Institute for Area Studies, as part of the new graduate school. The website, rather tersely, notes

> This institute will be newly formed from various institutes in the former faculty of Arts. Many researchers from the CNWS will join this institute, as will researchers from departments working in the field of languages and cultures from the Middle East and Asia.[21]

The brevity of the remarks suggests the intellectual and personal dramas inherent in any such reshuffling. Strong groups resist incorporation, fearing that their staff–student ratios will be driven into dangerous territory as their strength is used to pad the numbers of less popular courses. As in any business takeover, job losses seemed inevitable. In 2010, Indonesian studies was merged with Indian and Tibetan studies into a department of South and Southeast Asian Studies with one joint BA program, while still retaining – as of late 2011 – separate MA programs.[22] It is unclear if further forcible integration will be imposed; the more popular Chinese, Japanese

---

[21] http://www.hum.leiden.edu/research/area-studies.jsp. Accessed June 2008. For current programs, see http://hum.leiden.edu/lias.

[22] In 2007 the BA in Indonesian studies in Leiden had seven first-year students, in 2008 12, with a staff of seven. The MA students numbered seven, most in the contemporary Asean oriented project. In 2011 the staff included three professors (Ben Arps for language, David Henley for contemporary Indonesia, Marijke Klokke for art history) one associate professor in history and economics (Thomas Lindblad) and two senior language lecturers; Javanese is no longer compulsory in the BA program.

and Korean studies could be used to buttress study of their less fashionable Asian neighbours.

In 1935, the Dutch historian Jan Romein formulated the idea of '*de wet van de remmende voorsprong*', or the 'doctrine of the retarding lead' to describe how initial advantages could become liabilities, inhibiting the ability to adjust to change (1935, 9–64). As the political scientists have also discovered, path dependency ensures the survival of established patterns of behaviour, even after they have become inefficient or inappropriate. Breaking such dependency is extremely difficult, as it may require a paradigm shift. In situations of 'normal science', as Thomas Kuhn (1996) observed, researchers focus on filling in the gaps within an existing paradigm, rather than questioning the assumptions that frame their enquiries. This holds true not only for the ways scholars shape intellectual agendas, and are shaped by them, but also for academics' relationships with the structures within which they work.

A parade of plans, committees and reports marked the seemingly Sisyphesian attempts to restructure and rationalise (the Ministry of Education) or preserve (the academics) the traditions of Indonesian studies in the Netherlands. Looking back, it seems that the former have succeeded in achieving their main goals, which were to cut costs and to increase accountability (or political control) of teaching and research by centralising funding. The struggles of the latter, however, have proved a delaying tactic at best. Under threat, the Asianists mustered a familiar arsenal in their defence, combining references to the crucial role of Asia in the global future with evocations of past scholarship. But to little avail.

Three parallel processes have contributed to this crisis: the first was that of institutional politics, while the second was the logical result of decolonisation; the third was related to the second, and reflected the fundamental realignments in history and anthropology after the 1960s. The first process was fairly straightforward. The ramifications of expanding state intervention, and the concomitant imposition of simplified business models on the universities has been relentless. While many supported demands for more transparency, scholars have become increasingly bitter regarding the government's imposition of quantitative indices for productivity and petty administrative demands as revealing a contempt for core academic values (Lorenz 2008). Meanwhile, as decolonisation swept away the practical need for specialists in Indonesian studies, the job market shrank.

The relationship between university staff and policy bureaucrats has not been a happy one. Academics are the epitome of an epistemic community, 'a network of professionals with recognised competence in a particular domain and an authoritative claim to policy-relevant knowledge within that domain'. Such a community is characterised by shared norms, causal beliefs, notions of validity and common practice (Haas 1992, 3). Like other institutions (including ministries), universities develop sub-cultures, which shape the way their inhabitants view the world and can be very resistant to change. It could be argued that this applies *a fortiori* to academics: the nature of their work tends to convince them that they know best. However, while the professorial consensus of 'shared norms, causal beliefs, notions of validity and common practice' was once unchallenged, it has now been superseded by that of the bureaucrats who hold the purse-strings and hence have the power. Intellectual qualifications and experience in research and teaching is no longer regarded as constituting an authoritative claim to policy-relevant knowledge. But while policy-makers may have had (and have) little appreciation of the academic's frustration, they could see the potential political value of the Indonesia studies tradition. Because of this, it sometimes seemed that Asian studies enjoyed a privileged position in the Netherlands compared with other region-focused initiatives.

After the renewal of contacts with Indonesia after 1965, there were a number of praiseworthy government efforts to increase access by Indonesians to the Netherlands' scholarly resources. The Indonesian studies program (1975–1992) brought junior academics to the Netherlands for PhD training; since 1997 this effort has been successfully expanded in the wider TANAP (VOC) project, which resulted in 17 dissertations on early modern history. At the MA level, a similar initiative called 'Encompass' (Encountering a Shared Asian Past) brings future intellectual trend-setters from all over Asia to Leiden. Research funding also benefits from this desire to capitalise upon useful tradition: the Royal Academy of Sciences, or KNAW, has sponsored several cooperative research efforts specifically designed to unite scholars from Indonesia and the Netherlands, with some participation from other countries.

This internationally oriented sponsorship also resulted in one of the government's more successful initiatives, the creation of the International Institute of Asian Studies in 1993. The IIAS was intended to combine the resources of Leiden and Amsterdam to create a leading role for the Netherlands' Asian studies in the global arena by sponsoring research projects and the accompanying conferences and publications; current emphasis is on urban issues, globalisation in Asia, and heritage. External funds support networking activities, while new initiatives for summer-school-like programs are being developed. On the whole, the IIAS has been a success; the newsletter has established itself as an internationally useful reference. The IIAS has also tried to strengthen Asian studies teaching by supporting designated chairs at several universities. A branch office in Amsterdam was created to ensure that activities would not be too narrowly concentrated in Leiden but this will now close as the University of Amsterdam has withdrawn its funding. Such internationally oriented projects are seen as investments in Dutch status and 'soft power', and consequently enjoy some political support.

However, it could be argued that all this investment has had little positive influence on the teaching of Indonesia-focused subjects. Indeed, it seems that government generosity created a distorted structure: a relatively well-funded postgraduate sector enjoyed wide interest and high status, but this was not sustained by a strong undergraduate base within the Netherlands itself. Much of the money has gone to support conferences and visiting academics, and relatively little has trickled down to those most engaged in teaching. The PhDs and post-doctorates produced by the various projects have had dispiritingly little chance of permanent academic employment. On the other hand, there has been an expansion at BA level in East Asian studies, given that knowledge of China, Korea or Japan is seen as useful to a number of future careers, but this has not been the case for Indonesia. This suggests that the weakening of Indonesian studies is part of a rebalancing of the curriculum as a whole, reflecting the logic of the market. However, shifts in preferences are a result not only of changing assessments of job prospects, but also of developments in the intellectual climate of the last decades, which was referred to above as the third factor influencing the crisis in Indonesian studies.

In particular, the Leiden traditions in philology, history, archaeology and even anthropology often seem to be regarded as slightly dated and too demanding.[23] Amsterdam has fared somewhat better, as it is perceived as more open to influence from cultural studies and other popular trends. Nostalgia once provided a pool of potential students, particularly among those with a family background in the Indies, but this also has shrunk with time. For this constituency, the old interest in *ons Indie* or our Indies, was not so readily translated into a desire to study Indonesia. When students did choose for

---

[23] The compulsory study of Javanese has been one of the main obstacles for students contemplating a degree in Indonesian studies in Leiden; too difficult, and not really necessary for the students' interests.

Indonesia, most were drawn to either contemporary problems or the role of 'the Indies' in Dutch history, memory and culture.[24] Neither interest demanded the rigorous training (particularly in languages) characteristic of the old area studies approach. In short, it can be concluded that, despite the continuing international importance of the Netherlands–Asia-focused intellectual infrastructure, there is an ongoing and deepening crisis in Indonesian studies, caused by the loss of interest among Dutch students and a collapse in political support. Given the mathematics of the funding model (geared to the number of graduations), this has had inevitable and serious consequences.

History within Indonesian studies in the Netherlands and Australia

The Netherlands and Australia may both seem to have a natural commitment to Indonesian studies, but the reasons for that interest are very different. The legacy of the Dutch East Indies has left the former with an impressive infrastructure that enjoys international respect, and has proved to be a political resource worth exploiting. There remains within Dutch society a strong, if ambivalent, emotional involvement with the colonial era, but this has not translated into a significant interest in modern Indonesia. In fact, even the Indies' past is primarily used by contemporary political factions and public moralists as a convenient 'other', to create contrasts and parallels with current events.[25] The situation in Australia is much more straightforward: Indonesia dominates the 'near north', a source of cheap holidays and political anxieties, which occasionally combine in events like the Bali bombings of 2002 and 2005. It makes sense for the Australian government to invest in expertise on the region, and as a result Australia must have the highest concentration of Indonesianists in the world, outside the country itself. Indeed, there are probably more scholars working on Indonesia at the ANU alone than there are in the Netherlands as a whole. But even in Australia, despite the highly developed language teaching (even at school level), and

---

[24] The Dutch campaign to encourage reading chose a 61-year-old novel, *Oeroeg*, by Hella Haasse, as the book to be distributed free to millions of readers in 2009.

[25] Classic recent examples include the debate about the Dutch 'My Lai' massacre at Rawagede in 1947, finally accepted as a 'war crime' by Dutch courts in September 2011, or a well-known and still frequently cited 2006 reference by then Dutch Premier Jan-Peter Balkenende to 'the VOC mentality' see http://www.youtube.com/watch?v=L798qiQXVo4. Accessed October 2011.

the emphasis on in-country training, Indonesian studies was losing ground sharply: between 2002 and 2009 the number of students studying the language dropped by 30 per cent.[26]

Two separate issues must be distinguished: is there a loss of interest in Indonesia as such, or is the decline specifically in the study of Indonesia as institutionalised in the traditional area studies? Would a trawl through the disciplines and more fashionable fields such as cultural or post-colonial studies reveal that interest in Indonesia is alive and well, and that students are being turned off not so much by the subject, but by the presentation and demands of the region-focused programs?

As described earlier in this chapter, classic area studies were characterised by an emphasis on language, an interdisciplinary knowledge of the literature, and personal experience in the field. Disciplines, on the other hand, while superficially distinguished by subject (non-Europeans for anthropologists, the past for historians) always found their basic identity in methodology: fieldwork for the former, archives for the latter. Here I will focus on history. As mentioned earlier, many historians felt somewhat embattled in the later decades of the twentieth century. Paradoxically, there has also been a great expansion in the discipline as a whole and – at least in the Netherlands – an explosion of public interest in the field.[27] C. A. Bayley, in his *The Birth of the Modern World 1780–1914* concluded that 'the discovery of history as the essential mode of explanation for all phenomena, natural and human, was the most revolutionary change of the nineteenth century' (Bayley 2004, 484). It is claimed that 'history does dominate the public mind: its hold over the social imagination is total' (Davies 2006) and that 'history must not be just a subject matter but rather an epistemology' (Somers, 1996). This last comment goes beyond the relatively factual emphasis on methodology, arguing that historians must consider the relationship between knowledge, assumptions and belief, the questions of what is truth and how can we know it, and the reconciliation of different truth regimes.

If history is a way of knowing, then there is some justification for its claim to be a 'discipline', a field of study based on a mode of enquiry with acquired technical skills and controlled by institutions applying

---

[26] http://www.theaustralian.com.au/higher-education/plan-unable-to-save-study-of-indonesian/story-e6frgcjx-1226006527311.

[27] There were 1999 professional historians in British universities in 1980; in 2008 there were 2896; see Corfield 2008, 22.

acknowledged standards. The 'shared norms, causal beliefs, notions of validity and common practice' that form the foundation of the historians' sense of community are the social expression of this epistemological shared ground. While the institutionalisation of academic fields, discussed briefly in the first section, is shaped by politics at all levels, ultimately their academic legitimation depends on their claim to represent a specific epistemology, reflected in a body of theory and related methodologies. This legitimation has often been seen as strong for the long-established disciplines (history, language, natural and social sciences),[28] and relatively weak for newer subjects regarded as providing mere job-training (for example, in the media) or an over-inflated theoretical superstructure with little methodological rigour (for example, black or cultural studies). Generally, these new disciplines – like area studies – were created as a response to political pressures or market interest and, like area studies, have often had a reinvigorating influence on the academy.

Placing area studies in such an epistemologically based framework raises interesting questions. Are Indonesian studies, for example, simply a bundling together of useful practical knowledge into a conventional degree structure, or is there something special about the ways we 'know' Indonesia? Is knowing Indonesian history, for example, qualitatively different from the ways a colleague might know fourteenth century France or nineteenth century Peru? I think not. In each case there is a need for special skills ranging from an ability to access sources in other languages, to a general knowledge of context. But whereas a historian of fourteenth century France might be excused a lack of interest in modern French politics or the anthropology of Provence, he would probably be versed to some extent on contemporaneous developments elsewhere in Europe. However, a historian with a background in area studies would probably be familiar with current events, but much less well informed of similar thematic developments elsewhere in the world. The trade-off for the interdisciplinary strength of area studies is the parochialism noted by Manning (2003). This is reflected in a typically wide general knowledge of the region, but relatively little interest in theory, method or comparison. Inevitably, as the intellectual frontier has come to emphasise global trends, cultural exchange and academic self-questioning, area studies have tended to look provincial, old-fashioned and self-satisfied.

---

[28] This is not intended to imply that the established disciplines were neutral entities with a self-evident and natural right to existence; see for example (Jasanoff 2004).

The solution would seem to lie in a closer engagement with the disciplines as a whole. It is interesting that work on Indonesia is a natural part of the mainstream in some fields, as in prehistory, anthropology, archaeology or economics, while in others, such as history, the Indonesianists tend to operate in region-oriented organisations and have little or no interaction with the discipline as a whole. This reflects partly the compartmentalisation of the historical profession in general, but even in the explicitly global or issue-oriented journals, such as *Comparative Studies in Society and History*, *History and Theory* or the *Journal of World History*, Indonesia is sparsely represented. A more intensive dialogue with colleagues working on other themes or regions is, however, inhibited by two major factors. The first is the existing territorial institutionalisation and often parochial sub-cultures within area studies; the second is the lack of interest by colleagues in what the Indonesianists have to say.

Like any sub-culture, that of Indonesian area studies is to a large extent self-referring, with its own heroes, themes and fashions (Cribb 2005). While this can be comforting and rewarding for those involved, it does not necessarily translate into intellectual concerns of general interest. This has become painfully clear in the Netherlands, where salvation seems to lie in the embedding of Indonesian studies in wider programs focused on contemporary Asia or, in Leiden, in 'area studies', that is, the rest not the West. Such restructuring brings together a number of minority interests, the collective strength of which, it is hoped, will prove sufficient to be viable. This represents a choice for a middle way, between that of the more narrowly defined area studies and the open seas of the disciplines. The latter are seen, understandably, as much too threatening: non-Western subjects will always be first in line for sacrifice in hard times.

The choice for the middle way here, as in most cases, involves compromise. The rigour of the old area studies tradition will be sacrificed, as governments are disinclined to subsidise the most rarefied forms of expertise. This is a pity, as although this sort of BA or MA degree might be unsustainable, the subjects themselves need to be preserved and made available to the international select few who choose them.[29] This means staff must be trained and paid. An 'Asian'

---

[29] The organisation of pan-European or international summer schools or intensive courses is an obvious and necessary strategy; seven universities have participated in such MA programs initiated by Leiden University and organised by the IIAS. These have been held in Leiden (2006), Paris (2007) and Naples (2008). Europe can only retain this capacity if, for example, the Netherlands does Javanese, the UK Burmese. The IIAS is active in this regard.

framework is also somewhat arbitrary and unfocused, and may encourage a false confidence in the ease of cross-cultural comparisons. The Leiden preference for 'area studies', which effectively means non-Western societies, is even broader, but does offer the potential advantages and disadvantages of wider cross-cultural post-colonial perspectives. Both options perpetuate the risk of isolation from debate in the disciplines, and a consequent intellectual provincialism, without the students necessarily acquiring the compensatory depth of knowledge offered in the classic regional studies programs. The question is how to maximise the security provided by incorporation into new structures, while resisting the limitations imposed.

Institutionalisation is a prerequisite for participation in the professional knowledge establishment, and inevitably it creates vested interests and fosters the development of self-regarding sub-cultures. These resist change, and are typically only broken open through major changes in the social and political context (expressed most concretely in funding shifts), such as those imposed in the Netherlands over the past 25 years. The resulting enforced reorientation can have positive effects, as some of the alliances entered into for strategic or marketing reasons can bear real intellectual fruits. The KITLV in Leiden, for example, a symbol of Dutch colonial expertise, must increasingly compete in the open market by seeking research funds earmarked not for Indonesia, but for general themes, resulting in projects comparing economies in Africa and Southeast Asia, or on the heritage industry.

Conclusion

Indonesian studies in the Netherlands achieved its classic form over 80 years ago, in the Indology training for colonial officials. Only now does it seem that fundamental change has arrived, 50 years after decolonisation, and after decades of political pressure. Even so, we must wait and see what actually happens. As the Dutch say, the soup is rarely eaten as hot as it is served. In Australia the field seems to have encountered less turbulence. This is logical, given the greater continuity in the political context. The threats and opportunities offered by the powerful northern neighbour have remained, even if Indonesia's role in public rhetoric has fluctuated. The apparent security offered by this geopolitical environment could encourage a false sense of entitlement, with debilitating effects comparable to the colonial 'retarding lead' in the Netherlands. Indeed, the challenge posed by changing intellectual interests and declining student enrolment suggest that some re-assessment is overdue.

Ideally, in both countries, area studies scholars could use their specific insights into particular cultures in order to contribute to current debates within the disciplines. Political scientists could present themselves not as 'Indonesianists', but as experts on, for example, military regimes, democratisation, tensions between central and regional elites, or any number of other topics of wider interest. This would require familiarity with the priorities and sub-cultures dominant in the discipline as a whole, and also a broadening of interest by those disciplinary scholars to whom Indonesia, despite its size, seems peripheral in every sense. Journal editors, conference organisers, and curriculum planners would have to be willing to look further than they have in the past. For historians, a newly emerging field like world or global history offers relatively accessible opportunities to participate in emerging comparative themes (Manning 2003).

* * *

The courses I followed at the ANU in the early 1960s included four years of Indonesian and Malay, including the reading of classical literature in Jawi. I also studied Javanese for two years, as well as Minangkabau and basic Arabic. Looking back, I can safely say that I have never made use of most of this training but, at the same time, I regard it as having been of great value. The study of texts in their original languages provides an opportunity for a slow and careful appreciation of their intellectual significance, acquired not through second-hand summaries, but through the painstaking unravelling of concepts and contexts. Similarly, area studies scholars typically build up their knowledge of local societies through the cumulative reading of literature from a number of disciplines, combined with first-hand personal experience. This also fosters a useful skepticism, which, if tempered by a wider knowledge of theory and the potential as well as the pitfalls of comparisons, can provide an excellent point of departure for more ambitious work. It would be a great pity if these sober qualities were lost through a combination of government economising and changes in university organisation. The days of the area studies programs, including those on Indonesia, may seem numbered. But government policies and intellectual fashions are often cyclical, and it could well be that current obsessions with cultural difference, religion, local identities and globalisation will lead to a reinvention of area studies. If so, we should be there.

References

Bayly, C A. 2004. *The Birth of the Modern World 1780–1914*. Oxford: Blackwell.
Bonnell, V E; Hunt, L, editors (1999). *Beyond the Cultural Turn: New Directions in the Study of Society and Culture*. Berkeley, CA: University of California Press.
Burns, P. 2004. *The Leiden Legacy: Concepts of law in Indonesia*. Leiden: KITLV.
Campbell, I C. 1997. 'Culture Contact and Polynesian Identity in the European Age' *Journal of World History* 8 (1): 29–55.
Chakrabarty, D. 2002. *Habitations of Modernity: Essays in the Wake of Subaltern Studies*. Chicago: University of Chicago.
Chaturvedi, V, editor. 2000. *Mapping Subaltern Studies and the Postcolonial*. London: Verson.
Corfield, P J. 2008. 'How to get back', *Times Literary Supplement* (21 November): 22.
Cribb, R. 2005. 'Circles of esteem, standard works, and euphoric couplets: Dynamics of academic life in Indonesian studies', *Critical Asian Studies* 37 (2): 289–304.
Cumings, B. 1997. 'Boundary displacement: Area studies and international studies during and after the Cold War', *Bulletin of Concerned Asian Scholars* 29: 6–26.
Davies, M L. 2006. *Historics: Why History Dominates Society*. London: Routledge.
de Ridder, R; Karremans, J A J, editors. 1987. *The Leiden Tradition in Structural Anthropology: Essays in Honour of P. E. de Josselin de Jong*. Leiden: Brill.
Fardon, R, editor. 1990. *Localizing Strategies: Regional Traditions in Ethnographic Writing*. Edinburgh and Washington: Scottish Academic Press and Smithsonian Institution Press.
Fasseur, C. 1983. *De Indologen: Ambtenaren voor de Oost*. Amsterdam, Bert Bakker.
Fukuyama, F. 1992. *The End of History and the Last Man*. London: Penguin.
Haas, P M. 1992. 'Introduction: Epistemic communities and international policy coordination', *International Organisation* 46 (1): 1–35.
Heryanto, A. 1996. 'Beyond authenticism and academism: Priorities for future Indonesian studies'. Paper to Association of Asian Studies, Hawaii.
Hurgronje, C S. 2007. *Mekka in the Latter Part of the 19th Century*. Leiden: Brill.
Iggers, G G. 2005. *Historiography in the Twentieth Century: From Scientific Objectivity to the Postmodern Challenge, with a new epilogue by the author*. Middletown, CT: Wesleyan University Press.
Jasanoff, S., editor. 2004. *States of Knowledge: The Co-production of Science and the Social Order*. London: Routledge.
Kassimir, R. 1997. 'The internationalization of African studies: View from the SSRC', *Africa Today* 44 (2): 155–63.
Kratoska, P H; Raben R., editors. 2005. *Locating Southeast Asia: Geographies of Knowledge and The Politics of Space*. Singapore/Leiden: NUS Press/KITLV Press.

Kuhn, T S. 1996. *The Structure of Scientific Revolutions*. Chicago, Illinois: University of Chicago Press.

Kuitenbrouwer, M. 2001. *Tussen Orientalisme en Wetenschap. Het Koninklijk Instituut voor Taal-, Land- en Volkenkunde in Historisch Verband 1851–2001*. Leiden: KITLV Press.

Legge, J D. 1999. 'The writing of Southeast Asian history'. In *The Cambridge History of Southeast Asia: Early Times from c1500*, Vol. 1, Part 1, edited by Tarling, Nicholas. Cambridge: Cambridge University Press: 1–52.

Lorenz, C, editor. 2008. *If You're So Smart, Why Aren't You Rich?* Amsterdam: Boom.

Ludden, D. 2002. *Reading Subaltern Studies: Critical History, Contested Meaning and the Globalization of South Asia*. London: Anthem South Asian Studies.

Maier, H J M; Teeuw, A, editors. 1976. *Honderd Jaar Studie van Indonesie 1850-1950: Levensbeschrijvingen van Twaalf Nederlandse Onderzoekers*. The Hague: Smits.

Manning, P. 2003. *Navigating World History: Historians Create A Global Past*. New York.

Matsuda, M K. 2006. 'The Pacific', *American Historical Review*, 111 (3): 758–780.

McDonald, T J, editor. 1996. *The Historic Turn in the Human Sciences*. Ann Arbor: University of Michigan Press.

van den Muijzenberg, O. 1991. Krishna in de Delta: De Azie-studies op weg naar de 21ste eeuw, KNAW, Amsterdam.

Philpott, S. 2000. *Rethinking Indonesia: Postcolonial Theory, Authoritarianism and Identity*. London: Macmillan.

Piekaar, A J. 1949. *Atjeh en de Oorlog met Japan*. The Hague: W. van Hoeve.

Romein, J. 1935. *De Dialectiek van de Vooruitgang. Het Onvoltooid Verleden: Kultuurhistorische Studies*. Amsterdam: Querido.

Said, E. 1978. *Orientalism*. London: Routledge.

Sears, L J, editor. 2007. *Knowing Southeast Asian Subjects: Critical Dialogues in Southeast Asian Studies*. Seattle/Singapore: University of Washington Press/NUS Press.

Somers, M R. 1996. 'Where is sociology after the historic turn?', in *The Historic Turn in the Human Sciences*, edited by McDonald, T J. Ann Arbor: University of Michigan Press: 53–90.

Suny, R G. 2002. 'Back and beyond: Reversing the cultural turn?' *American Historical Review* 107 (5): 1476–1499.

Sutherland, H. 2003. 'Southeast Asian history and the Mediterranean analogy', *Journal of Southeast Asian History* 34 (1): 1–20.

Sutherland, H. 2007. 'The problematic authority of (world) history', *Journal of World History* 18 (4): 491–521.

Swellengrebel, J L. 1974 (Vol. 1); 1978 (Vol. 2). In *Leijdeckers Voetspoor*. The Hague: Martinus Nijhoff.

Tobin, J. 1994. 'Cultural construction and native nationalism: Report from the Hawaiian front', *Boundary* 2 21 (1): 111–133.
Weijts, C. 2004. 'Letteren op de schop', *Mare* (7 October 2004). Accessed October 2008. Available at: http://www.mareonline.nl/2004/06/0101.html.
Wills, J E. 1991. Review of *Leiden Oriental Connections, 1850–1940*, *The Journal of Asian Studies* 50 (3): 648–649.

Chapter 7

Shared Problems, Shared Interests

Reframing Australia–Indonesia Security Relations

Richard Tanter

Against a background of recurring crises in Australia's most sensitive security relationship, one new approach to the security aspects of relations between Australia and Indonesia could be based on the possibilities of new communities of shared interests emerging to deal with the challenges of global problems faced by both societies. On the basis of careful examination of the potential and limitations of existing policy currents, and with a mapping of existing networks of social relationships between the two countries, it may be possible to provide an empirical and theoretical foundation to a new set of policy approaches to Australia–Indonesia security relationships. The key hypothesis is that global problems manifest in the fabric of the two societies, and whose causes lie beyond their national systems, will not only generate deep security challenges but also new possibilities of cross-border communities of shared interest. The secondary hypothesis is that this process will enhance the capacity to manage the difficult bilateral problems already evident by placing them in a context of larger security collaborations, albeit largely of a non-traditional kind, and relying more than in the past on leadership from non-state actors.

The main argument here is that there is a need to rethink the analysis of relations between Indonesia and Australia, and equally, the kinds of politics that are conducted – and could be conducted – between the two states and social formations. It is concerned with the analytical underpinnings of the practical political processes of restructuring the boundaries of communities of shared interest and shared values. It is also derived from persisting limitations of much Australian and Indonesian media and academic commentary on the subject.

The very phrase 'the Australia–Indonesia relationship' has come to connote something discrete and reified, calling to mind a small furry animal-like object that can be prodded and poked on the consulting table, and have its temperature taken, and be pronounced – by a politically approved commentariat in both countries – as sick, damaged, critical, recovering, or in fine fettle. It is not that the political situations to which these labels were applied were not real – they often referred to situations with serious and all too often deadly consequences. But the phrasing and conceptualisation of 'the relationship' had the effect of carefully excluding both consideration of particular enduring problems and the voices of inappropriate would-be entrants into the discourse. But the question of how we in Australia think about Indonesia politically – not just analytically – is now very firmly on the agenda.

Let us begin with five concerns with the character of contemporary Australian relations with Indonesia. These are:

- the ongoing volatility and fragility of the state–state relationship
- persisting analytical deficiencies deriving from an unreflective commitment to methodological nationalism
- the emergence of new types of problems affecting both countries; namely global problems such as climate change
- declining resources in Australian society to understand Indonesian society
- the uneven and limited success of democratic reform in Indonesia, and, despite economic growth, the enduring likelihood of serious social and political conflict and regime instability
- an Australian strategic culture marked by persistent and endemic ambivalence towards Indonesia, fundamental feelings of geographically defined vulnerability, and a commitment to the use of armed force in international affairs.

Many of these political and analytical difficulties flow from the structures of the relationship between the two countries – their states and their societies – and from their historical and contemporary locations in the wider world system.

The characteristics of the Australia–Indonesia relationship

If Australia's relationship with the United States is the most important in Australian defence and foreign policy, then the almost equally important security relationship with Indonesia is the most sensitive and volatile. Crises are recurring and, because of their media treatment, are well known in Australia in iconic terms: East Timor, the Bali and Jakarta bombings, the drug possession and trafficking convictions of Schapelle Corby, Michelle Leslie and the 'Bali Nine', the Aceh tsunami, Papua, refugees, illegal fishing, people smugglers, ADF training of Indonesian forces and Kopassus in particular, Islamist terrorism, and most recently cruelty to beef cattle exported from Australia in Indonesian slaughterhouses. The raw material of these crises in the relationship is in large part generated from two sources. The first, as the live cattle trade, refugee, and drug-related incidents demonstrate, is a set of socially and politically mediated 'cultural differences', mixed with a good measure of Australian domestic political concerns, selective attention and double standards. Most of the rest, setting the tone for the overall relationship, are driven by the character of the Indonesian political system, its inherent contest between centrifugal and centripetal forces, and the lack of restraint on militarised solutions to what are otherwise quite common and normal political problems. Both of these sets of drivers will continue to generate conflict. To take the highly salient example of Papua, with its multiple linkages to border control, relations with PNG, Australian perceptions of Islam and ethnicity (Aspinall 2006), and concerns about human rights, the characteristics of the post-Suharto Indonesian political system operating on Papua will ensure continual potential for crisis (Chauvel 2006).

Yet the structure and character of the relationship between the two states also influences the structure of conflict. In conventional wisdom, the defining characteristics of the relationship between the states derive from geography and history. In the mid-1990s, Gareth Evans made the point colourfully:

> Australia and Indonesia are most unusual neighbours. More than any other two countries in the world living alongside each other we are different – in languages, cultures, religions, history, ethnicity, population size, and in political, legal and social systems. We might as well be half a world apart (Evans 1994).

The Secretary of the Indonesian Department of Foreign Affairs and former Ambassador to Australia, Imron Cotan, echoed these thoughts, seeing the two countries as, 'absolutely different from one another, notably in terms of history, culture and political orientation' (Cotan 2005).

This conventional wisdom has important elements of truth that should not be forgotten, but there are also elements of exaggeration or misperception. Moreover, these are not the only significant elements in the structure of the state-state relationship and may not be the most important sources of conflict. A number of themes are immediately salient.

Ambiguous asymmetry

In 2010, Australia, as a small rich country with a population of 22.6 million people, had a Gross Domestic Product of US$1219 billion (13th in IMF rankings), and a GDP per capita of US$54,869. In the same year Indonesia, as a large developing country with a population of 237.6 million people, had a Gross Domestic Product of US$695 billion (18th in IMF rankings), and a GDP per capita of US$2963 (International Monetary Fund 2010). While Australia likes to cultivate amnesia concerning the genocidal character of its settler colonial origins, both countries are largely the result of European colonialism coercing pre-existing societies to form complex social formations retaining structural and cultural qualities of both the pre-colonial and colonial periods.

The relationship between Indonesia and Australia is an asymmetrical one. The fundamental fact is that Indonesia is far more important to Australia's security concerns than is Australia to Indonesia's. However wounding the recognition may be to Australian narcissism, Australia is also much the less important in world affairs and world history in almost every respect, except through the size of its economy at this point in history. The past two and a half centuries of history have weakened the Indonesian social formation to the point where a country one-tenth its population size can see itself as its equal in world politics. However, this is unlikely to persist for a comparable time in the future.

As Nancy Viviani reminded Australians some years ago, the bedrock asymmetry in the relationship derives from size and geopolitics:

> Population size and military strength also matter in international relations. This means that, generally speaking, Indonesia carries more

weight among Asian countries, including China and Japan, and with the U.S. and Europe, than Australia does (Viviani 2000).

At root, geography and size mean that Indonesia matters a great deal more to Australia than Australia matters to Indonesia. One consequence of this asymmetry, as Viviani went on to say, is that 'in any dispute with Indonesia, Australia stands to bear disproportionate costs to the bilateral relationship'.

One mark of this recognition is the difference in academic, research and policy attention: the number of Indonesia specialists in Australian universities considerably outweighs the number of Australian specialist in Indonesian universities – in absolute terms, let alone proportionally to population. Moreover, in the Australian defence, intelligence and foreign affairs communities, deep knowledge and competence on Indonesian affairs is highly valued, ranking alongside or even above Chinese or Japanese competence.

For both countries, the United States is the key friendly country, although in both cases there are ambivalences and doubts. However, the ANZUS treaty notwithstanding, Indonesia is of much greater strategic importance to the United States than is Australia to the US, as demonstrated clearly during the 1959–1962 West New Guinea crisis, and recognised at the time by the Australian Minister for External affairs, Garfield Barwick. Viviani noted that, 'Some Australians are confused by this because of the importance they attach to their alliance with the US, always expecting the U.S. to support Australia, regardless of its own interests' (Viviani 2000).

This is not to say that Australia is not very much closer to the United States on almost every contemporary issue of international security. Australia willingly and indeed enthusiastically provided substantial combat support for the United States-led wars in the Persian Gulf and Iraq, and after almost 10 years of fighting, continues to do so in Afghanistan. Indonesia supported none in comparable fashion. Australia is host to a range of United States military and intelligence facilities under the rubric of 'joint facilities'. Several, especially in electronic and increasingly in space intelligence, are of great importance to the United States. The ANZUS alliance is of such importance in Australian strategic and popular culture that it is extraordinarily difficult, six decades after its establishment and even two decades after the end of the Cold War to conduct a meaningful debate in Australia on strategic options absent the US alliance.

On the contrary, successive Indonesian governments have pursued differing versions of a *bebas dan aktif* (free and active) foreign policy that has its roots in the formulation in 1948 by the country's first vice-president (and prime minister at the time), Mohammad Hatta: *mendayung di antara dua karang* – rowing between two reefs (Wuryandari 2008: 42–43). Leaning sometimes to left until 1965, sometimes to right during the Cold War, post-New Order Indonesian governments have moved closer to the United States as a result of the demands of the US-led Global War on Terror – and the prospect of an end to Congressional bans on certain forms of military cooperation. In 2008 President Yudhoyono proposed forming 'a comprehensive partnership' with the United States, and evoked a positive response from the United States (United States 2010).

Asymmetry of threat perceptions

Yet, this 'comprehensive partnership' is a long way from a formal Indonesia–United States alliance, or from the depth of the Australian attachment to the United States. Indeed, while Indonesia has drawn closer to the United States in the past five years or so, there is also an ambivalence about that shift among the Indonesian foreign policy and security elite. Novotny's study of threat perceptions of the Indonesian foreign policy elite based mostly on interviews conducted in late 2004 and early 2005, showed elite opinion divided and oscillating between 'love' and 'hate' – towards the United States, especially over the War on Terror. Novotny found that most of his interviewees:

> ... still consider the U.S. anti-terrorism campaign not as a direct threat to Indonesian national security but rather as an offence to the sensitivities and pride of the Indonesian people (Novotny 2010: 139).

Novotny's interviewees showed an updated sense of traditional Indonesian nationalist concerns when they identified three non-traditional sources of contemporary American threat to Indonesia: US power stemming from its prominent norm-building position; US power over information and manipulation of international media; and NGOs operating around Indonesia functioning as Washington's agents serving US interests (Novotny 2010:146).

Leaving aside the accuracy of these perceptions of threat, it is this type of threat cluster which, together with more conventional and traditional nationalist concerns, and the wider principle of a *bebas dan aktif* (free and active) foreign policy, with its residues of non-alignment, which distinguishes Indonesian and Australian policy elites attitudes to the United States. Indonesia will always remain more important to the United States than Australia will be, and consequently, not least for that reason, Australia clings closer to its American ally, eschewing the doubts Indonesia believes it can afford to have.

For Australian strategic culture and consequently for its defence planners, Indonesia is the primary source of threat. Two former senior defence recently summarised the place of Indonesia in past Australian defence thinking, referring to then recently declassified *Strategic Basis* papers (Frühling 2009a).

> The simple facts of geography dictate that Indonesia is a country of abiding strategic importance to Australia ... Australia has a permanent interest in Indonesia's friendship and stability. An Indonesia that became hostile could pose a serious threat to Australia's security. Australia's classified defence planning has long acknowledged that the most likely direct military threats would come 'from or through' the archipelago to our north (Dibb and Brabin-Smith 2007: 67).

Looking forward, their former Defence Department colleague Hugh White, in a sketch exploring possibilities of war for Australia over the next two decades, scrutinised two possibilities, both of which he considered highly unlikely: war with Indonesia and war with China (White 2002: 259). But for this discussion of asymmetry between Australia and Indonesia, what added significance was White's emphasis on the 'very distinctively Australian' characteristics of Australian strategic culture. These include:

> ... a strong predilection to alliances; an almost equally strong disposition towards self-reliance; a highly possessive approach to the islands in our immediate neighbourhood, often manifested as a kind of Monroe Doctrine; an acute sense of vulnerability in relation to our sparsely populated north and west, including a persistent anxiety about invasion; an endemic ambivalence towards Indonesia, and an instinct for what at one time was called forward defence. These elements in turn are based on a deeply held sense of separateness from our regional environment, an undiminished adherence to the idea of the state as the key actor in the security arena, a belief in the enduring significance of

armed force in the international system, and a strong apprehension of potential threats' (White 2002: 257).

Australians are often loath to see their security policy as a substantially militarised one – in contrast, many of them would think, to Indonesia, or the United States. But White's bravura insider's sketch of Australian security culture leads to that conclusion, as well as to an understanding of the multiple drivers in that strategic culture that lead to an asymmetry in threat perceptions with Indonesian strategic culture.

There is however, one symmetrical aspect of threat perceptions. Australian and Indonesian public opinion polls in recent years show that roughly half of the public in each country does not have a good feeling about the other country. The Lowy Institute has conducted public opinion polls in Australia every year from 2006 asking respondents to rate their feelings about other countries on a scale from zero (cold and unfavourable) to 100. In no year did Indonesia rate above 50 for Australian respondents. In 2009, '54 per cent of Australians trusted Indonesia "not at all" or "not very much" to act responsibly in the world, with almost one-quarter (23 per cent) of Australians trusting it "not at all"'. In 2006, the only year in which Indonesians were asked about their feelings about trusting Australia, respondents scored an average of 51 (Hanson 2010: 6–7). Both countries are at best lukewarm and mistrustful towards the other.

Returning to elite perceptions, in the aftermath of the Australian role in the independence of East Timor, including the Howard government's 2004 declaration of a pre-emptive strike policy and of a 1000 nautical mile Maritime Identification Zone which necessarily included Indonesian territorial waters, Australia's position in Indonesian elite security perceptions changed substantially. As one well-placed Indonesian friend put it in early 2007, 'For your information Indonesia's view of Australia has somewhat changed, from a harmless, though at times annoying, neighbour to a threat.'[1]

Conducted several years earlier, Novotny's interviews with his sample of the Indonesian foreign policy elite showed exactly this view, with Australia ranked as either the second or third most important threatening country – after the United States, and comparable with China. According to Novotny, three negative images of Australia 'overwhelmingly shared' by the Indonesian foreign policy elite gave rise to the sense of significant threat

---

[1] Author's personal communication, Anon. n.d.

from Australia: the Australian role in the independence of Timor-Leste; Australian embrace of the role of US Deputy Sheriff for Southeast Asia, and Australian-perceived designs on West Papua – and beyond that, a challenge to the Indonesian *negara integralistik (integrated nation)*.

Novotny provided no information as to whether the passing of time and subsequent events such as changes of government in Australia and the signing of the Lombok Treaty have assuaged the breadth and depth of these concerns. It is likely that the passing of time, the retirement of older political and bureaucratic players who built their careers in the New Order, reasonably successful cooperation over counter-terrorism, and increased aid after the Australian governmental and community response to the 2004 tsunami in Aceh, may have had some effect. But it is unlikely that the bedrock of mistrust has been eroded much.

Watching Australia assessing the costs of ongoing support for the independent state of Timor-Leste has given rise to a degree of Indonesian *schadenfreude*, seeing that commitment as a restraint on further Australian ambitions (Novotny 2010: 262). The signing of the 2006 Lombok Accord, with its declaration of mutual respect for existing territorial definitions indicated the intention and commitment of the Australian state to override the concerns of Australian civil society groups about the justice and validity of the historical process by which the territory of the former Dutch colony of West New Guinea was incorporated into Indonesia.

State–state relations dominant, business links weak, and transnational civil society absent

It is a commonplace that relations between the governments of Indonesia and Australia greatly outweigh all other components of the Australia–Indonesia relationship. The extent and intensity of government–government relations have greatly increased in recent years.

Trade and investment have increased in recent years, but remain lower than would be expected from comparable contiguous countries. Two-way merchandise trade amounted to $8.6 billion in 2009, roughly evenly balanced, making Indonesia Australia's 13th ranked trading partner, and Australia Indonesia's 8th most important export partner. (DFAT 2010: 83) Australian investment in Indonesia, which amounted $4.9 billion in 2009, is still low on the rankings of Australian investment abroad, while Indonesian investment in Australia was less than one-tenth the size at $339 million (ABS 2011).

Movements of people between the two countries show comparable disparities. While 16,000 Indonesian students were studying in Australia in 2008, less than 80 Australian undergraduates were studying in Indonesia for at least one semester in that year – and less than 60 the following year (Hanson 2010: 7–8). Australian tourists still flock to Bali, but only a trickle comes the other way.

The substantial and illuminating report of the 2004 parliamentary inquiry into Australian relations with Indonesia, titled *Near Neighbours – Good Neighbours*, maintains that the picture of the connections between the two countries is 'a richly textured and complex tapestry', yielding 'a multifaceted, multilevel, bilateral relationship'. It is certainly true that the relationship operates at different levels and has a number of facets, but as the report concedes, it is an uneven affair (Foreign Affairs Sub Committee 2004: paras 1.27–1.29). Moreover, there is little support for the case that the relationship is 'a richly textured and complex tapestry'. Indeed it is more like a poorly woven, ill-fitting and moth-eaten hand-me-down that needs serious repair if not replacing. The report began its chapter on 'people' by remarking

> At the heart of Australia's relationship with Indonesia is the relationship between the people of Indonesia and the people of Australia. One of the strongest themes that appeared in the evidence received during the course of this inquiry was the importance of the people-to-people links in building Australia's relationship with Indonesia (Foreign Affairs Sub Committee 2004: para 6.1).

Yet the report had remarkably little to say about the exact nature of those 'people-to-people links', other than to assert, without evidence, that 'the relationship at this level is reasonably strong' (Foreign Affairs Sub Committee 2004: para 6.3). The remainder of the chapter is devoted to demonstrating the contrary case by documenting the collapse of teaching of Indonesian language and Indonesian studies in Australian high schools and universities, preceded by a heroically optimistic account of the work of the government's Australia–Indonesia Institute.

There is little hard or systematic evidence to either support or contradict the Sub Committee's optimistic statement, but anecdotal evidence received informally from a range of Australians closely involved with Indonesia, in business, the community sector, academia and government confirms the impression that apart from tourism and government, Australians have very little to do with Indonesia – certainly nothing that would compare with what could be expected from equivalent situations – for example, the United States and Mexico (TBI 2011) or the interactions between Western Europe, and North Africa (Anheier and Katz 2004).

What is most striking, in comparison with data from the North American and European relations with less developed neighbouring countries, is an apparent almost complete absence of substantive transnational civil society relations between Indonesia and Australia – even on a hierarchical basis (c.f. Anheier and Katz 2004). Examples of such relations immediately come to mind to suggest the contrary case, but it seems very likely that hard evidence would confirm their relative absence in the Australia–Indonesia case. Put simply, the impression is that, apart from government and tourist connections, the two societies sit beside each other, do not know each other, do not like each other very much, and have relatively little to do with each other.

The scale of the problem for Australians becomes clear if we ask our colleagues who are not professionally concerned with Indonesia: what prominent contemporary Indonesians, leaving aside presidents, can they name? In my anecdotal experience, for people concerned professionally with international relations and politics, but not themselves Indonesian specialists, the list tends to be very short – perhaps the adviser to former President Habibie, Dewi Fortuna Anwar; perhaps the ubiquitous conference attender and former Opsus (*Operasi Khusus*, Special Operations group) associate Jusuf Wanandi; perhaps the late Pramoedya Ananta Toer – but I suspect not many more. Such a short list would be shorter still if the question was put to colleagues in other disciplines, or outside academia.

The proximate source of the problem, but hardly the real explanation, becomes clear when you ask yourself when was the last time you read an Indonesian opinion piece in an Australian newspaper? On Papua, on refugees, on problems of border control, on relations with Timor, on bird flu, on the status of the Aceh peace agreement, on the ongoing conflict in the Malukus, on the regulation of the Malacca Straits, on taxation or investment climates, or just plain Indonesian daily political developments, to say nothing of the systemic problems that Indonesia faces? In fact there are no Indonesian voices to be heard – all are filtered through Australian commentary and 'expertise'.

It is hardly surprising that the relationship becomes reified so readily, since it is so thin, so friable and fragile, so identified with government-government relations, and marked by the absence of deep transnational and inter-penetrating civil society and institutional relationships.

Dominance of leader-to-leader relations

Another consequence of the weakness of broad and deep business and civil society linkages between the two countries, when combined with the inherent capacity of the Indonesian political system to give rise to challenges to international norms of civil rights and human security, is a fragility in Australian–Indonesian relationships and over reliance on relations between necessarily transient leaders. In the absence of multiple and diverse institutional and community linkages and pressures, whispers in the ears of strong-minded leaders hope to carry the day. The dominance of the relationship by state-state relations, in the almost complete absence of substantive transnational civil society relations and the remarkably thin market relationship, in combination with the inherent capacity of the Indonesian political system to give rise to challenges to international norms of civil rights and human security, means inevitable fragility and reliance on the somewhat fanciful or labile characteristics of the putative relations between leaders.

Leaders are always important to some degree in such relationships, but they have been particularly so on the Australian side. The consequences of the personal relationships between Prime Minister Gough Whitlam and President Suharto between 1973 and 1975, or between Prime Minister Paul Keating and President Suharto two decades later immediately come to mind.

But there is a wider set of leadership connections, which can be identified following the model of David Lampton's analysis of the development of the China-United States relationship in the last decade of the twentieth century in his *Same Bed, Different Dreams* (2001). Lampton suggests that at least four sets of leaders are important in a bilateral relationship, each of which have capacity for personal influence on decision-making and policy execution. In all levels, there is much to be explored beyond what is possible here, and the examples below are highly selective, for illustrative and once again preliminary purposes.

The first and most obvious layer is that of the constitutionally empowered leaders: the presidents and prime ministers, and the members of their cabinets. In the present case, on the Australian side, in most crises the character, attitudes and frame of thinking of the leadership has been important. Among prime ministers, the most striking, and tragic, example must be Whitlam's forceful personal role in the formulation of policy towards the decolonisation of Portuguese Timor in 1974–75, with disastrous consequences for East Timor, and to a very considerable extent, for both Indonesia and Australia.

This pattern was repeated two decades later with Keating and Suharto in their six meetings, with his affection for Suharto, his intentional setting aside of the New Order's foundations of terror, and determination to personally establish a firm foundation for future relations. The results included the Australia–Indonesia Ministerial Forum, the secretly negotiated 1995 Australia–Indonesia Security Agreement, and a failure to foresee the end of the New Order and the shift of fortunes for East Timor, despite the best of intelligence resources.

The second layer, those Lampton describes as the controllers of the 'strategic passes' of policy-making, have had an equally large role on the Australian side of the relationship. Two generations before Keating, Garfield Barwick played a key role as Minister for External Affairs in deflecting Prime Minister Menzies' Anglo-centric racism concerning Indonesia towards a more pro-American position focusing on preventing a communist takeover in Indonesia rather than simply preserving the imperial construct of Malaysia. In this, Barwick was allied to a remarkable group of public servants in the Department of External Affairs, and to some extent in defence, exemplified by K. C. O. 'Mick' Shann, Thomas Critchley, Gordon Jockel and Robert Furlonger, whose role in the period of confrontation is told in Woodard's account of 'best practice in Australia's foreign policy' (1998). In earlier years, John Burton's role in External Affairs, and in later years Arthur Tange's in Defence, and Richard Woolcott's in Foreign Affairs exemplify, for better or worse, Lampton's controllers of the 'strategic passes' of Australian policy-making.

A third layer of leaders are informal power holders who maintain influence and access to decision-makers irrespective of their formal position at any given time, including 'wise elders'. In the Australian case concerning relations with Indonesia, these are not easy to spot. Woolcott has already been mentioned – and was, for example, tapped in retirement by Prime Minister Kevin Rudd to direct Rudd's ill-fated and inept campaign for a new Asia–Pacific community organisation. Allan Taylor, another former ambassador to Indonesia, and former head of the Australian Secret Intelligence Service (ASIS), was consulted by both sides of politics on matters Indonesian. But this is a category that requires closer scrutiny. Two other business figures and private sector advisers on Indonesian affairs to successive Australian governments were the first head of the ASIS Jakarta station, the late Murray Clapham, and the former foreign policy adviser to Gough Whitlam over East Timor, the late Geoff Forrester.

The fourth layer Lampton suggests are informal power holders. These are citizens who use their power to shape the broader context in which management of the relationship occurs, as well as those who have a capacity to intervene on specific issues. They may be in business, labour circles, NGOs, religious organisations, or think-tanks. One key Australian personal linkage to Indonesian politics for a time was the formateur of the Democratic Labor Party, B. A. Santamaria, through his connections with Father Joop Beek, a Jesuit priest and anti-communist activist. Beek often visited Australia in the 1960s, and had a strong relationship with Santamaria. Beek was very closely involved with Ali Moertopo's Opsus, particularly through the Center for Strategic and International Studies (CSIS) and his two most prominent proteges, Harry Tjan and Jusuf Wanandi (Liem Bian Kie) (Tanter 1992: 319–321). Another example, not unrelated, is the connection between Bob Hawke and Ali Moertopo. The latter told an entirely believable story of a drunken night getting to know 'my mate, Bob Hawke', then head of the Australian trade union movement, and subsequently prime minister (Tanter 1992: 448).

Australian security policy currents towards Indonesia

One useful framework for understanding the impact of elite politics on policy formulation is Franz Schurmann's concept of policy currents within and transecting the state (Schurmann 1974). These streams of policy advocacy may have tangible linkages to the wider society, but especially in the area of foreign and defence policy, are generally a matter of largely autonomous elite debate and division on matters of specific policy direction. These sit within a wider socially and politically structured consensus that sets the parameters of what is politically acceptable – beyond which alternatives are almost literally unspeakable. In the United States during the Cold War, the prevailing anti-communist orthodoxy, rooted in defence of the capitalist world system and specific interests of American capital, made support for revolutionary movements unspeakable in respectable policy circles. However, within those constraints, the choices of alternative policy frameworks between roll-back, containment and détente with the communist world were the subject of deep conflict within the United States foreign policy and security community elites. These distinct policy currents within the state gave rise to elite politics based on bureaucratic and budgetary power, articulated not only through policy positions on specific matters but also, over time, rather abstract outlooks and even ideological statements.

Australian policy towards Indonesia has covered a wide range of positions since 1945, ranging from the brief period of UN-centred support during the revolution through two periods of almost overt military conflict (Borneo and Timor) to the current close institutional intertwining. Very occasionally Australian policy reflected – or at least responded to – articulated public pressure. There were several substantial drivers behind Prime Minister John Howard's decision in early September 1999 to press President Clinton to at least not block moves in the United Nations Security Council to authorise the formation of a UN-mandated multinational intervention. Not least were his own concern for a resolution in East Timor, and his ambition for a larger regional role for Australia (Fernandes 2004; Pietsch 2009; Connery 2010).

Yet a crucial element often neglected was the fact that the former Labor Party shadow Foreign Affairs spokesman Laurie Brereton had, to the ire of his colleagues such as Kim Beazley and Gareth Evans, articulated an alternative Labor Party position in support of East Timorese self-determination, and in favour of external intervention to realise that possibility. This shift broke more than two decades of bilateral conservative and Labor agreement to support Indonesia over East Timor, and allowed Howard the political space to undertake his initiative to Habibie (Dorling 2010).

But the combination of massive media coverage of the Indonesian military-orchestrated violence over the preceding months, a quarter century of campaigning by Timor support groups, and the clarity of the result in the UN-sponsored vote for self-determination all aligned together with Howard's own tentative dispositions. The result was a shift in policy towards both East Timor and in the wider region towards what became known as the Howard Doctrine, best characterised as regional stewardship. But this was a rare exception.

Normally mass public opinion almost never has direct effects on foreign policy. Within systems of electoral democracy, foreign policy and security policy are the policy arenas most insulated from popular influence. This is not to say, however, that public opinion is irrelevant to the success or failure of policy currents within the state. On the contrary, one requirement for some types of policy initiative is that they resonate with the goals of a significant public constituency as perceived by, and literally mediated by, the mass media.

Existing Australian policy currents on Australia–Indonesia security issues broadly fall into four main groupings: the dominant strategic realist and liberal institutionalist approaches, the human security approach, and the aspiration to Australian regional stewardship. Each of these has a substantial history, a dominant implicit theoretical or analytical framework, and a set of virtues and vices that set the limits to their effectiveness.

	Key concerns and themes	Carrier groups	Key individuals	Limitations
Strategic realist	Power located in nation states, based on economic and military strength Nationalist, within imperial/alliance parameters Skeptical of multilateral institutions other than military alliances Compatible with both Forward Defence and Defence of Australia doctrines	Liberal Party Defence Department ADF Defence intellectuals	Frederick Scherger Arthur Tange Paul Dibb	How to assess threat claims and estimates How to avoid action–reaction cycles of regional and bilateral weapons acquisitions
Liberal–institutionalist	Maintain communication Avoid provocation Build bilateral and multilateral institutions Respect national sensitivities Compatible with Defence of Australia doctrines	DFAT Australian Labor Party AFP	T. K. Critchley K. C. O. Shann Richard Woolcott Gough Whitlam Paul Keating Mick Kealty	Inadequate realism Inability to judge the point where regime maintenance undermines both justice and security Willingness to ignore foundations of New Order state in terror Risks being undermined by US alliance forward deployment requirements Duped by 'Asian values' debate
Human security/human development	Maintains that Indonesian social conditions are a key security driver Critique of human rights abuses Moral cosmopolitan disposition	Aid community Australian Greens NGOs		Selective outrage Possible unreflexive self-righteousness that can itself generate unnecessary conflict Deficient realist understanding of actual degree of Australian influence Blindness to role of military security as a requirement of human security
Regional stewardship	Deal with failing states and abuses of human rights Accept alliance responsibilities for regional management Realise application of 'Australian values'	Liberal Party (2000+) Strands of DFAT and Defence	John Howard	Heightens association with imperial hegemon Legitimates regional bullying Counterproductive when applied to large country with strong nationalist tradition Encourages perception of Australia as a threat

Table 1. Australian security policy currents towards Indonesia

Strategic realism

Strategic realism has dominated military policy towards Indonesia for the entire post-war period. For most of the post-war period, the fundamentals of Australian defence policy were set out and explained periodically in a series of classified documents presented to cabinet generally known as the Strategic Basis papers. The purpose of the papers was:

> ... to prioritise possible and actual threats to Australia's vital interests, and to develop the outlines of 'a plan for continuing advantage' – or avoiding disadvantage – from which principles could be derived to guide the development and use of Australia's armed forces (Frühling 2009b: 6).

In these respects, Australian strategic realism was and is no different, apart from the consequences of the country's perceived strategic situation, resources and goals, from that of other countries. What is distinctive is the surprisingly militarised and alliance-dependent strategic culture in which it is embedded, as discussed above, and its oscillation over time between two poles, generally known as 'forward defence' and 'the defence of Australia'. Both phrases are overstatements, since there were always substantial common ground, and there have been variants of each.

However, Indonesia has always been a primary concern of all Australian military planning, whether that concern was derived from perceived contemporary potential threats, as during the crises over West New Guinea and confrontation, or in more distant and contingent terms as in the 1980s and 1990s. The heart of all Australian post-war military planning has been and remains the defence of the sea–air gap surrounding Australian continental territory. That in turn has always largely concerned assessment of potential threat from or through the Indonesian archipelago. Among security professionals, this is not a matter of the 'invasion from the north' phobia otherwise deeply embedded in Australian political culture derived from the country's origins in conquest by settler colonialism, so much as a calculation of what an antagonistic Indonesia could do by way of low-level military action to raise the costs to Australia of any given political or diplomatic position. In recent decades, Australian planners have identified 'the knowledge edge' (vis-a-vis Indonesia in particular) as the 'highest capability development priority' for the defence forces, especially to ensure military control of the approaches to Australia in the vent of conflict (cited by Ball 2001: 243).

The fundamental difficulties with the strategic realist approach to military policy have been twofold, and both have been salient to Indonesia. The first is a general one: in a properly democratic society, how is the government's stated assessment of threat itself to be assessed? Given the normal insulation of foreign and defence policy from public influence, how can civil society assess the claims of government security professionals of a need for very large public expenditure to guard against highly unlikely or remote threats? The requirement for 'the knowledge edge' leads directly to the need to maintain the alliance with the United States, since the alliance is the only basis on which the United States is prepared to give Australia preferential regional access to the requisite technologies (Ball 2001). The question then arises as to whether claimed potential, arguably remote, military threats from a future Indonesia warrant the political and budgetary price to be paid for 'the knowledge edge'.

The second problem with the strategic realist approach to military policy regarding Indonesia is that there is an inherent danger that military preparations for Australian defence will be perceived – presumably incorrectly – as preparations for military offence, and will in turn generate a responding round of Indonesian military preparations – the beginnings of a vicious action–reaction cycle. More specifically, particular Australian military preparations have been regarded by Indonesia as unfriendly acts in themselves. In recent years, these include the declaration of a 1000 nautical mile Maritime Identification Zone, and the planned acquisition of long-range ship-based cruise missiles. There can be little doubt that Australian military preparations, starting always from a technological base well in advance of the cash-strapped Indonesian forces, induce Indonesian military planners to consider, within the limits of their resources, matching technology and force structure.

Liberal institutionalism

Liberal institutionalist approaches have dominated Australian diplomatic policy towards Indonesia since its formulation in the context of Confrontation by Critchley, Shann and Barwick. The original Shann–Critchley stress on maintaining communication with the Indonesian leadership despite the external and internal pressures did have a realist basis in recognition of the difficulties that could be caused to Australian interests by a hostile Indonesia. Yet overall the emphasis was on informal and formal communication and institution building and the avoidance of conflict. The policy was devised and carried out by a highly skilled and creative set of External Affairs officers to deal with the White Australia Policy attitudes of Menzies, and, after Barwick's departure for the High Court in April 1964, the rigid, reflexive anti-communism of his successor as Minister for External Affairs, Paul Hasluck.

Over time, the liberal institutionalist emphasis on communication and compromise, especially with the military-dominated Suharto presidency and the occupation of East Timor in particular, lost its realist footing, and in the eyes of its critics, was dubbed 'the Jakarta lobby'. Four decades after its inception it is possible to see both the virtues of liberal institutionalism in Indonesia policy – its prudence and avoidance of provocation – and its increasingly severe limitation in a failure to deliver the strong security outcome that is the promise of a realist approach.

Richard Woolcott, the Australian ambassador to Indonesia in 1975, is infamous for his cable of 17 August 1975 advising the Australian government to accept the imminent Indonesian invasion.

> Policies should be based on disengaging ourselves as far as possible from the Timor situation. We should leave events to take their course; and if and when Indonesia does intervene, act in a way which would be designed to minimize the public impact in Australia and show privately understanding to Indonesia of their problems ... I know I am recommending a pragmatic rather than a principled stand, but that is what national interest and foreign policy is all about (Woolcott 1975).

This is usually taken to demonstrate, as Woolcott's final sentence would have it, a clear expression of realism in international relations in the national interest. In fact, Woolcott's recommendations produced a policy outcome that was neither realistic nor effective. In place of genuine realism there was a rhetoric of masculine toughness and brutality masking poor political judgement based on prejudice and poor intelligence.

This is doubly tragic, for not only was there a huge price to be paid over the next quarter century for this flawed and faux realism, but Woolcott misrepresented himself as a Realpolitik pragmatist. For the bulk of his career in relation to Indonesia, he was a faint echo of the earlier generation of Indonesianist liberal institutionalists. While he lacked their well-grounded realism and political judgement, Woolcott was in fact a genuine liberal institutionalist, and strongly supported closer bilateral institutional ties, as well as expanding the educational base for Indonesian language and Indonesian studies in Australia (Woolcott 2006).

The liberal institutionalist approach, dressed in power politics realist cloth, was best articulated by Paul Keating. In 1994, Keating famously said:

> No country is more important to Australia than Indonesia. If we fail to get this relationship right, and nurture and develop it, the whole web of our foreign relations is incomplete [and] ... the emergence of the New Order government of President Suharto, and the stability and prosperity which [it] has brought to [Indonesia] was the single most beneficial strategic development to have affected Australia and its region in the past thirty years (in Brereton 1998: 35).

Combined with his often mentioned personal respect for Soeharto, this attitude drove Keating to thicken the governmental relationship with the New Order, suppress concerns about Indonesian atrocities in East Timor and Papua, and to whitewash the manner in which the New Order was established. Ultimately intensely Realpolitik in his willingness to set aside his knowledge of the bodies and terror on which the New Order was built, Keating forged a series of institutional and cultural links with Indonesia as part of a reconstitution of what it meant to be Australian. The results were mixed, in part precisely because of the weak realist understanding of New Order Indonesia. A brief spasm of Asian language learning in schools passed quickly, aided by the early years of the Howard government. The security agreement with Indonesia collapsed in the aftermath of the decolonisation of East Timor. But in many respects, Keating's institution-building agenda was echoed in the later years of the Howard prime ministership – through the post-9/11 years of cooperation on terrorism and the 2006 Lombok security agreement.

Human security and transnational moral communities

The human security approach has its political roots in the antagonists to the liberal institutionalist – the critique of human rights abuses by the Indonesian state in Indonesia and East Timor. Analytically its roots lie in a blend of cosmopolitanism and a claim of the inseparability of internal state–society relations from foreign policy considerations. Its various proponents stress not only the degree of moral obligation brought by shared humanity, but that a realism informed by an understanding of social and economic pressures on the Indonesian state leads to an understanding that Australian national interest requires attention to the state of Indonesian society and human rights. The virtues of the human security approach to Indonesia policy are its recognition of transnational moral community and its realist conception of the social context of state action. Its vices, include 'selective outrage' (Aspinall 2006), a sometimes unreflexive self-righteousness that itself generates further conflict, and most importantly, as in the case of contemporary concern about Papua, a deficient realist understanding of the degree of influence to be expected.

The case of contemporary Papua illustrates the need for the human security approach, but also its limitations. As long as the Indonesian military and police are permitted to dominate policy towards Papua, to continue predatory economic activities in Papua, and to carry out violent abuses of human rights with impunity, there will be a need for a human security-centred approach from both within Indonesia and neighbouring countries. The problem in the case of Papua is not so much that human rights politics are exhausted – far from it – but that they have far fewer institutional handholds than in the case of East Timor. This dramatically lowers the likelihood that Australian-based human security approaches will have comparable influence in the Papuan case – even short of self-determination.

Three relevant differences between the Timor and Papua cases stand out. Firstly, despite the best efforts of the Indonesian and Australian governments, the question of East Timor as former Portuguese colonial territory remained on the agenda of the United Nations Decolonization Committee from 1975 until the independence of Timor-Leste. This ensured that the matter of East Timor could always be brought before the Security Council, and was never erased from the global institutional public agenda. Secondly, military, political and cultural resistance endured throughout the Indonesia colonial period at a level that, however much it ebbed militarily, always exacted a considerable price from Indonesia. Despite continued resistance to Indonesian occupation in Papua over many years, this has not to date attained the coherence, endurance and effectiveness of the Timorese resistance. Lastly, Australian church-based human rights campaigning over undoubtedly gross and continuing abuses of Papuan human rights are hampered by the appearance of, to use Aspinall's term again, 'selective outrage' and borderline – if not in some cases, outright – racism in the depiction of 'Javanization' (Aspinall 2006). For all these reasons, current human security approaches to the Papuan question in Australia–Indonesia relations need serious reconsideration, at the same time as being absolutely necessary.

Regional stewardship

The fourth approach has emerged most clearly in the years since the East Timor intervention of 1999, and subsequent regional peace keeping operations in the Pacific and East Timor. Justified in terms of concerns about failing states and abuses of human rights, the new approach is, with respect to the states of the south-west Pacific and East Timor, an aspiration for Australian regional stewardship. A realist approach to regional threats and the use of Australian interventionary power – military and civil – has been legitimated in terms of Australian values, local responsibilities within the wider context of the US alliance the War on Terror, and a fusion of national interest and moral responsibility (Brenchley 1999; Leaver 2001; Pietsch 2009: 295–300). A week after ADF forces landed in Dili in September 1999, John Howard announced the Howard Doctrine in an interview with *The Bulletin*'s Fred Brenchley:

> The Howard Doctrine – the PM himself embraces the term – sees Australia acting in a sort of 'deputy' peacekeeping capacity in our region to the global policeman role of the US. East Timor shows Australia as a medium sized, economically strong, regional power leading a peacekeeping force with other regional nations, and the US acting as 'lender of last resort'. Australia, says Howard, has a responsibility within its region to do things 'above and beyond', bringing into play its unique characteristics as a western country in Asia but with strong links to North America. East Timor peacekeeping shows Australia playing an 'influential, constructive and decisive role in the affairs of the region' (Brenchley 1999).

Howard went on to press the emotional and value-based core he was to emphasise in the coming months of radio talkbacks and sound bites:

> Gee, we were ourselves in Asia in the last few weeks. We were defending the values we hold as Australians. We were willing to be in dispute with our closest neighbour, to defend those values. And we were able to build up our associations with nations outside Asia in the course of that (cited in Brenchley 1999).

East Timor in 1999 and 2006 demonstrate both the attractions and limitations of this aspiration of a delegated regional steward (who is, however, not a regional hegemon): military overstretch, confusion about goals, host country antagonism towards perceived colonial rhetoric if not intention. Indonesia does not lie within the region to be stewarded by Australia, but against a background of Indonesian nationalism, emerging expressions of Australia as a threat, however unfounded, are unsurprising and have the potential for a downward spiral.

The way out: shared problems, shared interests

Thickening the relationship, giving it 'heft' via market and civil society, are clearly important. Much current government policy is unhelpful in this regard – especially the catastrophic consequences of long-term defunding of language teaching, which the Asian Studies Association of Australia (ASAA 2002; 2007) and David Hill's recent report on Indonesian language teaching in Australian universities (2012) have documented. But where then is this thickening going to come from? Very likely the market is going to fail us here: the potential generative factor, Australian investment in Indonesia, is limited by exactly those aspects of Indonesia that give rise to crisis: poverty, corruption, state incapacity and militarisation. The Indonesian direct foreign investment figures, as Indonesian government officials have pointed out, are dismal, and unlikely to improve quickly in the Australian case. So the most important element is civil society.

The way out of the present somewhat dangerous dead-end is to widen the argument, and to transform the entire character of the relationship, its framing and its dynamics by arguing that the problems of Indonesia and its society and of Australia and its, in fact intersect much more than we have been admitting to date. Paradoxically, I want to suggest to both Indonesians and Australians that because we are in even deeper trouble than we think there is more of a chance to find – at least in part – common cause to resolve some of the most violent aspects of the present mess.

The four existing Australian policy currents now face serious limitations, and need to be supplemented with a more broadly founded theoretical and policy approach. The recognition in the human security approach of at least the beginnings of a transnational moral community will find a sounder footing to the extent it is supplemented by discovery of transnational communities of interest. This may lie in an approach through the concept of 'global problems'. The well-known challenges to Australian security concerns from Indonesia indeed do have both an internal and bilateral dynamic as argued above, but they are also part of a wider pattern of global problems whose substantive causes largely lie at least as much outside the society in which they are manifest as within it. Islamist terror in Indonesia and the antipathy of its proponents towards the Australian government and Australian people is a manifestation of a much wider, global problem. The Bali bombings and the Corby conviction symbolise a strong Australian sense of religious and cultural difference with Indonesia, which has a long history, but which is periodically mobilised anew under novel structures of sentiments and prevailing global and regional political patterns (Tanter, 2000; Walker, 1999). Indonesian cultures – plural – are deeply inflected by their location in a framework of communicative and cultural and social and economic globalisation that empowers, diminishes, destroys and creates. The terrorist politics of some Salafi groups are inexplicable outside a framework of globalisation – as is the entire discourse of 'the politics of terrorism'. What is less often noted is the fact that similar global pressures are manifest in Australia: the Cronulla riots and the long-festering conflict between young men of Anglo and Lebanese backgrounds in Sydney also have a pattern of both local and global causes. The Cronulla riots and the Bali bombings are both regressive cultural responses to the intersection of globalisation with local contexts: they are both manifestations of the same global problem.

Global problems are not just important problems, or problems that affect many people. Rather they are those problems that affect the whole of the planet, and potentially all of the people who live on it. Climate change is one clear example that springs to mind. This is because the consequences of humanly generated changes in the atmosphere will, albeit in different ways according to region, affect everyone on the planet. In other words, the consequences are universal. Moreover, unless we profoundly change our collective behaviour, climate change may well result in irreversible changes in the climatic conditions of life – a measure of the deep vulnerability of human society in the face of this issue. And it is easy to see that there will be no easy solution to the problem. The causes of the present situation are clearly related to our economic system, our attitudes to nature, our political organisation, our technological capacities and preferences, and our uses of resources. Solutions will involve not just all communities and every country, but solutions will necessarily involve cooperation between all, rather than individual approaches. In other words, the example of climate change suggests that global problems are complex, intractable, and make human society as a whole very vulnerable.

Other examples of global problems of this scale and with these characteristics would include weapons of mass destruction; the violation of the human security of several billions of the world's poor, and the consequences of the conditions of their lives for the rest of the world; failures and deficits of global governance, especially when set beside the largely unregulated pressures of economic and cultural globalisation; resource depletion, especially that of energy resources, on a scale and in a manner that is both unsustainable and profoundly inequitable; the degradation of natural environments as a result of economic activities, including the oceans, forests and soils; the physical, social and psycho-cultural consequences of unprecedented and still accelerating development of megacities; and cultural collisions within and across national borders generated by globalisation and claims to the primacy or universal superiority of one version of reason and ethics (Hayes 2007; Tanter and Hayes 2008).

There are at least three major interrelated global problems that face both Indonesia and Australia with undoubted security implications: pandemics, climate change and energy insecurity. The salient key characteristics are inherently transnational in both their causes and their consequences. They are set to interact in ways we may well not anticipate, such as climate change and infectious disease; and they are already giving rise to perceptible new forms of threat to both societies.

As an illustration, Australian concern over climate change is one justification for the establishment of components of the nuclear fuel cycle in Australia – uranium enrichment, fuel fabrication, high-level radioactive waste storage, and possibly nuclear power generation. A parallel debate in Indonesia, mainly fostered by concerns over declining position in hydrocarbon reserves and longstanding economic nationalist policy currents, is promoting nuclear power generation. Irrespective of the economic and political realities in each case, security elites in both countries have registered developments in the other with degrees of alarm, especially since both countries have records of secret nuclear weapons development, which even then were in part responses to fears of each other (Walsh 1997; Cornejo 2000).

Climate change, energy insecurity and pandemics will certainly interact with existing conflict patterns. To take but one plausible example, global warming will influence already massively degraded fishing stocks in the seas of eastern Indonesia, which provide the basic protein requirements for most of the population of that large region. The implications for migration into Papua and further pressure on the fishing grounds of north-west Australia are easy to imagine – as are the political consequences.

All three global problems foreshadow deep threats to the fabric of Australian and Indonesian life, and all require, for their even their partial amelioration, cooperation between the two countries – and between the two societies. This in fact offers both a challenge and a chance to restructure the pattern of conflict into which we are increasingly locked by the dialectic of Indonesian militarisation and Australian community-based concern about human rights.

Reframing Australia–Indonesia security involves an approach to Australian–Indonesian security dilemmas that refocuses on the common threats to both countries rather than traditional concern with possible threats to each other. Inherently the approach involves a challenge to methodological nationalism to develop policy prescription in empirical and theoretical examination of national, regional and global systems beyond conventional state-based security analysis.

The key hypothesis is that global problems manifest in the fabric of the two societies, and whose causes lie beyond their national systems, not only will generate deep security challenges but also new possibilities of cross-border communities of shared interest. The secondary hypothesis is that this process will enhance the capacity to manage the difficult bilateral problems already evident by placing them in a context of larger security collaborations.

The fundamental hope is that there is a potential Australian–Indonesian bilateral component of global civil society that can form around shared interests in the resolution of questions of climate change, energy insecurity, and pandemics. This approach seeks to explore a realist or interests-based foundation to the intra- and inter-national generation of norms and normative communities. This civil society emphasis also takes the conceptualisation of the policy consequences of these global problems beyond the 'securitisation' of 'human security' issues and the utilisation of global public goods (Caballero-Anthony 2004), both of which remain largely state-focused, and with an ambiguous attitude to interest-based political formations across borders.

The work has six long-range goals:

- to map the existing social relations between Indonesian and Australian society
- to document the manifestations and interrelated impacts on the two societies of global problems such as climate change, new infectious diseases and energy insecurity
- to map the articulation of these shared global problems on the security relations between the two countries, both in terms of 'hard' military security and human security
- to develop policy responses by both government and civil society

- to map the existing social and ecological relations between Indonesian and Australian socio-ecological systems as a prerequisite to understanding the impacts of climate change on security issues
- to develop a model of bilateral policy responses to shared global problems potentially applicable to other cases.

Mapping the set of relations between social formations

Mapping the existing relations – in ideal type, the set of total social relations between the two social formations – is a logical requirement for any assessment of the effect of climate change or any other variable: unless the base line is known, it is difficult to determine the presence and causation of change. Yet remarkably, there is no documentation of the full range of interactions (even in their thinness) between the two societies. Mostly we are content with trade and investment data, gross data on tourism and migration, and not much more. Some sense of the full depth and complexity of the relationship could be gained by the following approaches:

- individual-level formal and informal cross-border interactions, measuring frequency, volume, extensity and intensity of connection
- geo-spatial network analysis of relationships between formal and informal social entities and organisations in Australia and Indonesia, including relations of state, market and civil society
- geo-spatial mapping of relations between the two countries – by region and city
- mapping of Australian and Indonesian diasporas in the other countries and mediation via third-country presences
- documentation of value-based cross-border relations and expressions of identity and joint moral purpose – for example, religion, environmental protection.

Layered frames of analysis

Before looking at the security impacts of climate change, it needs to be understood that there are series of layered frames for thinking about the relationship between 'Indonesia' and 'Australia'. The first, although by no means obvious, focuses on the bio-physical and social-ecological systems under consideration. There may appear to be some contradiction or impediment involved in excising a bilateral unit of analysis ('Australia–Indonesia') based on political–territorial conceptions from a set of much larger complex systems. But clear and viable modelling is possible: not all parts of 'Australia' and 'Indonesia' are equally closely related bio-physically and socio-ecologically Tasmania–Aceh linkages are less important than Northern Territory–Nusa Tenggara linkages. But what is important is to establish ways of understanding the bio-physical and socio-ecological bases. Most modelling to date is either global or national in character. What is now needed is an overlapping set of regional, bilateral, national, and sub-national models.

The second layer is the historically formed relationship between the two societies and states: this is much closer to the conventional sociological and historical understanding, but still requiring mapping of complex interactions of the socio-technical systems of the two societies, including energy and materials transfers, as well as human interaction.

The third layer involves intentional collective efforts to address actual and expected climate change through mitigation of greenhouse gas generation and release, and adaptation to specific patterns of climate change. It is already clear that 'mal-adaptation' is a possible and indeed likely outcome of climate change adaptation policy. Nuclear power is likely to be one such example – either when it is an inappropriate answer to a country's energy needs compared to other alternatives; or when the risks of the particular nuclear power plant are inadequately assessed; or when the follow-on security consequences – real or erroneous but still anticipated – take the form of nuclear weapons proliferation.

Climate change and common security

One strong conclusion to date of collaborative work with Indonesian and Australian specialists on complexity and climate change impacts on Indonesia and Australia was that climate change impacts are a shared problem (Nautilus Institute 2008). This may appear unremarkable, except that there is a noticeable and regrettable tendency in bilateral relations between Indonesia and Australia to assume that one side has the problems and the other side has the answers. In the case of climate change it is evident that both societies are in deep trouble and both will be unable to solve all the problems to which climate change is already beginning to give rise on a national basis: cross-border collaboration, cooperation and policy coordination will simply be essential.

One product of this collaboration may give a sense of the intellectual and policy outcomes that can be expected from the approach of this project. Allan Behm, former Assistant Secretary of Defence, addressed the question of the security consequences of climate change for both countries. Behm argued that:

> ... the geophysical and ecological forces that are currently (re)shaping the physical environment add another layer of complexity to the political and economic forces that have hitherto determined the longer-term strategic prospects of Indonesia and Australia. How competently – and proactively – Indonesia and Australia deal with this complexity, inter alia, will largely determine the vitality of the bilateral strategic relationship over the next four decades or so (Behm 2009).

Behm continued, 'If climate change is inherently non-linear, changes in the strategic environment are inherently discontinuous' (2009). After setting out integrated policy recommendations at national, bilateral, regional and global levels, Behm concludes by stressing the need for:

> ... a diplomatic and scientific strategy that deals with the issue proactively. To address the consequences of climate change in a piecemeal and reactive manner would almost certainly create the preconditions for misunderstanding and consequent miscalculation (Behm 2009).

Responding to climate change has already come to be an immensely difficult task for national governments. It clearly cannot be resolved by national governments alone, and there is good reason to think governments per se in their present mode of thought and action cannot resolve them at all without immense inputs from civil society. But certainly, neither the Indonesian nor the Australian governments are applying themselves adequately to any of those problems, and in several cases – the energy–nuclear proliferation nexus for example – are actively making matters worse.

Climate change and other global problems offer deep threats to the fabric of Australian and Indonesian life, and all require, for their even their partial amelioration, cooperation between the two countries – and between the two societies.

This in fact offers both a challenge and a chance to restructure the apparently endlessly repeating pattern of crises disrupting a fragile and volatile relationship. The key task – on a scale vastly greater than anything attempted in the past by Australian community groups and social movements, is to find common cause with Indonesian community groups and social movements on specific aspects and angles of these shared, globally rooted problems. On issues of environment, climate change, food resources, energy, nuclear proliferation, cultural fears, rights, obligations, migration and labour, resources, food stocks and biodiversity, Australian and Indonesian organisations and voices need to find their partners, build relationships and work out new forms of cross-national collaboration, mutual support and political tactics.

As is normal in politics, alliances and antagonisms will be built on mixtures of interest and value. Some will be temporary and some enduring. Some may be partial and some may be wide-ranging, some fragile and some robust. They will be built on identifications that are thin, and on those that are thick. They will cross-cut, fluctuate, collapse, expand and contradict.

These ties will come, but they will not be built without the will to do so. We need to think politically as well as analytically. There is good analytical reason to think that such ties, such expansion of our moral and political community, are both necessary and feasible, but not without great effort and commitment. This is a political project unlike any other that Australians have attempted – across borders, across boundaries of culture, language, and more than most Australians are willing to admit they care about, across ethnicity and religion.

References

ABS. 2011. *International Investment Position, Australia: Supplementary Statistics, 2009*, Australian Bureau of Statistics, Catalogue no. 5352.0, Tables 3 and 5. Accessed 5 March 2012. Available from: http://www.abs.gov.au/AUSSTATS/abs@.nsf/DetailsPage/5352.0Calendar%20year%202009?OpenDocument.

Anheier, Helmut; Katz, Hagai. 2003. 'Mapping global civil society', in *Global Civil Society 2003*, edited by Kaldor, M; Anheier, H; Glasius, M. Oxford: Oxford University Press.

Anheier, Helmut; Katz, Hagai. 2004. 'Network approaches to global civil society'. In *Global Civil Society 2004/5*, edited by Kaldor, M; Anheier, H; Glasius, M. London: Sage.

Aspinall, Edward. 2006. 'Selective outrage and unacknowledged fantasies: Re-thinking Papua, Indonesia and Australia', *Austral Policy Forum*, 06-15A (4 May). Accessed 5 March 2012. Available from: http://www.nautilus.org/publications/essays/apsnet/policy-forum/2006/0615a-aspinall.html/?searchterm=aspinall.

Asian Studies Association of Australia (ASAA). 2002. *Maximizing Australia's Asia Knowledge: Repositioning and Renewal of a National Asset: A Report.* Bundoora: Asian Studies Association of Australia, 2002.

Asian Studies Association of Australia (ASAA). 2007. *Suez to Suva: ARC Asia Pacific Futures Research Network.* 'Suez to Suva' website, Bibliometric data. Accessed 3 March 2008. Available from: http://www.sueztosuva.org.au/biblio.

Ball, Desmond. 2001. 'The US–Australian alliance: The strategic essence', *Australian Journal of International Affairs* 55 (2) (July): 235–248.

Behm, Allan. 2009. 'Climate change and security: The test for Australia and Indonesia – involvement or indifference?' *APSNet Special Report* 09-01S, (12 February). Accessed 5 March 2012. Available from: http://www.nautilus.org/publications/essays/apsnet/reports/2009/climate-behm.pdf.

Brenchley, Fred. 1999. 'The Howard defence doctrine', *Bulletin* (28 September): 22–4.

Brereton, Laurie. 1998. 'A Labor perspective', in *Development Issues Number Ten: Bridging the Arafura Sea: Australia–Indonesia Relations in Prosperity and Adversity*, edited by Smith, S L; Sofyan, G H; Sulaiman, I F. Canberra: Asian Pacific School of Economics and Management, Australian National University.

Brereton, Laurie. 1999. 'Australia and East Timor', speech to the Queensland Branch of the AIIA, 4 February.

Caballero-Anthony, Mely. 2004. 'Revisioning human security in Southeast Asia', *Asian Perspective*, 28, 3: 155–189.

Chauvel, Richard. 2006. 'Australia, Indonesia and the Papuan crises', *Austral Policy Forum* 06-14A 27 April 2006. Accessed 5 March. Available from: http://www.nautilus.org/publications/essays/apsnet/policy-forum/2006/0614a-chauvel.html.

Connery, David. 2010. 'Crisis policymaking: Australia and the East Timor crisis of 1999', *Canberra Papers on Strategy and Defence* No. 177, Strategic and Defence Studies Centre, Australian National University.

Cornejo, Robert M. 2000. 'When Sukarno sought the bomb: Indonesian nuclear aspirations in the mid-1960s,' *The Nonproliferation Review*, (Summer).

Cotan, Imron. 2005. 'Indonesia–Australia relations: East Timor, Bali bombing, Tsunami and beyond'. Duta Besar Republik Indonesia, Canberra (1 March). Accessed 5 March 2012. Available from: http://www.kbri-canberra.org.au/speeches/2005/050301e.htm.

DFAT. 2010. 'Australia's trade with East Asia 2009' (August). Market Information and Research Section, Department of Foreign Affairs and Trade.

Dibb, Paul; Brabin-Smith, Richard. 2007. 'Indonesia in Australian defence planning', *Security Challenges* 3 (4) (November): 67–93.

Dorling, Philip. 2010. 'Player Rudd knew the game', *Canberra Times* (7 August).

Evans, Gareth. 1994. 'Australia and Indonesia: Partnership in diversity'. Address to the Research Institute for Asia and the Pacific (RIAP) and the Indonesian Centre for

Strategic and International Studies (CSIS) Conference, Jakarta, 2 July.

Fernandes, Clinton. 2004. *Reluctant Saviour: Australia, Indonesia and the independence of East Timor*. Carlton North: Scribe Publications.

Foreign Affairs Sub Committee. 2004. *Near Neighbours – Good Neighbours: An Inquiry into Australia's Relationship with Indonesia* (May). Joint Standing Committee on Foreign Affairs, Defence and Trade, Canberra: Parliament of Australia.

Frühling, Stephan. 2009a. *A History of Australian Strategic Policy since 1945*, Canberra: Defence Publishing Service, Department of Defence.

Frühling, Stephan. 2009b. 'Australian strategic guidance since the Second World War', in *History of Australian Strategic Policy since 1945*, edited by Frühling, S A. Canberra: Defence Publishing Service, Department of Defence.

Hanson, Fergus. 2010. *Indonesia and Australia: Time for a Step Change*, Policy Brief (March). Sydney: Lowy Institute for International Policy.

Hayes, Peter. 2007. 'Global problems, global solutions', Nautilus Institute (9 May). Accessed 5 March 2012. Available from: http://www.nautilus.org/gps/understanding/probs-solutions-PH-text.

Hill, David T. 2012. *Indonesian Language in Australian Universities: Strategies for a Stronger Future*. National Teaching Fellowship: Final Report, Murdoch University, February, (http://altcfellowship.murdoch.edu.au/Docs/ALTC_NTF_Indonesian_in_Australian_Universities_FINAL_REPORT.pdf).

International Monetary Fund. 2010. World Economic Outlook (WEO) database (October 2010). Accessed 5 March 2012. Available from: http://www.imf.org/external/pubs/ft/weo/2010/02/weodata/index.aspx.

Lampton, David. 2001. *Same Bed, Different Dreams: Managing U.S.–China Relations, 1989–2000*, Berkeley: University of California Press.

Leaver, Richard. 2001. 'The meanings, origins and implications of "the Howard Doctrine" ', *The Pacific Review* 14, 1 (March): 15–34.

Nautilus Institute. 2008. *Mapping Causal Complexity in Climate Change Impacts and Responses: Australia and Indonesia*. Accessed 5 March 2012. Available from: http://www.nautilus.org/projects/reframing/cc-security/mapping.

Novotny, Daniel. 2010. *Torn between America and China: Elite Perceptions and Indonesian Foreign Policy*, Singapore: Institute of Southeast Asian Studies.

Pietsch, Samuel. 2009. 'Australia's military intervention in East Timor, 1999', PhD thesis, Australian National University.

Schurmann, Franz. 1974. *The Logic of World Power: An Inquiry into the Origins, Currents and Contradictions of World Politics*, New York: Pantheon.

Tanter, Richard. 1992. 'Intelligence agencies and Third World militarization: A case study of Indonesia, 1966–1989, with Special Reference to South Korea, 1961–1989', PhD dissertation, Monash University. Accessed 5 March 2012. Available from: http://www.nautilus.org/about/associates/richard-tanter/richard-papers/indonesian-intelligence/thesis/thesis%20-%20toc.

Tanter, Richard. 2000. 'After fear, before justice: Indonesia and Australia in the long haul, as if ethics mattered', *Inside Indonesia* 61 (January–February). Accessed 5 March 2012. Available from: http://www.insideindonesia.org/edition-61/after-fear-before-justice.

Tanter, Richard; Hayes, Peter. 2008. *What are Global Problems?* Nautilus Institute. Accessed 5 March 2012. Available from: http://www.nautilus.org/gps/intro.

TBI. 2011. *Border Resources: Border Information and Statistics*, Trans-Border Institute University of San Diego. Accessed 5 March 2012. Available from: http://www.sandiego.edu/peacestudies/tbi/resources/information_and_statistics.php.

United States, Department of State, Bureau of East Asian and Pacific Affairs. 2010. *Background Note: Indonesia* (3 November). Accessed 5 March 2012. Available from: http://www.state.gov/r/pa/ei/bgn/2748.htm.

Viviani, Nancy. 2000. *Australia–Indonesia Relations after the East Timor Upheaval*, JPRI Working Paper 64 (January). Accessed 5 March 2012. Available from: http://www.jpri.org/publications/workingpapers/wp64.html.

Walker, David. 1999. *Anxious Nation: Australia and the Rise of Asia – 1850-1939*, University of Queensland Press.

Walsh, Jim. 1997. 'Surprise down under: The secret history of Australia's nuclear ambitions', *The Nonproliferation Review* 5: 1–20.

White, Hugh. 2002. 'Australian defence policy and the possibility of war', Australian Journal of International Affairs, Vol. 56, no. 2: 253–264.

Woodard, Garry. 1998. 'Best practice in Australia's foreign policy: 'Konfrontasi' (1963–66)', *Australian Journal of Political Science* 33 (1) (March): 85–99.

Woolcott, Richard. 1975. Cable to Alan Renouf. 17 August.

Woolcott, Richard. 2006. 'Our relationship is like a rope', in *Good Neighbour, Bad Neighbour: Australia's Relations with Indonesia*, Kings Cross: Uniya Social Justice Centre.

Wuryandari, Ganewati, editor. 2008. *Politik Luar Negeri Indonesia Di Tengah Pusaran Politik Domestik*, Pustaka Pelajar with P2P-LIPI.

Index

academic freedom 91
academic activism 1, 5–7, 26–34, 49–50, 71, 89–92
'administrators and solidarity makers' 84, 86
Almond, Gabriel 79, 83
Andaya, Barbara xxvi
Anderson, Benedict R.O'G x, xi, 5, 11–12, 54, 58, 82, 85–86, 92, 99
Anwar, Dewi Fortuna 133
Apter 83
area studies xxv, 19, 59, 73, 98–105, 114–116
Arndt, Heinz 2, 68
Asia Foundation 63
Asian Studies Association of Australia (ASAA) xix, 145
Aspinall, Edward
  debate with Peter King 78–79, 89–92, 93
Australia Indonesia Institute (AIA) 132
Australia West Papua Association (AWPA) 91
Australia-Indonesia Governance Research Partnership 62
Australia-Indonesia Ministerial Forum 135
Australia-Indonesia Security Agreement 135
Australian Consortium for 'In-Country' Indonesian Studies (ACICIS) 27, 63
Australian Institute of International Affairs (AIIA) xiv
Australian Research Council (ARC) xix, 60, 62
Australia-Netherlands Research Collaboration (ANRC) 62
Australian-Indonesia relations
  East Timor 55, 68, 130, 131, 134, 137, 141, 144–145
  popular perceptions 53–54, 66
  West Papua (Papua) xxi, 55, 125, 130, 143
  Australia as 'middle power' 58
  in Australian media 67
  security policy 123–130, 137–149
  leaders 134–136
  trade 131–132

civil society 131–133
climate change 149–152

Bali bombings (see terrorist bombings)
Ball, William McMahon xiv, xvi-xvii, xviii
Barwick, Sir Garfield 127, 135, 140–141
Bayly, C.A. 114
Beek, Joop 136
Behm, Allan 151
Berg, C.C. 106
Binder, Leonard 83
Blainey, Geoffrey 47
Brereton, Laurie 137

Carr, E.H. 40–42
Castles, Lance 82
Chase-Dunn, Christopher 79
Clapham, Murray 135
climate change 146–147, 149
Cold War xv, 69, 70, 98–100, 127–128, 136
Colombo Plan xv
community of assessment xxi
consulting 24–26, 63
Coppel, Charles A. xviii
Corby, Schapelle 125, 146
Cornell 'Preliminary Report' 11–12
Cornell Modern Indonesia Project xii, 9, 99
Crawford, Max xiv
Cribb, Robert xx, 49–50
Critchley, Tom 135, 138, 140
Cronulla riots 146

Department of Foreign Affairs and Trade (DFAT)
  travel warnings xx

East Timor
  Indonesian occupation 137, 143
Emmerson, Donald 56
Emy, Hugh 80–81, 92

Feith, Herbert

as role model xxii, 17
first engagement with Indonesia x–xiii, xvii–xviii, 7–9
background 2–4
at Monash University 10, 17
peace studies xii
as scholar-activist 9–12, 14
values in his scholarship 7–14, 80
Decline of Constitutional Democracy 82–85
Fernandes, Clinton 79, 88–89
fieldwork 21–23, 65–66
Forrester, Geoff 135

Garnaut, Ross 88
Garran, Sir Robert xiv–xv
Geertz, Clifford ix, xv, xvii, 6, 9–10, 83
Goldsworthy, David 77, 79–80, 81, 87, 91–92

Habibie, B.J. 133
Hadiz, Vedi 70
Hamilton, Neil 93
Harry, Benda 83, 99
   debate with Herb Feith xii, 80, 86–88
Harvard Department of Social Relations xvii
Hasluck, Paul 141
Hatta, Mohammad 128
Heryanto, Ariel xxii
Hill, David xix, xx, 145
history
   writing of 38–46, 102–104; uses of 46–48
Howard Doctrine 61, 137, 138, 144
Howard, John 137

IIAS (International Institute of Asian Studies) 111–112
IISG (International Institute for Social History) 105–106
Indonesia, the study of
   in USA ix, xvi, xvii, xix, 56, 58, 98–99, 100–101
   in Netherlands 105–118
   in Australia xiii–xx, 60–61, 113–114, 127
   with leftist sympathies 70, 80, 87–88; bans 72
   at Melbourne University xvi, xviii, 9
   at Monash University 10, 17
   at Australian National University 62, 68–69, 97, 99, 113, 118
'Indonesia lobby' (see 'Jakarta lobby')

Inside Indonesia 65
Iswanto 27–28, 29, 30, 32

Jackson, Karl D. 83
'Jakarta lobby' 55, 67, 91, 141
Johns, Anthony 2
Josselin de Jong, J.P.B 106

Kahin, George McT. 10, 11, 82, 85, 99
Kalidjernih, Freddy xxi, 88–89
Keating, Paul 60–61, 101, 134, 138, 142; relationship with Suharto 134–135
Kelly, Paul 68
Kiefer, Ed 27
killings
   anti-communist 11
King, Peter
   debate with Edward Aspinall 78–79, 89–92, 93
KIT (Royal Tropical Institute) 106
KITLV (Royal Netherlands Institute for Southeast Asia and Caribbean Studies) 105–106, 117
KNAW (Royal Netherlands Academy of Sciences) 108

Lampton, David 134, 135
Lane, Max 70 (fn6)
Legge, John D. x, xiv, 2, 5, 47, 86
Leiden (see also KITLV and IIAS) 116–117
Lev, Daniel xxi, 10, 13
Liddle, William 82
Lindsey, Tim xx
Linklater, Andrew 80–81, 92
Lombok Accord 131
Lowy Institute 130

Mackie, Jamie xii, 2, 10, 12, 86–87
Manilowski, Bronislaw 83
Manning, Chris 88
Manning, Patrick 99–100
Maritime Identification Zone 140
McDonald, Terrence 103–104
McGibbon, Rodd 79, 89, 90–91
McVey, Ruth 11–12, 82, 99
Moertopo, Ali 136
Mohamad, Goenawan 1
Mortimer, Rex xii, 5, 70

NIOD (Netherlands Institute for War Documentation) 106

Novotny, Daniel 128, 130
nuclear power 147
NWO (Netherlands Organisation for Scientific Research) 108

Osborne, Robin 88

Pausacker, Helen 57
Philpott, Simon ix, xvi (fn8), 6, 97 (fn2), 99 (fn5)
political science
 and Indonesian studies 55–57, 79–82
Purdey, Jemma 85, 88
Pye, Lucien 83

Reid, Anthony 1, 6
RMIT Globalism Institute 93–94
Robison, Richard 70
Ross, Ian Clunies xiv
Rudd, Kevin 135

Said, Edward 102
Santamaria, B.A. 136
Schurmann, Franz 136
Scott, Joan 103
Sears, Laurie 6
Sewell, William 103
Shann, K.C.O. 135, 138, 140
Shepard, Jack xiv
Sheridan, Greg 68
Smail, John 6
Snouck, Christiaan Hurgronje 106
Social Science Research Council (SSRC) 100–101
Somers, Margaret 104
Staal Report 107
Strauss, Leo 79
Subaltern studies 102
Sukunan 27–33

Tanter, Richard 14
Taylor, Allan 135
Taylor, Jean Gelman 7
terrorist bombings 61, 66, 113, 125, 146
Thomas, Paul xiv
Tjan, Harry 136
Toer, Pramoedya Ananta 133

United Nations Decolonization Committee 143
United States foreign policy
 relations with Australia 127, 129, 136, 140
 relations with Indonesia 127–129

van Vollenhoven, C. 106
Vietnam War 11
Viviani, Nancy 126–127
Volunteer Graduate Scheme x, xvi-xvii

Walker, David xiv, xv
Wanandi, Jusuf 133, 136
War on Terror 100, 128, 144
Waterside Workers xvi
West Papua (Papua)
 Australian scholarship on 71–72, 77, 78, 88–90, 93, 143
White Australia Policy 58, 141
White, Hugh 129–130
Whitlam, Gough 134
Women's Barefoot Bank 26–27
Woolcott, Richard 68, 135, 141–142